IN SEARCH
OF THE
DEAD

IN SEARCH OF THE DEAD

JEFFREY IVERSON

BCA

LONDON · NEW YORK · SYDNEY · TORONTO

TO

TEGWYN HUGHES

This edition published 1992 by BCA
by arrangement with BBC Books,
a division of BBC Enterprises Limited.

First published 1992
Reprinted 1993

© Jeffrey Iverson 1992

CN 8740

Photoset in Garamond by Redwood Press Limited, Melksham, Wiltshire

Printed and bound in Great Britain by
Butler & Tanner Ltd, Frome and London
Jacket printed by Belmont Press Ltd, Northampton

Acknowledgements

This book and the television series on which it is based were possible because of the efforts of many people, most of whom are mentioned in the text. Special thanks must go to Dr Ian Stevenson of the University of Virginia, USA, who helped lay the ground plan for the project and was never too busy with his own *magnum opus* to give advice and help. There was real assistance too from the Society for Psychical Research, London, and the American Society for Psychical Research, New York, whose officials were kindness itself.

The talents of many went into the television programmes, which BBC Wales had the courage to support. Mr Bill Pearce, head of Channel WXXI, Rochester, New York, was the man who finally made it all happen.

My own small team in Cardiff was director Dick Vigers, researcher Gitti Coats, and assistants Tessa Cordle and Lindsay Davies, who made it physically possible for me to complete the programmes and this manuscript. My thanks go to everyone.

Picture credits

Courtesy of the Dalai Lama nos 23 & 24; Mary Evans Picture Library no. 11; Emma Michell no. 27; Viresh Narain no. 25; National Maritime Museum no. 9; courtesy of Marion E. Nester, New York nos 13, 14, 15 & 16; Scott Pfundt no. 2; Smithsonian Institution no. 7; courtesy of the Society for Psychical Research (BBC photo) nos 12, 20 & 21. The remaining photographs were provided by the BBC.

Contents

Introduction

There is more evidence for life after death than is generally realised. Carefully pieced together over many years by individual scientists, it has led some to believe that a new science of Mind is necessary, if we are to understand the nature of our consciousness and how we fit into a universe whose ultimate reality is still a mystery.

The majority of scientists are sceptical about such claims, but in most cases they have not studied the evidence. Classical science preserves the blinkered neutrality it adopted 300 years ago, when the founding fathers, Messrs Galileo, Descartes and Newton, decreed that Science should analyse objective realities only; subjective studies, like consciousness, were non-scientific and beyond the pale. Since then, the powerful probes of science have been generally pointed away from our interior selves – but nowadays parapsychologists and others say it's time for a change, for the boundaries to be re-drawn. In the words of the British consultant neuropsychiatrist Dr Peter Fenwick:

> The old science describes brain only in terms of structure and function. We know about the red wavelength of light but have no science to tell us why we see redness. We need a science of subjective experience because today's science explains only half the truth about our nature. We need a science of Mind.

A subjective science of Mind would be a scientific revolution, made possible in part by the disarray of traditional physics. Newton's idea of the universe as a great machine, obeying precise cause-and-effect rules, like balls on a billiards table, was shown to be inadequate almost a century ago by Albert Einstein's Theory of Relativity. Also, the true nature of matter is no longer perceived as particles, playing by these same rules of billiards, but as fields of energy which seem to behave in outrageous ways: quantum physics has shown, on the smallest scale, that matter appears able to be in two places at the same time, and sometimes the experimenter, by his presence, seems to affect the outcome of his own experiments. Science seeks an overall theory to make sense of all this, and Newton definitely no longer has all the answers – the universe is a place of infinite mystery.

One speculation is that the universe might be composed of thought, which could explain how an observer might appear to interact with his experiment. If matter is a 'frozen thought' in a universe composed of 'mind-stuff,' then almost anything is possible – including the paranormal, Survival (survival of the mind after death), and all the as yet imperfectly understood phenomena mentioned in this book.

For many years the theories of the world's leading physicists have sounded strangely like old-fashioned mysticism. The notion that reality might be thought is quite similar to the Buddhist concept of the world as a place of karmic illusion. A Nobel Prize winner for physics, Professor Brian Josephson, talked to me about these new possibilities:

> In the last decade, there has been a lot of talk about connections between science and mysticism. The reaction of a vast number of scientists has been that this is nonsense, it's pseudo-science. I think this is a wrong conclusion and we will in future see this kind of thing becoming routine science. A statement often made is that when something unorthodox comes up, scientists first ignore it, and then say it's nonsense. Eventually, they say it's obvious and was obvious all the time. I think we'll get that happening in the areas you are exploring.
>
> There are all sorts of things scientists claim which are really acts of faith, as much as any religious belief. When a scientist says we understand how the brain works, or how man came into existence through natural selection, these are enormous extrapolations. The sort of thing that happens is somebody writes a computer programme which can understand simple sentences and says, 'We now understand the principle of language and how our minds work.' Or somebody else produces a theory which explains a little piece of evolution, like changes in the colour of a moth as the background changes, and scientists say, 'We understand how evolution works.'

A new, subjective science of Mind might seem a heresy to some, but they should reflect that the classical demarcation lines of science might have been much more soft-edged from the outset if Galileo and Descartes had not lived with the Holy Inquisition looking over their shoulders. Seekers after truth in the seventeenth century, who dared to advocate the study of man's inner thoughts, might quickly have been hauled off to a heresy trial and burned at the stake. Galileo came close to the flames simply by looking through his telescope at the movement of planets around the sun –

his objective observation that the earth circled the sun had the subjective implication that man's home planet was not at the centre of God's universe. In those intolerant times, subjective science was out of the question, even had they wished it – let's hope it's not the same today.

Before examining the evidence for life after death, there was an obvious preliminary question: is there any scientific sign of some quality or force within us which might be capable of surviving death of the body? Science teaches that our body is a machine made of meat, our brain a sort of computer. Everything vanishes without trace at death, or is there some alternative explanation? In the first part of this book, we scrutinise the evidence that there might be more to us than this – there might be mind as well as brain. Dr Fenwick defined the rules of this classical scientific debate:

> To talk about mind and brain being different, you have to show mind can exist on its own, is able to pass on information without the use of brain's five senses. You have to put someone in a box, seal them up so they can't get information, and somehow information is then transmitted to them by none of the known physical causes.

That's a good description of Remote Viewing, a type of experiment parapsychologists have been doing for years. We filmed a remarkably successful Remote Viewing test, where a person, shut away in a sealed room in New York, visualised a scene someone else was telepathically trying to transmit. She described and drew on paper a secret location in the city as precisely as if she had been standing on the same spot as the observer. This was done by the power of psi, the modern name for telepathy or extra-sensory perception, still sometimes known as ESP. The existence of psi has been demonstrated statistically by parapsychologists who have analysed hundreds of tests at scientific institutes in various parts of the United States.

For psi in the community, we looked at the psychics who from time to time help police investigate serious crime such as murder. The book reveals the remarkable, untold story of a Canadian psychic working on the manhunt for the murderer known as 'Son of Sam' back in the 1970s. A parapsychologist, Dr Karlis Osis, and a New York detective supervised a team of psychics trying to pinpoint the killer.

Evidence which seemed directly to support the idea of Survival came from people revived from apparent death by the techniques of modern medicine. Millions of people have had Near Death Experiences – usually they claim to leave their bodies, float through a black tunnel and enter a world of brilliant light.

Dr Melvin Morse of Seattle has studied NDEs in children and has a collection of wonderful colour drawings of the next world, made by youngsters close to death. Dr Morse is critical of scientific explanations that NDEs are either hallucinations in a dying brain or a reliving of the birth experience. He seemed to find support in the case of a woman, suffering a heart attack, who found herself floating around outside the hospital, where she noticed a tennis shoe on a distant window ledge. Her out-of-body experience might have been written off as hallucination if a hospital social worker had not recovered the shoe from the ledge!

Scientists have done surveys of apparitions which appear at times of crisis, sometimes to give a warning. A newly discovered case was on board a British warship in the Second World War, where there was an invisible presence in an operations room and a voice that warned of approaching enemy aircraft. Apparitions sometimes manifest themselves to the dying: scientists have questioned doctors and nurses in the United States and India about the experiences of dying patients. Shortly before death, many patients claim to have a visitor – a dead friend or relative who comes to take them away to the next world. Most go willingly.

Much good evidence for Survival comes from a lifetime's work by Professor Ian Stevenson of the University of Virginia. He has done thirty years of research into reincarnation cases and has files of 2500 children who claim to remember previous lives. Stevenson always considers alternatives, like fraud and hallucination, before making a judgement. He has a nucleus of about twenty-five cases where reincarnation clearly seems the likeliest explanation, and told me:

> Science should pay a lot more attention to the evidence we have pointing towards life after death. Looked at fairly, the evidence is impressive and from a variety of sources. The prevailing orthodoxy is when your brain dies your mind perishes also. That is so deeply believed that scientists fail to understand it is an assumption only and there is no reason why aspects of the mind should not survive death of the brain. But to shake this belief amongst scientists of today is extremely difficult.

Stevenson hopes to make an impact on this entrenched belief with publication of four volumes of a major scientific work – a study of birthmarks and birth defects in children who remember other lives. His new evidence is compelling: children who remember living before sometimes carry marks and deformities suffered in a previous life. In India, a boy with no fingers on his right hand remembered a life as a child whose fingers on the right hand were cut off in a fodder-chopping machine. Another child, born with almost no chin, recalled the life and death of a bandit who was hanged twice – it seems the first execution was bungled and the murderer's jaw was smashed in the process. In many of the cases Stevenson has documents and photographs confirming the injuries suffered in previous lives.

These young children sometimes start talking about another life with almost the first words they speak, and for Stevenson this is significant. Infants are unlikely to be able to concoct a story about another life from something they previously had heard or read about. This is a problem with all such adult memories, including hypnotic regressions. In some of the cases examined here, particularly of children, their precise identity has not been revealed, usually at the request of the family.

One aim of this book is to interest non-scientists in the somewhat neglected and maligned work of parapsychologists. Some have published studies of their own cases and these are listed at the back of this book. The evidence they have uncovered is startling and of value to non-scientists and scientists alike. It should cause us all to pause and think more deeply, and optimistically, about what we truly are and what may be our destiny. With television colleagues from Britain and the United States, I followed the trail of the parapsychologists across the continents of Europe, America and Asia. It was an enlightening journey 'in search of the dead.'

PART ONE

Powers of the mind

Nowadays, most people identify themselves almost exclusively with their consciousness and imagine they are only what they know about themselves. Yet anyone with even a smattering of psychology can see how limited this knowledge is. Rationalism and doctrinairism are the diseases of our time; they pretend to have all the answers. But a great deal will yet be discovered which our present limited view would have ruled out as impossible. CARL JUNG

CHAPTER ONE

A green man with wings

*Man also possesses a power by which he may see his
friends and the circumstances by which they are
surrounded, although such persons may be a
thousand miles away from him at that time.*
**PARACELSUS
(SIXTEENTH CENTURY GERMAN PHILOSOPHER)**

I s there truly some power of the mind, some inner eye which allows people to see what is happening miles away from them? In September 1990, we recorded a Remote Viewing experiment in New York which suggested that people do have such an ability.

In a tightly controlled scientific test, a stranger to New York somehow managed to beam in on Dr Nancy Sondow, an American psychologist, at a secret location in the vast city. She described telepathically what Dr Sondow was looking at – including something very individual: a statue of a large green angel with wings, which Dr Sondow happened to be standing in front of!

The scientists running the experiment were delighted, but said they would need to run more tests before they could scientifically say the subject had proven psi ability.

They were not particularly startled because they have seen similar results before and know from the statistics of many trials that Remote Viewing really works. Together we had recorded a spectacularly successful experiment, but a hit, even an absolute bull's-eye, does not in itself prove the existence of the paranormal to scientists concerned chiefly with the statistical average of many tests.

The most surprised person was the subject of the experiment, Tessa Cordle, my production assistant. In a library miles from the target site, with all of New York City and Manhattan to choose from, Tessa saw a typically English park dominated by a statue of a man with wings, an angel made of metal which was turning green. She drew pictures of this figure and other very specific aspects of the scene – all of which were found to exist at the secret location. It was a success that would have impressed a hardened cynic.

Tessa, who is from Wales, had not previously regarded herself as psychic but the scientists were keen to have an independent subject, a stranger provided by our team of outsiders. The scientists believe that Remote Viewing can be done by anyone and someone to whom New York was entirely unknown made the experiment even more convincing.

As to the filming, we recorded the full scientific experiment as it happened. There were no short cuts for television. The assessment of the Remote Viewing test was done by Dr Keith Harary, Research Director of the Institute for Advanced Psychology, San Francisco. He was unaware of the true location and compared Tessa's descriptions with four possible sites in New York, which he was told about after Tessa had recorded her test. With Tessa's drawing in one hand and notes of what she had said in the other, he had no difficulty in correctly identifying the target site, a small park next to a church.

Only if the assessor gets it right, does a Remote Viewing score scientifically as a hit. This prevents possible collusion or wishful thinking by the subject and the sender. It also means there is a straightforward one-in-four possibility that the judge may correctly select the target by chance alone.

In this case, more impressive than the odds against Dr Harary making a correct judgement, was Tessa's precise description of the target. She correctly described five different aspects of the scene, including a small building with a pointed roof and a row of small shops, one with a red and white striped awning, on the road which ran alongside the park.

Just as remarkable, she drew the major features of the scene on a single sheet of paper. There were no drawings of elements not found at the location, nor did she make any spoken references to anything not present at the target site – it was just as if Tessa had been there in person, standing alongside Dr Sondow!

Also, the location was very different from any stereotyped image of a city famous for skyscrapers and hustle and bustle. That would have been Tessa's idea of New York and yet, when she was afterwards taken to see the target site for the first and only time, she said, 'This is incredible. This is the place I saw.'

Dr Harary's verdict on her success was, 'Results like this are why people are interested in this area. There is a lot to explain, a lot to study.'

❈   ❈   ❈   ❈   ❈

We began the experiment at the headquarters of the American Society for Psychical Research (ASPR) on 73rd Street. Our volunteer was introduced to Dr Harary, a small dynamo of a psychologist with much experience of psi experiments. The two sat quietly in the library and began some conditioning exercises, a preparation for what was to come.

'I'm thinking of an object outside this room,' said Harary. 'Think of it. Draw its shape.' Tessa drew what looked like a tennis ball, slightly flattened at the top and bottom.

'Anything else about it?' asked Harary.

Tessa drew an extension near the top. It now resembled a teapot with a spout but no handle.

'Good,' said Harary. 'Let me show you what I was thinking of.' On the wall outside the room was a round light-fitting, a globe mounted on the wall by a bracket attached to its underside. It was like Tessa's spoutless teapot, but upside down!

'Let's do another,' said Harary. 'Hold out your hand, I'm going to give you something.' He placed his empty palm over Tessa's outstretched hand and said, 'There's something in my hand. What does it feel like?'

'It's soft.'

'I'm going to turn it over. What does the other side feel like?'

'It's soft too.'

'What is it?'

'It's a sponge!'

And so it was. In the kitchen, Harary showed Tessa a small sponge, used for washing dishes, which he'd put to one side. Those were the preliminaries. Now we were ready for the main event.

We set up a locked-off camera in the library, loaded with a tape that ran for twenty minutes. With no one else in the room, it recorded everything the pair said and did during the experiment, which lasted fifteen minutes. Elaborate precautions were taken to prevent any leakage of information to Tessa and Harary, shut away on the first floor.

At 2.30pm, the psychologist Dr Nancy Sondow gave me a copy of a list of four possible target sites she had drawn up with the acting Director of the ASPR, Patrice Keane. This copy, unopened, remained in my wallet until the experiment was over. I stayed on the ground floor and never went near the library. Then Nancy Sondow left the ASPR to get a cab. She numbered the sites one to four, and used a random number generator to select site three.

Tessa and Harary, isolated in the library, knew only that Nancy was going somewhere within half-an-hour's drive of the ASPR and would be on site by 3.15pm. No one inside the ASPR, not even Patrice Keane, knew exactly where Nancy had gone.

At 3.15pm Tessa began talking and drawing the things she felt she could see. Harary prompted by asking simple questions such as, 'What can you see?' At 3.30pm the core of the experiment was finished.

Tessa remained in the library to await Nancy Sondow's return. Harary joined me and the rest of the television crew on the ground floor. We drove to each site on the list in my wallet, going first to the nearest, an order worked out by our director, Jack Kelly, who was familiar with New York. At each of the four locations – Lincoln Center, Trump Towers in Manhattan, a boat-dock, and the small park – Harary recorded his assessment of how they compared with Tessa's description. A few hours later, at the final location, Harary rated the sites in order of probability. The park was his clear choice.

During the 'blind' judging of the four sites, Harary's verdict on each went as follows:

At Lincoln Center, a lively plaza dominated by a fountain, he said 'There's no statue. The buildings are fairly large, as opposed to the small structure Tessa saw. I don't see a T-shaped path here, but we have shops and an awning. There are lots of people here and she didn't see lots of people. She didn't have water and the thing she described did not look like this fountain. Not really a lot of tall trees either. I'm not powerfully gripped by this place, but it's got some subtle aspects. Let's go check on the other stuff.'

Site two was Trump Towers, a glass-fronted skyscraper reflecting the frenetic activity of a Manhattan main thoroughfare. 'I don't see any relationship to this drawing. It's very noisy, very crowded. It's not peaceful that's for sure. I don't see any statues. It doesn't really fit.'

Site three gave us another change of mood. It was the water's edge at the 79th Street boat basin. 'We're in a park-like place, and it's quiet getting here. There's no statue here, and there was no water, nothing about boats, in her description. If this were the site and you were to look for correspondences with her description, they are not here. There are a lot of people around, and I would not be big on this as the likely site.'

Finally, we visited a small park dominated by a statue called 'Peace' alongside the Cathedral of St John the Divine. We came to it last by pure coincidence, and the impact on Harary was immediate. 'It's very hard to ignore having somebody describe a statue with wings, when you find a statue with wings!'

    *   *   *   *   *

At the outset, at the ASPR, Harary gave Tessa these instructions. 'Take a deep breath, and just kind of relax. It's quite straightforward really. We'll take you to a place where you haven't been before and Nancy is there right now. So you can focus on Nancy and what she's experiencing, the sound and the smell. Just imagine yourself with her in a way, and yourself there later . . .'

The remote viewing – in the library

TESSA It's not noisy. It doesn't seem to be noisy, as if the noise is at a distance. A path I think, yes, a concrete path or a gravel path.

HARARY You kind of look around. What surprises you about it?

TESSA That it's quite peaceful considering it's surrounded by noise and traffic and goings on. Like tranquil, a small piece of quiet.

HARARY You said there was a path.

TESSA Yes.

HARARY Can you tell me anything about that path?

TESSA I think it's like a T, I think it may be a path like that (*draws a T-shaped path*).

I think there are tall trees there, but they're not close. If you look up you can see the branches coming over, but quite tall.

The assessment – at the target site

HARARY Okay, the first thing I notice as I come up this path, that does come to a kind of T – there is a statue with wings . . . there is a cement or stone walk here and there are trees around and it is peaceful here, very peaceful. It's the statue of Peace . . . tall trees are up above us because they're on higher ground.

I don't know if there's a stand down one end, the far end of the path. Maybe like a summer stand, bandstand or something white, with railings and a pointed roof ...

I think the roof is wooden and the railings are all metal and the steps are wooden ...

Well it must be a park ... it's sort of like where people go to eat their lunch, their sandwiches in the city ... you could think your own thoughts there ... it does seem vaguely British or European ... it's like one of the small parks you might come across walking through central London.

HARARY What's Nancy doing here?

TESSA Enjoying the quiet I think. It feels to me as if she's standing right here (*draws a figure on the path*).

HARARY Look around, turn around in some new direction.

TESSA I can see small shops off to the left hand side. Across, out of the park, but not that far away, there's like small delis (delicatessens) and one looks as if it's got a red and white striped canopy over it. Just a little row of shops ... sort of between the trees, but not that far away ... I'm trying to stand where she is and look around, which is not easy.

(*Looks at drawing.*)

There is a structure like that right over there in the corner of that building, sort of with that pointy wooden roof ... there is metal fencing, although not exactly the way she described it. There's another small structure over there that could also relate to this. It has steps going up.

... this is a park.

... she also described having the city sort of surrounding this park-like area ...

... and then having shops across the street, and a red and white striped awning, which I see there's a red and white striped awning. And this is definitely more red and white than the awning we saw at Lincoln Center. This is really red and white.

HARARY It's also where you're going to be. You're going to be there.

TESSA There might be a statue, like a bronze or a metal with a concrete base ... it's either something with wings, I don't know, like an angel or something. It looks like a butterfly (*points to her drawing*). It's not a butterfly, it's like something with wings and a long robe, where the metal turns a sort of green, greeny colour ... it could have been a man. This is quite tall.

HARARY (*pointing to drawing of structure with pointed roof*). Is that the same general location?

TESSA It could be directly in front of that. I'm not really sure where that is. It's somewhere there.

HARARY What do you think it's about?

TESSA Just a small park that was built when the residential area around it was built, as a recreational ground for the early century ... you don't feel closed in by the sky-scrapers or any buildings there ... just a plane going across the sky. It's quite unobstructed.

HARARY You've never been here before.

TESSA No.

HARARY Good. Are there any people around?

TESSA A couple walking dogs, but not a lot of people.

... well, it's very hard to ignore having somebody describe a statue with wings and finding a statue with wings! In fact, I would have to say the statue is a very prominent feature of the site. It is a park, the statue is turning green, and she did mention the statue had green to it ... Look at those wings. God, really striking! (*looks at drawing*). Here we have a picture of wings, this could be the head. Obviously, this would have to be the first choice.

So we have the trees, the wings, the awning, the stores, the park-like setting, the statue, green on the statue, the sort of small T-shaped walk coming into this place.

I'm going to have to rate this number one. Lincoln Center would probably be number two, the boat basin three and Trump Tower fourth.

But this is a big number one. I mean this has so many correspondences that it will be interesting if this is not the place!

After the judging, Jack Kelly telephoned Dr Sondow at the ASPR to ask where we should meet. She said the park was the target site. Only then were we sure the experiment had been successful. Tessa arrived at the park with Dr Sondow, and had not been told this was the target site. Immediately, Harary asked, 'Does this look familiar?'

'Yes', said Tessa, physically standing in that park for the first time in her life. 'It looks very familiar ... the wings – it's quiet – that looks like my bandstand!'

Dr Sondow confirmed that she had stood in the spot marked by Tessa on the drawing of the path. She had also looked further afield, at peacocks in another area, but they were not visible from where we were standing. All three participants in the Remote Viewing experiment, viewer, sender and judge, compared notes.

Harary remarked on the small pointed structure, separated from where they were standing by a metal fence. There were steps in the foreground, as described by Tessa. Tessa noted that the statue and the small building were in a direct line with the point where she had seen Dr Sondow standing on the path. This was as she had predicted.

Tessa was standing on the path, on the spot where she had drawn Dr Sondow looking at the statue, when Harary again asked Tessa to turn around and look the other way, as he had done earlier in the ASPR library. 'I have something interesting to show you. There's something behind you that you ought to see.' She turned round and was visibly startled. 'Oh my goodness, that's incredible ... the shop with the red and white striped awning ... the canopy ... that's incredible!'

Twenty-four hours after the test, Harary summed up the experiment.

It's always tempting when you get a particularly striking result, or set of results, to jump to conclusions and make extreme statements about the nature of consciousness and reality. I don't want to do that. What we have here is something very suggestive of some additional level of communication or perception, beyond that with which we are familiar. Our experiment with Tessa was carefully done, but it's not appropriate to draw gigantic conclusions from one trial.

Of course, there were really striking features, like the statue with wings and the shop with a red and white striped awning that she described. But the really important thing about what we did was that we did not bring in one of our own people, or somebody who has been doing this for years. Apparently, whatever is going on in this area of perception is not limited to some special, unique group of people, different to the rest of us, called psychics.

What we are looking at here is some aspect of our psychological functioning. Some way we respond to other people and to the world around us. Psi is apparently a kind of information process, an ability we don't understand at this point. As to who has this ability, the answer is 'us' – human beings.

I was intrigued by Harary's reference to psychics. Not many years ago, he had some reputation himself for psi ability, and here he was insisting it was a skill we all might have to a greater or lesser extent. But if psychics are individuals in whom psi is particularly highly developed, might they not provide good evidence of this power of the mind that appears capable of transcending the normal range of our five senses?

The ASPR in New York turned out to be the perfect place to study psychics in action, on a project recorded by trained observers. It had been at the centre of a manhunt by a team of psychics searching for one of the most wanted murderers of modern times – the Son of Sam!

CHAPTER TWO

The psychic and the Son of Sam

Spontaneous psi experiences have been of practical value in daily affairs. PROFESSOR J. B. RHINE

The search for the killer known as Son of Sam was at its frantic peak in the summer of 1977. New York City was gripped by the same hysteria as Victorian London in the days of Jack the Ripper. The murderer seemed able to strike at will, killing and maiming young people, usually as they sat in parked cars. As Son of Sam continued to gun down his victims, a Canadian psychic, Terry Marmoreo, gave details about him in a series of telephone calls to a New York detective, Rodney Roncoglio, and a parapsychologist, Dr Karlis Osis, who were working as a team on the fringe of the official manhunt.

The psychic claimed Son of Sam was a postman, white and aged about thirty. She described where he worked and marked the place on a street map of New York. She said he drove an old Ford and made two attempts to read the number on the licence plates.

None of this information directly helped to catch David Berkowitz, better known as Son of Sam, who was arrested outside his home on 11 August 1977, after a routine police check on a parking ticket issued near the scene of one of the murders. However, in hindsight it is interesting to note the extent to which Berkowitz resembled the psychic's description. He was a postman, white and in his mid-twenties. The post office where he worked was within ten blocks of the pencil dot on the map – very close considering the size of New York. Even the outside of the building was as the psychic described: what she had seen as a huge bird hovering over the killer's workplace turned out to be a giant logo of an eagle, symbol of the US postal service.

Berkowitz's car was a Ford as predicted. The number plate given by the psychic, although not absolutely correct, was a good match to the number of the killer's car – so close the detective says any experienced officer who had that information and saw Berkowitz's car near the Bronx or Queens districts would probably have requested police back up and stopped and interrogated the driver!

Might the police have caught Son of Sam months or even victims earlier if they'd listened to the psychic? There were extenuating circumstances, good reasons why detective Roncoglio wasn't able to rush out, find the right post office, check the staff lists and identify Berkowitz from his car number plate.

For one thing, all the pin-point, accurate information was buried in a mass of psychic outpouring that was often irrelevant and mostly wrong. Roncoglio and Dr Osis, Research Director of the American Society for Psychical Research, were dealing not with one psychic but with seven! Only when Berkowitz was caught and the facts of his life known, could Dr Osis and the detective see clearly that the Canadian housewife, Terry Marmoreo, was the one psychic producing 'real psi.' The descriptions from the other six were mostly wide of the mark.

Another handicap was that the police chief leading the investigation was barely tolerant of psychics being allowed near the case. Roncoglio and Dr Osis were kept informed, had access to evidence, and were given limited help, but they were essentially on their own. No manpower was available to help check possible leads thrown up by the psychics. Sorting the psi-wheat from the chaff was a monumental task.

Despite the difficulties, Dr Osis and Roncoglio were closer to the killer than they knew. While Berkowitz was still driving his Ford every day to his post office in the Bronx, Roncoglio was checking out another post office in the same area, closer to the dot on the map.

If the detective had chanced to visit the true location he might have noticed the building matched not only Terry Marmoreo's description but that of another psychic, Irene Beckman, who also said Son of Sam was a postman! If the detective had caught sight of Berkowitz's car outside the building, the search might have been over – but that's an awful lot of 'ifs.'

Millions of words, in books and articles, have been written about the investigation, capture and trial of David Berkowitz. None tells the story of Detective Roncoglio and Dr Osis's team of psychics – in particular, Terry Marmoreo the housewife from Canada who tried to unmask Son of Sam.

It was too good a chance for our television series to miss. Psi ability, outside the laboratory, could be measured against the records of one of the most intensive police investigations of the century. We studied photocopies of the detective's original note-books of statements Terry

Marmoreo made before Son of Sam was apprehended. There were also the research notes of Dr Osis, a respected scientist, vastly experienced at working with psychics and police.

In September 1990, we interviewed Dr Osis and ex-detective Roncoglio, who had left the force four years earlier to start his own business. Later that day, Terry Marmoreo flew down from Canada to the New York headquarters of the American Society for Psychical Research, where we reconstructed some of the dramatic telephone calls she had made to that building.

First, Dr Osis introduced her to the detective she knew as a friend, but had never met – he had always been just a voice on the telephone. A hug and a kiss, and the Canadian psychic said the burly ex-cop was exactly as she had imagined.

✳   ✳   ✳   ✳   ✳

Son of Sam's reign of terror began on 29 July 1976, when eighteen-year-old Donna Lauria, a medical technician, was shot dead in a car outside her home in the Bronx. Her boyfriend was wounded in the leg.

Over the next year, a further six young people, four women and two men, were killed and seven others wounded. Most were couples in parked cars. The girls were usually shot first, at point-blank range in the head, always with bullets from a .44 Bulldog revolver. Of the victims who escaped death, a number were seriously hurt. One is in a wheelchair for life, another has a metal plate in his head, and one young man was blinded. In all, there were thirteen victims killed or wounded.

At first the New York murderer was known at 'the .44 killer', until he began writing letters to New York columnist Jimmy Breslin of the *Daily News* and signing them 'Son of Sam.'

> I'm just dropping you a line to let you know that I appreciate your interest in those recent and horrendous .44 killings ... You can forget about me if you like because I don't care for publicity. However, you must not forget Donna Lauria and you cannot let the people forget her either. She was a very sweet girl but Sam's a thirsty lad and he won't let me stop killing until he gets his fill of blood.

There are echoes of Jack the Ripper in these letters and a book about the London killer was eventually found in Berkowitz's apartment. Son of Sam was an exhibitionist, who loved to play to the gallery.

Mr Breslin, sir, don't think that because you haven't heard from me for a while that I went to sleep. No, rather I am still here. Like a spirit roaming the night. Thirsty, hungry, seldom stopping to rest, anxious to please Sam. I love my work. Now the void has been filled.

New York panicked. The number of police working full-time on the manhunt, Operation Omega, built up to 300. Discos in the Bronx and Queens districts, scenes of all the early shootings, were deserted. The killer seemed to move with impunity, always a jump ahead of police stake-outs. Policemen in the Bronx were ordered to bring in their weapons for inspection – Son of Sam was so elusive, it was feared he might be a lawman!

In the *New York Post*, columnist Steve Dunleavy wrote, 'We had pure panic. The city was exploding around us.' Telephone calls from the public to the police about Son of Sam rose to 1800 a day. Newspaper headlines spoke of 'a city under siege.' Many young people were afraid to leave their homes. Son of Sam kept up the psychological pressure.

The killer wrote to Breslin:

... You will see my handiwork at
the next job.
Remember Ms Lauria. Thank you
In their blood
and
from the gutter.
Sam's Creation .44

Not since the Boston Strangler murdered thirteen women in the 1960s had a city been so obsessed with a serial killer. Detective Roncoglio of the New York Police Department lived in the Bronx and was as keen as anyone to catch the murderer. Donna Lauria, the first victim, was a friend and Judy Placido, seriously wounded in June 1977, was the sister of a friend.

The detective, as part of a police training course, was writing a paper on Psychic Phenomena, and met parapsychologist Dr Osis in April 1977. They discussed the murders and Dr Osis suggested his team of psychics might join forces with Roncoglio in the search for the killer.

A meeting was fixed with Deputy Inspector Timothy Dowd, the police chief in charge of the investigation. It was not a success. Dowd's view was that if psychics had any real powers, they'd be in Las Vegas making a fortune at roulette!

But the Mayor's Department and the Press were clamouring for an arrest and there was an air of desperation at police headquarters. The psychics never became part of the official investigation, but Roncoglio was allowed to carry on liaising with Dr Osis and there was limited co-operation from the police department.

To give the psychics a direct link to the murders, Roncoglio arranged for them to handle clothing worn by victims. Dr Alex Tanous, a psychic with whom Dr Osis frequently worked, was taken to police headquarters and handled bullets from one of the bodies. Rolling them in his palm, Dr Tanous described the killer, while a police artist drew a sketch. It led nowhere. One of the psychics enlisted was the Canadian Terry Marmoreo, after a district attorney's officer said she had helped solve an arson case in the Bronx, where a night club burned down and people died.

Psychometry, the technique of using an object as a psychic link to the killer and the victims, produced dramatic results. Terry Marmoreo was sent a small, blood-soaked fragment from the inside of a victim's purse. She was also given a street map of New York, and a photograph of a murder scene.

We filmed a re-enactment of the relevant telephone call, using dialogue from notes taken at the time. Dr Osis was adept at motivating the psychic, just as he had been in 1977. His voice was insistent, full of purpose.

'Come on Terry, that is the blood of an innocent girl you are holding in your hand. Can't you feel it? Can you see her? You see him now, don't you? What is he doing?'

Terry's face, in close-up, was viewed through the camera lens by videographer Doug Steffer, who said afterwards, 'I got goose bumps watching her face. It changed like she was seeing him all over again.' She confirmed that the compelling voice of Dr Osis had recreated the atmosphere of those 1977 calls when receiver in one hand and a small piece of bloodstained cloth in the other, she had tried in her mind's eye to catch sight of the murderer.

'You see him, Terry – where does he go?' persisted Dr Osis. 'Take the map that's in front of you – look at the map – where is he now?'

She ran her finger-tips across the surface of the map, making circles that became smaller. Dr Osis repeated his demands. The finger stopped.

'He's here!'

'Take a pencil and mark it on the map,' said Dr Osis. The psychic did as she was asked.

'Now Terry, be very sure. Is this where he lives, or where he works, or where he has committed murder?'

'It's where he works!'

When the map reached Dr Osis a dot was pencilled in an area of the Bronx, one of the five boroughs that comprise New York, one of the world's largest cities, with a population of eight millions. The Bronx was certainly the district where most of the shootings occurred. A likely place to choose perhaps, but the Bronx covers over 40 square miles, and had one and a half million inhabitants in 1970. That pencil mark was a needle in a haystack, but it was closer to the true location than anybody realised.

Working from the map and Terry's belief that Son of Sam was a postman, a view independently put forward by Irene Beckman, another psychic, Roncoglio in 1977 visited a different post office in the Bronx. It was on the corner of Jerome Street, and he went there because Jerome was a name Terry had once mentioned. But the detective could make no other connections between the location and the psychics.

And then, suddenly in the summer of 1977, Roncoglio and Dr Osis were told it was all over – the police had captured Son of Sam with no help from the psychics.

On 31 July, the killer had changed tactics. As police intensified surveillance in the Bronx and Queens, he struck in Brooklyn. He shot dead Stacy Moskowitz, aged 20, and blinded her boyfriend. It was Son of Sam's undoing.

That day a police patrol in Brooklyn had put a ticket on a cream coloured Ford Galaxy, illegally parked by a fire hydrant, close to the scene of the killing. A routine follow up on the ticket took ten days, but led to Berkowitz's car, parked outside his apartment building in Pine Street, Yonkers, on 10 August.

Peering through the car window, a policeman saw the stock of a machine gun protruding from a duffel bag on the back seat. Detective Zigo let himself into the car and found a letter in the glove compartment, addressed to Police Chief Dowd, head of Operation Omega. Handwritten, it promised an attack by Son of Sam at an exclusive summer resort in Long Island.

The car was kept under observation for hours. The police operation was nearly ruined when a neighbour looked at the car and was instantly surrounded by officers with drawn revolvers. But Berkowitz, in his seventh floor apartment, was unaware of all this.

At ten o'clock that night, he came down and sat behind the wheel, ready to drive off. He was ringed by police pointing guns at his head. Reports of his arrest say he smiled and said, 'Well, you've got me.' In the back of the car was a sub-machine gun. Son of Sam, as his letter made clear, was on his way to a discotheque, to kill as many youngsters as he could. It was intended to be his most spectacular crime so far.

His Bulldog .44 revolver was in the car, so was a pile of newspaper cuttings about his exploits, a toothbrush, a deodorant spray and a pair of dirty underpants. Reporter Breslin wrote, 'The inside of his car was like the inside of his head.'

When Roncoglio and Dr Osis heard the news that the captured suspect Berkowitz was a postman at the main post office on 148th Street in the Bronx, they decided to make a visit, out of curiosity.

'It was only a short walk from the post office I'd seen already,' Roncoglio said. 'When we got there, we were stunned. I'd never understood Terry's references to a peacock and a brightly coloured bird. But there on the wall was a huge logo of the postal service – an eagle in red, white, blue and gold. Karlis kept slapping his knee and saying "There it is – that's Terry's peacock, our big bird!"'

In numerous telephone sessions, Terry had referred to a peacock, a large brightly coloured bird, towering over Son of Sam. She once said in her stream of consciousness way, 'Screaming peacock – maybe his logo – very dark colours – don't tell my mother – a peacock – gold ankh – stream of light – pictures on walls – peacock or some other emblem sewn on his clothes.'

The huge eagle is there today, although not quite as colourful as in 1977. Early in 1990, the post office took away the circle of gold stars that had surrounded this enormous picture which looms over the main entrance. The likeness to a peacock, with colours streaming from its tail, is reinforced by a golden statue of an eagle, mounted on top of a flag pole in the forecourt – from this bird's tail stream the stars and stripes of the American flag.

Terry had given them other information about Son of Sam's job. Roncoglio said, and his notes bear him out, 'Almost from the very beginning, Terry believed the killer was a postman. When I asked her why, she said she could hear keys jingling and there was an emblem or insignia on the man's sleeve. People were pushing things like golf carts about.'

Roncoglio and Dr Osis took our television team inside the post office where Berkowitz had worked sorting letters. Some post office workers had insignia on their sleeves, and carts full of letters and parcels trundled about. Bunches of keys jingled on the belts of postmen who came and went at collection times. The keys open mail boxes around the city.

Dr Osis told me that another psychic, Irene Beckman, had in some ways been more accurate than Terry Marmoreo in describing where Son of Sam worked. She correctly said there was a garage opposite, and described the post office in some detail.

Beckman said that on the outside was a statue of 'a hero' coming out of a wall. Today, there is still, on the front of the post office, a huge white stone figure in bas-relief: Noah releasing a dove. This is another symbol of the postal service, and the mood of the sculpture is certainly heroic. Beckman said that her 'hero' appeared to be holding a gun, pointed at the sky. Noah has one arm bent at the elbow with two fingers pointed at heaven – it looks like a man holding a revolver!

This meant that two psychics had said the killer was a postman. Each had picked out singular, different features of his place of work, and one had marked its approximate location on a map. This seemed remarkable to me, but, according to the detective, the most potentially useful information was the number plate given by Terry Marmoreo.

When captured, Berkowitz was driving a six-year-old cream-coloured Ford Galaxy. Terry had said he had an old 'green' Ford – there is some debate now whether, over the telephone, the word 'cream' was mistaken for 'green.'

More significantly, the number of the licence plate on Berkowitz's Ford in August when he was arrested was 561 XLB. This compares with 650 XL, visualised by Terry for Dr Osis on 24 June. This means Terry had given two of the three letters with perfect accuracy, and two of the three numbers, the 5 and 6, although they were transposed.

On 2 July, she tried again for Roncoglio and said it was 366 XLA. One of three numbers, the 6, was now perfectly placed and so were two of the three letters. All three licence plates were obviously fairly similar, but what inferences can we draw from that?

Outside Berkowitz's old apartment block, where they have changed the street numbers to try to live down the notoriety, I asked Roncoglio: if the killer hadn't been trapped by something as simple as a parking violation, could the psychics have led police to his door?

The best chance, he said, was the number plate. The other hits were interesting but their relevance was realised only after the killer was caught. Taking the number 366 XLA and comparing it with the real 561 XLB, he said a trained officer would treat Terry's version as a partial sighting by a witness. He would know that 3 can be mistaken for 5, the lower half being identical. Also, A and B are similar, and would be possible alternatives in his mind.

'The plates are so alike that if I had seen Berkowitz's car in the Bronx or in Queens, I'd have immediately requested back-up. I'd have stopped the car and questioned the driver. Any experienced officer would do the same,' said Roncoglio.

Statistically, it is impossible to compute the odds against Terry coming up with her versions of the number plate by pure chance. There are so many imponderables. The odds would be high if one assumed she had no preconceived ideas about what numbers or letters could appear in a New York plate of three numbers and three figures. But was that the case?

Contrary to what some New Yorkers told me, New York number plates in 1977 were not created on a random basis. Perhaps Terry Marmoreo, on previous visits to New York, had unconsciously noted some typical combinations of letters and numbers used in the city. The system used is that the first two letters denote the district where the car was registered. Terry had those two letters XL absolutely correct and that is the mark of Westchester County, which contains Yonkers, where Berkowitz lived.

It should be remembered that no one had known Son of Sam lived in Yonkers, until he was caught. None of the killings took place there. Remember too, no one had previously speculated that he drove a Ford. Indeed, the police for months were looking for a yellow Volkswagen, according to the newspapers.

In one sense, anyone trying to guess the number of a car in New York City in 1977 had eight million cars registered in New York State and one and three-quarter million, registered in the city, to choose from – a total of almost ten million vehicles.

Thomas D. Appleton, a communications officer at the Department of Motor Vehicles, explained the licensing system and said it was a popular misconception amongst New Yorkers that plate numbers were randomly turned out by a computer. In 1973 there had been a major re-organisation of new and existing numbers, indexed by county. Had Berkowitz's car been registered in the Bronx, the favoured location for the killer, the first two letters would have been in the range XA to XJ. So the letter X was perhaps guessable. With a little knowledge of the registration system, the odds against getting close can be much reduced.

On the other hand, no one knows if Terry had access to that information, and she was making her forecasts remotely from Canada. Her number plate was close enough to the real one to impress a seasoned detective.

There are other aspects of the Marmoreo calls worth keeping in perspective. Too much should not be made of her correct statement that Berkowitz was a white man, five feet ten inches tall, aged about 30. There had been a few published eye-witness accounts of Son of Sam at the scene of murders. It was quite well reported that he was believed to be a young white.

Despite these reservations, it was impossible not to be impressed by the accurate overall picture Terry Marmoreo gave. She knew he was a postman and she marked his post office approximately on a map with a good description of his car and its number plate. Other details too, from the notebooks of the witnesses, supported the strong impression that by a paranormal way of seeing, she had homed in on the man they called Son of Sam. Compare some of her other recorded statements with the facts that subsequently became known about the killer.

Terry Marmoreo's statements	Facts about the killer
There is a police file on him ... a picture in a small brick station house ... an auxiliary policeman.	Berkowitz was an auxiliary policeman at the 45th Precinct, the Bronx, in 1970. This building is partially red-brick.
I see him running down Broadway ...	Berkowitz lived in a loop road just off North Broadway.
There is an apartment building. The number is 89 Maple Avenue.	He lived in an apartment building on Pine Street.
Two small children are involved with this man, they trigger his emotions. He has a sister.	He had a sister, who had two small children. Berkowitz was said to have shown real affection for these children.
He has a fear of dogs. He is involved with demons.	Berkowitz disliked dogs and had shot several, close to where he lived, killing some and wounding others. He said demons spoke to him through a large dog owned by a man called Sam Carr. They gave him instructions about the murders.
The house is in a middle class, residential neighbourhood – taxi stand, yellow cabs on the corner, Co-op on the cab ... some slum areas around, but not any close by. There's a school not far from him, also a Baptist church in the area, slanted roof, wood ... near a park on an incline, fixed up with grass, there's a river that's very wide near the park, trees that are very short but bushy ... he lives across the road from that park.	Berkowitz had worked as a driver for the Co-op cab company in the Bronx, before joining the postal service. He then lived in Co-op City, a middle-class residential area of the Bronx with slum houses nearby. He had joined the Baptist Church near his home. 'A good description of Co-op City where Berkowitz had lived,' Roncoglio wrote in the margin of his transcript of this telephone conversation.

He was white but a member of a minority group ... 'Shalom.'

He has been in a child shelter ... he is a loner ... has Swastika and Nazi symbols at home.

Berkowitz was Jewish.

Berkowitz was illegitimate, put up for adoption and eventually brought up by adoptive parents. He was regarded as a very solitary person with almost no close friends. He possessed Nazi symbols.

There were other minor correspondences, such as correctly stating the killer had held numerous jobs in recent years. There were also plenty of inaccuracies – times when Terry was wide of the mark, as with her repeated suggestion that Son of Sam was somehow connected with a hospital.

Dr Osis says all this is to be expected. 'No one has ever been known to produce only pure ESP information. It is always a blend of correct impressions, along with memories, fantasies and guesses. True statements do emerge in the rubble of trivialities and erroneous ideas that can mislead the investigator.' In the Son of Sam case, Dr Osis believes Terry Marmoreo produced enough correct information amongst the rubble, to demonstrate that real psi was at work.

Ex-detective Roncoglio is more sceptical about the paranormal and the possibility of psi being of much practical help in police work. But one incident, from the days with Dr Osis and the psychics, sticks in his memory.

Roncoglio had called at the American Society for Psychical Research to talk to Dr Osis, but found him engaged in an experiment with Dr Alex Tanous, a psychic who was helping in the Son of Sam case. From a soundproofed, windowless cubicle some distance away from Dr Osis in the control room, Dr Tanous was attempting to project himself out-of-body into a laboratory where various electronic instruments would try to detect his presence.

It was fascinating to watch and Roncoglio stood in the open doorway watching Dr Osis. Over the intercom he heard Dr Tanous say, 'Right, I'm leaving my body now ... I'm coming along the corridor ... excuse me Rodney ...'

Roncoglio politely stepped to one side. Then he realised what had happened! Dr Tanous might have somehow known the detective was in the building, but how could he have known, from his windowless room, that Roncoglio was blocking the way to the laboratory? The detective has never forgotten the incident.

He also recalls, with a laugh, what it was like to work with Terry Marmoreo. Sometimes she would ring him at two o'clock in the morning to say Son of Sam was in a car cruising near Roncoglio's home in the Bronx! The detective always dressed hurriedly and prowled the streets in his car. Roncoglio has an open mind about psychics, but was always certain how much he wanted Son of Sam behind bars. No effort was ever too great.

Today, David Berkowitz is safely behind bars, not very far into a 315-year prison sentence. But we may not have heard the last of the Son of Sam.

The detective gave me a book, published in 1987, *The Ultimate Evil* by Maury Terry, a respected investigative journalist, who claims Berkowitz did not act alone, but was part of a Satanic cult known as 'the Process.' The evidence persuaded Queens District Attorney, John J. Santucci, to re-open the Son of Sam case. Roncoglio too takes the content of this book very seriously.

At the time of the killings, Terry Marmoreo told the detective and Dr Osis that Son of Sam was part of a Satanic cult and was involved in devil worship and ritual murder. She even attempted to put names to some of Son of Sam's accomplices. If there truly was a cult, the Canadian psychic might have been even more accurate than she has been given credit for. So too might some of the other psychics.

CHAPTER THREE

A casebook of psychic detectives

*On the pure assumption that a few ESP subjects may
be able to develop conscious control of their ability
... crime on any scale could hardly exist with its
cloak of invisibility thus removed. Graft, exploitation
and suppression could not continue if the dark plots
of wicked men were to be laid bare.*

PROFESSOR J. B. RHINE

Psychics, seers, sensitives, mediums, call them what you will, have
been around a long time. In the Bible, Joseph was a psychic who
predicted famines for the Pharoah of Egypt, and became wealthy
and powerful by his visionary powers or psi.

Today, such people occasionally help police with major crimes. Some
have been credited with more success than Terry Marmoreo had in the Son
of Sam murder hunt. Their cases are worth study. If there is such a thing as
second sight, some paranormal way of knowing, a dimension beyond the
range of our normal senses, can these psychic detectives provide the
evidence to prove it to the rest of us?

Most people probably believe they have little or no psychic power – in
the land of second sight, we are mostly blind. Not so, says Dr Osis, who
agrees with Dr Keith Harary, the judge in our successful Remote Viewing
experiment, that we all have some psi powers. We just don't realise it.

Dr Osis has worked on thirty major investigations in a six-year study of
psychics involved in solving serious crimes or finding lost aeroplanes. He
says psi powers occur in everyday life as telepathic insights – something as
simple as knowing who is on the telephone before you answer the call. In
police work, a detective who follows a hunch or relies on instinct may be
demonstrating psi.

Amateur psychics sometimes triumph where professionals have failed.
Dr Osis was once asked to help find a lost plane, presumed crashed,
carrying businessmen from Bridgeport, Connecticut, to Albany, New

York. Psychics scoured the scene from the air – one pinpointed a mountain, which was painstakingly searched, but nothing was ever found. Then an office worker, who believed he had some psi ability, predicted that in the autumn, the plane would be found, miles off course, between Bridgeville and Zoar in north-east Massachusetts. That is exactly what happened – the wreckage became visible from the air five miles east of Bridgeville once the leaves were off the trees.

Over the years, there have been many such claims of paranormal powers and sometimes there are witnesses whose scientific standing and personal integrity are so widely acknowledged that it would be foolish to treat the case lightly.

In November 1884, for example, one of the founding fathers of American psychology, Professor William James of Harvard University, stopped his open carriage at Shaker Bridge, a wooden structure over a river at Enfield, New Hampshire, where he witnessed a strange and dramatic scene. Standing on the bridge, staring at the dark surface of the river, was a middle-aged woman and a group of police officers. Suddenly the blackness of the water was broken by the head of a police diver, who surfaced, gasping for air.

'Yes,' he told the sheriff, 'the girl is down there, trapped on the bottom, face down, arms spread.' He looked at the woman and said, 'The body is just how she said it would be.' Professor James was watching the climax to a three-day search for Bertha Huse, a missing girl. A hundred searchers had combed the banks of a lake, into which the river ran, without success.

The woman on the bridge was Mrs Titus, a psychic from Lebanon, five miles from Enfield. The previous night, in a dream, she had seen the girl's body under Shaker Bridge, floating face down, below the surface, arms and legs spread-eagled, hair caught in branches on the river bottom. She hurried to Enfield, took the sheriff and his men to the bridge and pointed out where the body was 'to within an inch.'

The diver was particularly impressed. 'Corpses in the water don't frighten me, but I feared the woman on the bridge. How can she come five miles and tell me where the body is? And it was in a deep hole, head downwards and in the dark – I could hardly see it.'

James wrote up his account in the very first volume of the Proceedings of the American Society for Psychical Research. Mrs Titus had convinced him of the reality of psychic phenomena and set him off on a lifetime of research, including his famous investigation of the American medium Mrs Leonore E. Piper.

Of course, if all psychics managed to hit the jackpot the way Mrs Titus did on Shaker Bridge, the debate about psi might have long since ended in their favour. The fact is many get it wrong and even psychics who make correct predictions can also produce reams of incorrect information. Sceptics might say Mrs Titus was an eccentric who had a dream that coincidentally turned out to be true. Against that, there have been many others like Mrs Titus.

In general, psychics are called in by police as a desperate last resort in the investigation of serious crime where conventional methods are not getting results, like the Son of Sam case. On the other hand, it is also true that psychics, although not called in regularly, are used more often than the public is told. If a medium helps locate a body or murder weapon, the police avoid courtroom complications by saying simply that 'acting upon information received' they recovered the weapon or found the body. Prosecutors and policemen don't encourage the belief that unorthodox methods of detection are used. In court, the evidence of a psychic might be open to challenge and could even be inadmissible.

There have been famous psi-detectives in recent times, and Dr Osis has worked with several. His favourite was the Dutchman Gerard Croiset, who died in 1980 at the age of 71, and was perhaps the most celebrated of all.

Shy and not well educated, Croiset was brought up at Enschede, Holland. He showed some clairvoyant ability as a child, but his talent could not earn him a living in his early years. He was a bankrupt ex-grocer, aged 36, married with a family, when he was discovered in 1946 by two eminent parapsychologists, Professor W. H. C. Tenhaeff of the University of Utrecht, Holland, and Professor Hans Bender of the University of Freiburg, Germany.

Tenhaeff did several months of psi tests on Croiset in Utrecht and said he was one of the most remarkable subjects he had met. A notable career was about to take off. He recommended Croiset to the Dutch police, who tentatively used him to trace missing children and catch minor criminals. He was soon invited to help solve major crimes like murder.

One of Croiset's early successes was at Wierden, Holland. This was a case of a girl who had been savagely attacked at night and beaten unconscious with blows from a hammer. Croiset never met the victim but was given the hammer to hold. He grasped the handle and said the man who struck the blows was aged about thirty, tall and dark, with a deformed ear – he said the hammer belonged to an older man, living in an old cottage frequently visited by the attacker.

This was almost Croiset's first major case, and no one took him too seriously. On the say-so of an unknown psychic, no real search was launched for a man with a deformed ear – it was too melodramatic to be true!

Months later, police arrested a twenty-nine year-old man on a different charge. An alert policeman noticed his deformed left ear and recalled Croiset's description of the assailant in the unsolved hammer case. Under questioning, the suspect admitted attacking the girl with a hammer, taken from the cottage of an older friend. Exactly as the psychic had said!

Croiset gained initial fame for locating missing persons. He was once consulted by telephone about a lost child, and predicted her body would be found in a canal near Eindhoven in three days' time. Three days later the girl's body was fished from the Eindhoven canal.

Dr Osis said some of Croiset's greatest successes were over the telephone, just like Terry Marmoreo. An American academic was given proof of Croiset's long distance ESP. Dr Walter Sandelius, Professor of Political Science at the University of Kansas, telephoned Croiset in Holland. He was concerned about his daughter who had disappeared from a hospital in Topeka, Kansas, a week earlier. From thousands of miles away, the psychic correctly described the hospital grounds and said the girl had left there, hitching lifts in a car and lorry. She was now in a city, looking at boats bobbing on the water – and would return home in six days. She was safe and well.

Six days later, the impatient Professor was making another call to Holland, when his daughter walked through the front door. She had hitched rides, as described by Croiset, and six days earlier had been watching boats bobbing on the ocean at Corpus Christi, Texas.

In the early 1960s, Croiset, already a celebrity, was brought to America to try to catch the Boston Strangler. He attended a meeting at the Waldorf Astoria Hotel, New York, with Dr Osis and Lieutenant Cronin of the Bureau of Missing Persons. Dr Osis recalls, 'Croiset was trying to impress us with his philosophy, which was just watered down Spinosa. Then he said to the policeman, "You have some interesting objects in your briefcase".'

Croiset said the documents in the case involved state security, part of a very recent crime, the murder of an important man. The policeman was astonished. He had just come from Central Park, where a professor of physics at Columbia University had been shot dead. The professor had been working on a secret project for the government and bloodstained papers, scattered on the ground from his open briefcase, were labelled 'Top Secret.' US intelligence agencies were already fearful of KGB involvement and a spy scandal.

Croiset was asked to assist this murder hunt. He said jealousy was a possible motive, and he spoke of the professor's involved social life. He described in great detail a restaurant in New York, where the physicist might have met his murderer. The restaurant sounded European and very unusual, with archways and a courtyard. A sceptical Lieutenant Cronin, born and raised in New York, said he was sure there was no such restaurant in the city.

Croiset, unperturbed, set off in a police car, on a tour which ended precisely at the restaurant as described. This turned out to be a regular rendezvous for the physicist and some of his friends! The psychic seemed to be picking up lots of leads and gave a dramatic account of the dead professor's personal life, including the idea that he might have been held prisoner at an address in New York, before escaping. It all came to nothing. There were suspects, but Croiset's snippets of information, sometimes startlingly accurate, did not pinpoint a killer.

Then, two years later, two black youths, arrested for something else, confessed that they had shot the professor for money. It was a straight-forward mugging.

Dr Osis says this is typical of the problems faced in working with psychics. Much of the information is imagination and only a certain percentage is pure clairvoyance. Croiset had some real insights into the life of the professor, but they had not been relevant to finding his killers. The psychic had led police along a false trail.

Croiset was not regarded as a professional psychic. He never demanded a fee for police work, usually he even paid his own travelling expenses, but he charged for private consultations, and ran a spiritual healing clinic to support his family – being a psychic detective was almost a sideline.

He gained a reputation for being able to see the future by a series of experiments known as 'chair tests'. Chairs were numbered around a table for a conference and Croiset would write a description of the person he thought would occupy each chair in a few days' time. Seating arrange-ments were always random. His notes were sealed in envelopes to be opened after guests had seated themselves in any chair that took their fancy. Croiset's descriptions were read aloud, and Professor Tenhaeff said the psychic was often remarkably accurate.

Precautions were taken to make sure the notes in the envelope were not tampered with, nor the seating arrangements rigged. Croiset made his predictions at times varying from one hour to 26 days before a meeting. In one successful test, Croiset wrote, 'I see nothing'. This was for one chair out of thirty which ended up vacant because a guest failed to turn up.

He once predicted a chair would be taken by a woman with a scarred face – the woman who sat down had facial injuries from a car crash a few months earlier. Sometimes, Croiset's notes included information about a person's past, present or future, and were said to be uncannily accurate.

But chair tests were not always successful. They worked in Holland, Austria, Italy and Switzerland, but in New York the experiment flopped. Croiset's descriptions matched only a handful of cases. Witnesses said the psychic was undismayed and spent a long time trying to work out what had gone wrong.

Perhaps it is that psi cannot be turned on and off like a light switch, even by the acknowledged best in the world! Some psychics, of course, claim complete control over their ability. Dr Osis says the celebrated psychic Eileen Garrett scoffed when asked what states were favourable to psi. 'I can sit on the George Washington Bridge and do it,' she said, referring to the busiest bridge in New York. Dr Osis observed that her performance could vary from excellent to nil, depending on health, mood, motivation and state of consciousness, as well as compatibility with those she was reading or working with – a long list of variables.

Several other well known psychics have worked with police in fairly recent times, and no list would be complete without Peter Hurkos, another Dutchman, born in Dordrecht in 1911. He was a merchant seaman at the outbreak of the Second World War, and joined the resistance movement against the Nazis. In 1941, working as a house-painter, he fell from a ladder and woke up in hospital. The bump on the head seemingly caused him to develop clairvoyant powers, which nevertheless failed to prevent him being arrested by the Germans. He was liberated by American and Canadian troops from Buchenwald concentration camp at the end of the war.

In post-war Holland, his new sixth sense brought him local fame. He could locate missing people, describe what had happened to them, usually by holding some personal item – the skill known as psychometry.

Hurkos never claimed spiritual motivation. He demonstrated ESP on stage and on television, and accepted money for what he did, with one exception: he never asked to be paid for helping the police.

He was brought to America in 1956 by millionaire Henry Belk, owner of a chain of department stores. Apart from getting the psychic's advice on business matters, Belk used him as a clairvoyant store detective, to uncover embezzlement and large-scale theft. Belk said this was all part of a programme to test the range of the psychic's gifts, but the partnership ended in tragedy and acrimony, according to the written accounts of Hurkos's career.

Belk's ten-year-old daughter disappeared from the family home in North Carolina, so he telephoned Hurkos in Miami to ask for help. Hurkos promised to call back. Minutes later he rang and said Belk's daughter had drowned in a river near the family home. The body would be found near a clump of bushes. It is said Belk went to the river and found the body of his dead child. It was the end of his relationship with Hurkos. Belk said, 'If he could see the future, why couldn't he tell me what was going to happen in time to save her?'

In Miami in 1958, Hurkos was credited with a key role in bringing a double murderer to justice. The head of Miami Homicide Department, Lieutenant Tom Lipe, called Hurkos to the murder of taxi-driver Edward Sentor, found shot in his cab. Hurkos sat in the cab and put his sixth sense to work. He described the killer and is said to have told police that a few hours before the slaying, the killer had shot another man in the Keys area of the city. Checks were made and officers found there had been another shooting earlier. John T. Stewart, a retired naval commander, had been shot dead at his home in Key Largo.

Hurkos linked the two killings before police thought they were connected and gave a clear picture of the killer: tall and thin, walks like a sailor, has a tattoo on his right arm, has been in trouble with the police and is known in Havana and Detroit. He was called 'Smitty.' The police cross-checked with their colleagues in Michigan and found a merchant seaman and ex-convict, well known in Detroit. His name was Charles Smith, nickname 'Smitty.'

A photograph of Smith was wired to Miami and shown around the murder district. A waitress said it was a man who boasted one night of killing two men. She hadn't believed him at the time. Eventually, Charles Smith was sentenced to life imprisonment for double murder. Partly as a result of publicity from this case, Hurkos was asked to help find the Boston Strangler by the Deputy Attorney-General for Massachusetts, John Bottomley. As with the other psychics in the hunt for the Strangler, Hurkos was not totally successful. He always acknowledged that at least a fifth of what he saw would be either irrelevant or inaccurate – an underestimate, according to Dr Osis!

In the Strangler case, Hurkos surprised police with his insights about suspects. Eventually, he led police to a man with a pointed nose and a scar on the right-hand side of his face. For a moment this man was thought to be the Boston Strangler, but later, the real killer turned out to be another man, Albert De Salvo, who also had a pointed nose and a scar on the right side of his face! De Salvo confessed to the crimes, but was found through normal police work, not through the psychic powers of Peter Hurkos or any of the other psi detectives.

Like other psychics, Hurkos was often criticised for confusing police with wrong or misleading information, but his work was also praised by senior policemen in major investigations. Inspector Jack Hall, working on the Jackson murders in Virginia in 1960, said Hurkos led police to two different suspects, either of whom could have been the killer. Hurkos also astonished the police chief with a flow of personal information about his family: he knew all about Hall's bad back, and the death of Hall's son from leukaemia. He predicted, to the day, when Mrs Hall would give birth to a child – 24 June 1961. Hall said, 'It was enough to make you believe in Almighty God.' The policeman gave Hurkos credit for helping to establish which of the two suspects was the real killer.

Dr Osis has always conceded that psi, in its practical application to police investigations, is 'a blend of correct impressions, memories, fantasies and guesses'. He also knows there are many scientists who say the evidence for psi is anecdotal and deals with the activities of charlatans and kooks. But over the years, so many of these anecdotes have been attested by eminent men and women. Were they really all deceived?

Dr Osis told me how psychics are normally used in police investigations. Usually they visit the site of a murder or abduction. They are often taken to explore a search area, to try and locate a victim's body or the wreckage of a plane, or to trace the escape route of a criminal as he flees the scene.

Two of the psychics Dr Osis worked with, the late Dr Alex Tanous and Beverly Jaeger, are said to have led police directly to corpses. More often, says Dr Osis, the psychic can provide only a few clues – previously unknown details of the murder, characteristics of the getaway car, or perhaps information about where the killer lives.

A psychic may tune in to the killer, but mostly there is so much going on at the scene of a murder or plane crash that he becomes confused. 'The psi practitioner on these occasions is exposed to a great amount of sensory input, some of which can be distracting. The small voice of ESP may be drowned in the noise of ordinary perception,' says Osis.

On site, psychics often cannot work at their own pace. Driving along a road, trying to sense the getaway route, they may be forced into snap decisions about where to turn, because of traffic or the impatience of a sceptical police driver. 'With most psychics, accurate impressions occur in spurts, often fragmented, and with large gaps. If the questioner is impatient or aggressive, the spontaneous flow can turn into story-telling.'

Getting the best out of a psychic is a skilled business. Dr Osis has seen opportunities wasted because of police scepticism. 'I have watched officers who first of all must test the psychic. They spend an hour having the psychic prove himself or herself by giving information that is already known. The psi practitioner will oblige, some enjoy impressing people. They may describe the victim, his house, the murder scene, in such detail the officers are delighted – they think this is great! But I am dismayed. I know the peak time for psi has passed, and nothing valuable will be produced concerning the real target – the unknown aspects of the crime.'

Today, most scientists and policemen have little faith in psychic detectives. Perhaps scepticism would be diminished if scientists, working with psychics, could devise a way of detecting when information truly comes from the inner eye of psi, and is not a guess or fantasy. Is there some subtle variation in speech rhythm, skin temperature or brain-wave measurement waiting to be identified as the hallmark of real psi? Osis is doubtful. He believes a laboratory setting, where psychics are wired up to machines which monitor them, is usually counter-productive. 'Repetitive laboratory procedures diminish psi, which occurs spontaneously in some people in response to real-life situations.'

Dr Osis has plenty of experience of such experiments. One of the psychics on the Son of Sam case was Dr Alex Tanous, a medical doctor with whom Osis closely worked for many years until Tanous died in 1990. Tanous was the man who held the bullets from the Son of Sam victim and produced a sketch of a killer.

His preferred method of working was to go 'out-of-body' to the scene of a crime and describe what he saw. He often did this from Dr Osis's research laboratory at the ASPR. This was a sound-proofed cubicle, where he was wired up to an electro-encephalograph (EEG) machine to measure electrical changes in his brain as he attained an altered state of consciousness.

To test the validity of Dr Tanous's claims, Dr Osis would ask him to move out-of-body from the cubicle into another room, five doors away down a corridor. In this room, known as the 'soul trap', was a special box equipped with electronic sensors, strain gauges, light beams and other gadgets to detect any disturbance in the box. Tanous was supposed to go inside and look through a special lens. Only through this lens could anyone see a picture randomly selected of a symbol and a coloured background – in other words, Tanous had to be 'inside' the box to identify the picture.

Dr Osis says Tanous succeeded in naming these randomly produced images more frequently than should be possible by lucky guesses. There were also weight changes on the strain gauges indicating some presence in the box, at the times when Tanous said he was 'out-of-body'. Other sensors such as a television camera and a temperature gauge did not detect any change.

Once Dr Osis tried another kind of measurement. Without telling Tanous, he put another psychic in the room with the apparatus, to see if she could sense anything. Tanous was five closed doors away, when during this experiment, the psychic suddenly began laughing uncontrollably – she said she could see a man floating about near the ceiling, with arms and legs waving. It looked hilarious.

Afterwards, Tanous told Osis he had been unable to complete the test because he became 'stuck near the ceiling', and could not project himself any lower. Struggle as he might, he said, he could not get down to the box to identify the target picture. The test, he thought, was a failure.

Tanous, a star performer for Dr Osis, preferred to work from inside his booth because in this way he was free from all eyes of observers and could more easily enter into a state of consciousness he found conducive to psi.

Not all psychics are visualisers like Tanous, who scanned the scene of a crime with his mind's eye. Some are verbalisers, who repeat words and phrases which just pop into their minds. Others are 'doers', who express themselves in gestures and actions – paper and pencil are key aids for them. Some are map dowsers who hold a pendulum over a map to identify a target. The pendulum moves in small circles above the correct spot. Dr Osis says the movement of the pendulum is caused by slight muscle actions in the hand. Controlled by the subconscious mind of the dowser, it can be as valid a method of expression as speech.

Psychometry is another useful link between psychic and target, using a token object which has been in close contact with the person about whom information is wanted. This object could be a piece of clothing, a watch, a pocket-knife. Handling this gives the psychic a connection to the past and to that person. 'Ideally, we would like objects from both the victim and the perpetrator. In most homicides, the clothing of the victim has been touched by the killer and so can be a link to both persons.'

And when it works, says Dr Osis, the psychic often witnesses a scene of great horror or brutality. The effect can be as traumatic as for any other witness. Sometimes a psychic unconsciously delays seeing acts of brutality in a murder. 'When finally confronting the events, they become overwhelmed with emotion, moved to tears. Such work is, to say the least, very taxing. At times the trauma is so strong that either the flow of imagery halts, before the final event is visualised, or the psychic avoids the spectacle by switching to fictional ESP which, like day-dreaming, does not have a powerful impact,' says Osis. 'Some psychics are so disturbed, they need therapy before they are ready to tackle another case.'

Today, although many scientists deny that psi is real and say any successes are due to coincidence, exaggeration or plain trickery, Dr Osis stands by his belief that psi has a potential value in fighting crime. However, he knows its limitations. 'The state of the art is still incomplete – a disproportionate amount of misses as compared with successes was apparent in our casework.'

Before ESP can be effectively used to solve crimes, he says, improved methods and procedures are needed: new equipment, and better trained psi practitioners and police investigators. 'When methods of applying ESP become operational, there will be no walls for the criminal to hide behind, no location that could not be seen. Could there be a better deterrent than that?'

Dr Osis' view is that murder could be significantly reduced if the use of psychics led to the arrest and conviction of more murderers. 'There are 25 000 murders in America each year, a huge total. If as many people died in avoidable accidents there would be a public outcry. In my opinion this annual slaughter can be reduced by developing the psi techniques we have talked about. The same benefits can be gained in other parts of the world.'

CHAPTER FOUR

Rubbing strange stones together

Unless there is a gigantic conspiracy involving thirty university departments all over the world, and several hundred highly respected scientists in various fields, many of them originally hostile to the claims of psychical researchers, the only conclusion the unbiased observer can come to must be that there does exist a small number of people who obtain knowledge, existing either in other people's minds or in the outer world, by means as yet unknown to science. PROFESSOR HANS J. EYSENCK

The overwhelming majority of scientists do not believe in the paranormal. They reject the idea that part of a person's mind may exist outside the body, can pluck thoughts from another mind, or see things remotely, sometimes even into the future.

And yet there is hard scientific evidence, from hundreds of repeatable laboratory tests, computer analysed, suggesting such things may be possible.

Most scientists who dismiss psi phenomena out of hand as superstitious nonsense have almost certainly never read Charles Honorton's analysis of fifteen years of Ganzfeld tests in fourteen different laboratories. His statistical conclusion to this vast series of remote viewing tests is that the odds against the high success rate being due to chance or lucky guesses are 'trillions to one'.

A Ganzfeld test, like the Remote Viewing described in the first chapter, is an experiment in seeing at a distance. The difference is that in Ganzfeld everything happens within the laboratory. Nobody ventures into the outside world, and the aim is to thought-transmit an image from one room to another in a totally scientific setting.

No one with an open mind should be deterred from learning more about these remarkable experiments just because scientific orthodoxy rejects the findings in advance. A 1982 survey of top scientists in America showed that even the minority who accept the possibility of the paranormal do so mostly without having read the volumes of scientific evidence produced by their colleagues in parapsychology. Their belief is mainly due to personal conviction or seemingly paranormal incidents in their private lives. Most scientists know little of modern psi research.

Naturally, as part of our television series, we tried a Ganzfeld experiment for ourselves. Again, the BBC's Tessa Cordle was the subject and the result was once more strange and quite striking. The outcome was a 'miss' to the parapsychologists, but to us laymen of the television team it certainly looked as if there was some psychic force at work, almost enough to persuade us to set up my assistant in a small tent with a crystal ball – 'Madame Tessa, Clairvoyant'.

Four picture slides were randomly selected as possible targets, all quite unknown to Tessa. A sender tried to communicate one of them telepathically to Tessa from another room. He was not successful. Scientifically the experiment seemed a total failure, but more had happened than at first we realised.

When all four chosen slides were looked at, it was found that Tessa had precisely named two of them and had given an accurate general impression of the third! It was as if, instead of telepathically seeing the one picture in the sender's mind, Tessa had clairvoyantly picked up images of the other three! Parapsychologists know this result well. They call it ESP displacement.

Following normal Ganzfeld procedure, Dr Nancy Sondow had placed Tessa in the soundproof room at the ASPR in New York. Relaxed on a couch, Tessa was fitted with headphones down which 'white sound' was played, a soothing noise like surf. Over her eyes, half ping-pong balls were taped and a red lamp was switched on, producing a red haze. Tessa's perception was reduced to a bland, dream-like uniformity.

This weird-looking environment is thought to be conducive to good psi. 'Ganzfeld' is a German word meaning 'whole field', and is a technique which deliberately cuts down input from the normal five senses in order to focus the mind upon receiving ESP information.

In our experiment, in another part of the building, John La Martine, a volunteer from the staff of the ASPR was handed a randomly chosen set of four slides in an envelope. Without looking at them, he projected one against a screen. For half an hour, La Martine stared at the chosen slide while Tessa recorded her mind's eye impressions from her windowless, rose-tinted cubicle down the corridor.

The judging procedure is that, after the test, Tessa is shown all four slides and is invited to say which she thought she saw and to place them in ranking order. Only if she picks the correct target as number one is the experiment judged a success. The odds for getting it right by chance are one in four.

The target slide, a flock of birds, Tessa placed last, as the picture she was most sure she had not seen. The surprise was that she named two of the other three slides and described the third in recognisable, general terms!

One picture was of a wooden, Viking longboat sailing towards camera. Tessa talked about surf and then said 'The front of a ship ... like a Viking ship ... the pointy bit, which I think used to be a bird ... just the front of it.'

A second slide was the head and shoulders of a statue of a meditating Buddha. Tessa's words were ... 'eyelashes, long eyelashes ... a very big eye, like when you are right up close ... It's a Buddha's eye, and they are closed.'

The final slide was of soldiers and Tessa described various aspects of warfare. Dr Sondow gave her verdict.

This has to be considered a direct miss. Even if she had got it right, we would have wanted to do a series of say thirty trials to correlate it to other variables, like how she was feeling or who the sender was. But, having said that, it was an interesting miss. Although the target was birds, Tessa talked about a wooden Viking ship with a bird, which seemed almost to combine two of the pictures. And she talked about a Buddha with closed eyes, which very directly named another picture.

The other slide was of a group of African soldiers with fixed bayonets, all fiercely grimacing and running through a jungle. Dr Sondow's comment was, 'Tessa seemed to have caught aspects of this picture. She had a lot of aggressive images – a shark's mouth and metal points and explosions and war imagery. Although, of course, that is weaker than naming something directly, like the wooden ship or the Buddha.'

Dr Sondow then performed a test parapsychologists sometimes use if they feel a subject may be clairvoyantly viewing a set of slides rather than telepathically getting the individual target – she compared Tessa's descriptions to another set of slides. She put photographs of Tessa's four slides – the birds, the long-boat, the Buddha and the soldiers – side by side and randomly drew another envelope from the large box of possible targets. We put these four new pictures alongside the others and looked for any resemblances to Tessa's Ganzfeld utterances. There were almost no similarities between the two packs, and the slides in Tessa's test matched up well with her descriptions – the new set did not.

Dr Sondow stressed that we had not done enough tests to reach scientific conclusions.

> There are various ways to think about it. You might consider Tessa got information clairvoyantly from the entire pack of pictures, which means there was no sender involved. There have been experiments like that, where a target is designated electronically and no one sees it. Some have been successful, and it's not really clear we need a sender in these experiments, but the subjects are often more comfortable with the idea of telepathy than clairvoyance.
>
> Another possibility, with results like Tessa's, is that she could have gotten the information precognitively from the future, by going forward to the time when she sat with all four pictures in front of her.
>
> A third possibility is she might get the pictures telepathically from my mind, since I knew the possible pictures that might come up in the different sets. Then again, none of these possibilities might be the right category. It might be something else.

Dr Sondow showed me other examples of ESP displacement from her collection of Ganzfeld experiments. In some tests, all four target pictures were more or less precisely named. There were numerous orthodox Ganzfeld hits, where subjects beamed straight in on the target picture in extraordinary detail. For instance, some fruit on a table was described right down to the pattern of the table cloth.

As a student, Dr Sondow was a volunteer subject in successful Ganzfelds. In view of the general scepticism amongst scientists for claimed ESP phenomena, I asked for her assessment of the evidence for psi.

> To me there really are phenomena. You can demonstrate it experimentally, you can see it happening, but the interpretation is very foggy. It's as if we're back in the sixteenth century studying electricity. I think it's a universal human ability which most of the time happens below the level of conscious awareness. I think it's everywhere, and it's more like gravity than like a meteorite. It's happening all the time and we're just not looking at it.
>
> We don't understand what is going on, but it has to do with the physical world – with how consciousness interacts somehow with matter and energy and time. Physics is incomplete, but this is a physical phenomenon. It has an explanation. It is tremendously exciting, but I wish more people were working on it. You need a mass of critical minds to think about a problem before you really get a breakthrough and not enough people are thinking about this question.

Ironically, in the last year four of eight research institutions studying psi in the West closed down for lack of funds. One of these was the Psycho-physical Research Laboratory in Princeton, USA, run by Charles Honorton, an acknowledged Ganzfeld pioneer since the 1970s, when the technique developed out of experiments in dream telepathy at the Maimonides Medical Center, Brooklyn, New York. Experiments there seemed to confirm the ancient belief in psychic dreams – dreamers picked up thoughts from other minds, from senders who targeted images to sleeping subjects. The trouble was that an experiment took all night.

Honorton knew there were other altered states of consciousness where psi powers seemed strong, such as hypnosis and meditation. He reasoned that dreams, meditation and hypnosis had two things in common – physical relaxation and sensory deprivation. From that observation, Ganzfeld evolved. 'When we are dreaming, our brains are essentially shut off from our normal senses and so information from other sources might leak in,' Honorton told me. 'The stars are always in the sky, but we can only see them at night when it's not heavily overcast. It means we have to clear the mind to unmask psychic impressions.'

Honorton looked at Hindu meditation techniques, where a yogi sets out to obtain intuititive knowledge by shutting down normal sensory input until 'the mind is dissolved and self-illumination begins.' Ganzfeld's aim, by a similar technique, is to intuitively obtain knowledge of what is going on in someone else's mind in another room. Judged by the video tapes Honorton played for me in Princeton there have been numerous startling successes where subjects describe pictures as accurately as if they were standing in front of them.

One woman, eyes covered by ping-pong balls in a remote cubicle, was trying to home in on a clip from a television documentary film – a cheetah bounding across an African plain. She began seeing a cat, but within a few seconds saw the scene so vividly she correctly identified it as part of an episode from the *Life on Earth* series presented by David Attenborough.

Honorton found he got excellent results by targeting moving film clips, instead of static slides. A famous newsreel clip of a suspension bridge swaying and buckling in a strong wind, before collapsing, was described remotely as 'something swaying in the wind. Some thin, vertical object – a ladder-like bridge over some kind of chasm that's waving in the wind. It's not vertical, it's horizontal, and I see it opening in the middle' (as the bridge collapses!) Another example was a spider spinning a circular web. This was seen first as 'basket weaving' and the web as 'a shape like the vanes of a windmill,' before being correctly named.

A still photograph of a fire-eater expelling a torrent of flames from his mouth, was remotely viewed as 'a volcano with molten lava – I have an image of water for putting out flames – suddenly I'm biting my lip as though that is something to do with it – the lips I see are bright red, reminding me of the flame image earlier.'

Sometimes the viewer is both precise and impressionistic. In a scene from a movie, a gladiator battles with a huge figure, half man, half beast. This is described as 'looks like a centaur, like a man-horse combination – but not a man sitting on a horse.' Then, as the towering figure raises a club above its head 'something like the Statue of Liberty's hand holding a torch.' This is remarkably close to what the silhouetted figure looked like at that moment.

Some images are perceived gradually. A black and white American eagle swooping with outstretched wings was 'something that will fly – a parrot with long feathers going onto a perch – a great, huge eagle, wings spread out – head of an eagle, white head and dark feathers.'

At times, an image is captured in spirit but apparently never seen directly. The head of George Washington, the famous portrait used on US postage stamps, was described as 'The Lincoln Memorial – Abraham Lincoln sitting there – it's the Fourth of July – all kinds of fireworks – bombs bursting in air.'

There seemed no universal law applicable to these varied Ganzfeld hits. Some viewers got an impression, sensing the mood of the image without seeing it clearly, some built up from an impression to a precise picture, and some homed in on the target almost at once.

Some were especially dramatic. Film of a fiery inferno was followed by a bright shot of the sun which suddenly became a black disc, surrounded by a glowing corona, as a total eclipse occurred. The remote viewer said, 'I see the colour red. Red, red, red, red, red, red, red – I have a sunburn – a kind of cartoon sun, where you can see each spike around the sphere.'

In another movie clip, a group of young men in forties-style suits and trilby hats roll an old car into a lake. To their horror they see a girl's face appear at the back window. She screams soundlessly as the vehicle sinks below the water. The opening shot is of a young man in a rakish hat, brim turned up. This is seen as 'Fedora hat turned up very much at the back – a type of car – a big roundish car from the 1940s – seen from the back window – bumping up and down – car's standing still – a big mouth opening, yelling but no sound.'

Honorton has many examples like this. As I watched a dozen, one after the other, the explanation at the back of my mind, that these are co-incidences, thrown up occasionally in a large number of tests, began to appear increasingly unlikely and ultimately quite foolish. These 'viewers', with every subject under the sun to choose from, describe the targets in such fulsome and precise detail that they must either be part of an elaborate hoax or are truly 'viewing' the scene or object by some process unknown to our five senses.

Not that Honorton bases any claims for his work on individual experiments. His overriding concern is statistics and the results are certainly thought-provoking. In 1200 individual trials over the last fifteen years, where random guesses would statistically be expected to produce a success rate of 25 per cent, the Ganzfeld average has been 34 per cent – a 9 per cent mark-up on chance. 'The mathematical odds against chance are in the trillions to one, and even critics of parapsychology now acknowledge the results cannot be due to chance,' he says.

Over the last decade, there has been a lively academic debate about the scientific value of the Ganzfeld results. One suggestion is that overkeen parapsychologists have somehow been exaggerating the figures of their success rates. In answer to this, Honorton has computerised Ganzfeld as far as possible and recently published an article in an American scientific journal, jointly with one of Ganzfeld's major critics the sceptical parapsychologist Dr Ray Hyman. 'We agreed the results so far cannot be due to chance and are not likely to be due to improper selections of favourable data. However, we still disagree over whether this data constitutes evidence for psi or for some form of error that has not been detected.'

In his most recent series of computer-controlled tests, 355 trials over six years, Charles Honorton again produced a 34 per cent success rate. He estimates the odds against chance at 20 000 to one for this series. 'We feel now the burden of proof is on the sceptics to say why these results should not be accepted', he said. 'The evidence for psi is very strong but is still not generally accepted by the scientific community, mainly because they are not aware of the better research going on.'

In some Ganzfeld tests, Honorton's subjects have scored higher than 34 per cent. Working with students from the New York College of Performing Arts, a highly intelligent group with a high degree of rapport between sender and viewer, there was an average success rate of 50 per cent – doubling the one in four ratio ascribed to chance.

After years of research, Honorton's verdict on psi is this:

If psi is real, it would appear we have capabilities that extend beyond the nervous system. That we are able, in some way, not correctly understood, to obtain information from a distance, sometimes even from the future. This begins to sound like science fiction, and at this stage we are very much like people rubbing strange stones together and getting sparks. We need a theory and we also need the kind of resources that will allow us to develop these sparks into a higher level of functioning.

If claims made for psi are correct, and we believe some of them are, this casts an entirely different light on how we view the nature of man and his place in the physical world. That's really the important thing about parapsychology in my view – it stands as a bridge between science and philosophy.

CHAPTER FIVE

The dream laboratory

In the end, the only events in my life worth telling are those when the imperishable world irrupted into this transitory one. That is why I speak chiefly of inner experiences, amongst which I include my dreams and visions. CARL JUNG

In 1962 Dr Montague Ullman, a New York psychiatrist, launched a scientific experiment at the Maimonides Medical Center in Brooklyn – a dream laboratory to test popular beliefs about telepathy and precognition. Can dreamers really see what is happening elsewhere and can dreams foretell the future?

His verdict was that such ancient beliefs might well be true, according to the evidence of more than a hundred published scientific tests at the centre. By the time the dream laboratory closed its doors six years later, it had paved the way for future Ganzfeld and Remote Viewing experiments. It had also set the scientific world alight with controversy. Orthodox science claimed most efforts to repeat the dream-lab results for telepathy were failures, but some negative results were obtained in dubious circumstances, as we shall see later in this chapter.

In New York in the summer of 1990, Dr Ullman told me he thought the dream laboratory had at least demonstrated that dream telepathy and precognitive dreams could be reproduced and studied under tight experimental conditions. 'It's a difficult experiment, time-consuming and expensive, and perhaps that's why it hasn't been pursued as extensively as it merits,' he said, a little sadly.

Today the question of whether our dreams can put us in touch with the paranormal is still unresolved. Dr Ullman certainly believes that our dreams can tune us in to a level of consciousness he calls 'transcendental.' Is this the dimension that suggests an aspect of mind which may be capable of surviving physical death? The story of the dream-lab experiments and the history of that fascinating human pastime, the dream, are highly relevant to the possibility of survival after death.

Dr Ullman told me we all begin to dream about an hour and a half after falling asleep and have about four periods of dreaming each night. Ullman believes our dreams reflect four dimensions of human existence: biological, psychological, social and a fourth dimension that can be called cosmic, transcendental, or even spiritual.

People would benefit by listening to their dreams and working with them. Dreams are a terribly under-utilised natural resource in civilised society. All of us are dreamers and dreams should be universally accessible, but they are not. Work with dreams stops at the clinician's door. A dreaming consciousness does not play tricks. It reflects honestly where we are emotionally, not where we like to think we are or would like others to think we are.

The first part of our dreams is about our immediate personal life, our vulnerability. But dreams are open-ended and can take us into this other realm of the paranormal or cosmic. This dimension, perhaps more important than the personal, occasionally breaks through, typically at times of crisis, when someone is ill, in danger, or experiences an accident or sudden death.

We know this dimension exists, but don't know much more about it. It manifests itself in strange ways. Mystical experiences and perhaps the paranormal are going to be our guide into this area, but at this point it's a vast unknown.

Today's debate about the nature and meaning of dreams is as old as civilisation. In Babylon, ancient Egypt, Greece, Rome and China, thousands of years ago, dream diviners and mystics interpreted dreams for rich and poor alike. In those days, they had no doubt dreams were paranormal events. In some cultures, sleep was regarded as a secondary life and a dream was a memory of that existence.

The twentieth century debate about telepathy and dreams began in antiquity. Of the ancient Greeks, Aristotle said dreams sprang naturally from the dreamer's everyday life, whereas Pythagoras believed dreams could have a supernatural origin. The late Roman philosopher Macrobius said there were five categories: ordinary dreams unworthy of analysis, symbolic and mysterious dreams requiring an interpretation, dreams that were communications from gods, phantasms or nightmares, and visions offering glimpses of the future. Visionary dreams were much valued. In ancient Israel, for example, visionaries encouraged them by sleeping amongst tombstones. The Bible contains several instances of prophetic dreams.

Not all supernatural dreams belong to the distant past; there is a substantial literature of more modern dreams. In the nineteenth century several newspapers reported that an unnamed gentleman in Cornwall, England, dreamed of the assassination of the British Prime Minister, Spencer Perceval, eight days before it happened on 11 May 1812. He dreamed he was in the lobby of the House of Commons and saw a man in a brown coat approach a small man in a blue suit and shoot him in the chest. The dreamer questioned a bystander and was told it was Perceval who had been shot.

Next day he discussed it with his wife and a circle of friends, but was dissuaded from trying to warn Perceval by the argument that it was only a dream, and he would be regarded as a fanatic. Perceval's assassin, a Mr Bellingham, a deranged bankrupt with a financial grudge, was later hanged for the crime. Unfortunately, there were no newspaper reports of the dream before the assassination, but Dr John Abercrombie, a turn-of-the-century parapsychologist, traced the dreamer and was assured in writing that the claims were true.

A better attested example of a precognitive dream occurred on 28 June 1914, to the Balkan Bishop of Nagyvarad, a Monsignor Joseph de Lanyi, who was also tutor in Hungarian to the Archduke Francis Ferdinand, ruler of the Austro-Hungarian empire.

In the early hours of the morning, the Bishop dreamed he was sitting at his study table reading a black-edged letter which bore the coat of arms of the Archduke. The letter said:

Your Eminence,
My wife and I have been victims of a political crime at Sarajevo. We commend ourselves to your prayers.

In his dream, de Lanyi saw the Archduke and his wife seated in a motor-car, along with a general and another officer next to the chauffeur. Two young men stepped up to the car and fired at the royal couple.

The agitated churchman woke his mother and told several friends of his dream. He also wrote down the details. That afternoon a telegram arrived with news of the assassinations that day at Sarajevo, the direct cause of the First World War.

This dream was reported by a famous French parapsychologist, Dr Charles Richet, who enhanced his reputation as a scientist in 1913 by winning the Nobel prize for medicine.

The well documented world of crime and police investigations has many examples of dreamers who seem to know the unknowable. Around the beginning of this century, an American woman, a Miss Loganson, aged 19, dreamed in her Chicago home that her brother Oscar had been murdered by a neighbouring farmer at Marengo, fifty miles away.

Miss Loganson sent a telegram to her brother and received a reply saying that he had disappeared. She made a great fuss and accused a farmer named Bedford of murder. Eventually, Miss Loganson, with police and another brother, visited Oscar's home at Marengo. They found blood-stains and the sister showed police where to dig. Under some stones in a yard, they found the brother's body just as she had seen it in her dream. The neighbouring farmer, Benson, was subsequently hanged for murder.

Famous individuals have had impressive dreams, although not necess-arily supernatural in origin. The epic poem *Kubla Khan* came to Samuel Taylor Coleridge, according to his own account, in a dream induced by laudanum. Next morning he was writing down all he could remember when he was disturbed by a knock at the front door. Later he was unable to recall the end of the poem which remains unfinished.

The German writer Goethe says he got poetry from his dreams and also solved scientific problems whilst asleep. Robert Louis Stevenson says plots for novels came to him in dreams, and Charles Dickens acknowl-edged that some of the characters of his novels appeared fully formed in his dreams. The American chess genius, Frank Marshall, used to take paper and pencil to bed every night, to write down chess combinations that came to him in his sleep. The famous Marshall Variation was invented in this way.

There are many more examples of strange dreams, yet what inspires them is as uncertain today as ever. Opinions are as varied as the views of three of this century's most celebrated psychoanalysts, Adler, Jung and Freud. Alfred Adler was sure dreams were only a reflection of events in the dreamer's life. He regarded the paranormal as superstition. Carl Jung accepted the reality of both telepathic and prophetic dreams and wrote with great insight of his own remarkable dreams. Sigmund Freud, more equivocal in some of his utterances about dreams, nevertheless wrote that it was incontestable that sleep created favourable conditions for telepathy.

Freud speculated that telepathy might have been the original archaic method of communication – the way individuals understood one another before telepathy was pushed into the background by better methods of being understood, such as sign language and speech. Under certain con-ditions, said Freud, older methods of communication, like telepathy, might still manifest themselves. In a sense, it was to test the truth of such statements that Montague Ullman set up his dream laboratory. He wanted to see if telepathy could manifest itself in modern dreams.

The dream laboratory came about partly because of Ullman's early experiences with the paranormal. He stressed that scientifically there was no significance to this part of his life, but his brushes with psychic phenomena as a student set him on his path in life. At college, a friend claimed to have had poltergeist experiences, and they set up a small group to study psychic phenomena. For two years Ullman and five other students met every Saturday night around a bridge table in a darkened room.

> We tried out many of the things we read about in the classic literature and ultimately things began to happen. I won't go into it in any great detail because it may sound rather incredible, but they did include levitation of the table at one point.
>
> There was also writing that occurred without any of us holding the pencil. Also so-called thought photographs, where something appeared on an enclosed photographic plate, which was not exposed and which pertained to something we were thinking about.
>
> We weren't scientists performing under controlled conditions, but out of those days a solid friendship evolved that lasted to the present day. As to what it meant, reviewing our experiences thirty-five years on, we each came to the conclusion that we weren't clever enough to have fooled ourselves by inventing the range of phenomena that seemed to occur.

Dr Ullman put these youthful experiences behind him while he trained as a psychiatrist and served overseas in the Second World War. Later, as a practising psychoanalyst in New York, his active interest in strange phenomena was revived by certain patients, lying on the couch in his consulting room. Telling him about their dreams, some described images and events from Ullman's life, which he did not believe they could have known through any normal channels.

> When you're at the receiving end of something like that, it carries a wallop, it really touches you. It is less convincing to a sceptic because it's not occurring under controlled conditions and I can't guarantee these patients weren't somehow privy to what was happening in my private life. But it was a powerful experience for me.

In 1948, he joined a small group of New York analysts and psychiatrists to form a medical section of the American Society for Psychical Research. They met regularly for several years, and spontaneous examples of telepathy by dreaming patients were regularly discussed. Then in the 1950s two developments paved the way for dream telepathy experiments. Research at the University of Chicago established that a sleeper's brainwaves, measured on an electro-encephalograph (EEG), changed when he was dreaming. It was also noticed that in dreams, a sleeper made rapid eye movements (REM), as if the eyeballs were scanning from side to side under closed eyelids.

Although most people find it difficult to recall their dreams the following morning, someone who is awakened immediately a dream has finished has little difficulty in recalling it. By monitoring a person's REM and EEG reading, it was now possible to wake someone the moment a dream had finished and have him recall the dream fully. The stage was set for dream telepathy experiments, but Ullman needed an EEG, a sleep laboratory and some suitable assistants.

A renowned psychic, Mrs Eileen Garrett, an Irish woman who played a leading role in parapsychological research, came to the rescue. As President of the Parapsychology Foundation, she saw the value of dream telepathy experiments and put two rooms at the Foundation at Ullman's disposal. One was fitted out as a sleep room and the other had an EEG installed. Two parapsychologists were assigned to help, one of whom was Dr Karlis Osis.

The first subject for the experiments was Eileen Garrett herself, who had achieved considerable fame as a medium when she apparently communicated with the spirit of the dead captain of the R101 airship, after it had crashed in France in 1930, but before the news became known.

One of the early tests was particularly successful. In October 1960, Garrett retired to the sleep room with a few electrodes attached to her head. A target pool of pictures was selected by Dr Osis and sealed in separate envelopes. Dr Ullman was to choose one at random and try to send the image to the dreaming Eileen Garrett in her soundproofed room.

Waiting for Garrett's first dreams to begin, Dr Ullman was thinking about the book *Spartacus* by Howard Fast, the story of a slave rebellion against ancient Rome. Doodling, he drew some crucified figures representing the eventual fate of the leaders of the rebellion, according to the book, which was made into a successful film.

Woken up after her first dream, Garrett said, 'I went to see a Roman picture – I think *Spartacus* was the thing I was going to see, but I never went inside. I was standing on the outside looking at pictures of Roman soldiers.'

The target in Ullman's sealed envelope was a photograph of a doctor examining a patient. After his apparent success in transmitting his own thoughts, Dr Ullman decided to continue to improvise. He sketched the outline of a sword for Spartacus and a stethoscope for the doctor. He tried to transmit these images along with the photograph.

Mrs Garrett's fifth dream seemed to contain these various elements. 'I saw my doctor yesterday and he was at the Olympic games. We talked about the Olympic games and Rome – then I saw a picture of two men and they were swordsmen, but that again may be something to do with him because he is a fencer.'

Other promising experiments so encouraged Dr Ullman that in 1962 he opened the dream laboratory in part of Maimonides Medical Center, Brooklyn. The first dream laboratory devoted entirely to ESP experiments was made possible by funding obtained by Dr Gardner Murphy, a distinguished psychologist who became President of the ASPR. Two years later, Dr Stanley Krippner, a psychologist with an interest in the paranormal, joined as Director and tests proper began in the summer of 1964. The story of the next four years is told in Ullman and Krippner's most readable book *Dream Telepathy – Experiments in Nocturnal ESP*.

In the first tests, a dozen enthusiasts, seven men and five women, were the dreamers. Each separately underwent six nights of tests over a period of months. With electrodes attached, each was invited to fall asleep and dream. Eye movements and EEG readings showed when dreaming had begun, and a signal was flashed to an agent or sender in a remote part of the building, whose job was to transmit an image of an art print, randomly selected after the subject had fallen asleep. This could be any picture from a set of twelve, chosen for emotional impact and vividness.

When it was seen that dreaming had stopped, the sleeper was woken up and invited to dictate the dream into a tape recorder. This process, using the same target was repeated throughout the night and sometimes up to six dreams were recorded.

Next morning, transcripts of all the dreams and copies of the twelve prints from which the target was chosen were sent to three independent judges. Their job was to number the pictures, one to twelve, in the order each felt best matched the content of the night's dreams. The dreamer was also asked to judge which picture had been the target. At this stage, only the sender had any idea which picture had been used. If the judges all picked the correct target, the night's experiment was a direct hit. If they placed the picture among their top six choices, it was a hit of sorts. A place in the bottom six was a miss. The odds for guesswork meant there was a fifty-fifty chance the target picture would end up in this top six. To suggest telepathy, a series of experiments had to score significantly more hits than misses.

The first two subjects, tested for a total of twelve nights, scored eight hits and four misses. Telepathy was 'a possible hypothesis, but not demonstrated statistically.' However, when the two subjects' own rankings of the pictures were taken into account, the score improved to ten hits with only two misses. Statistically, this was evidence that the subjects had elements of the target pictures in their dreams.

It became clear that the dreamers were better than the independent judges at identifying the target picture. The dreamers seemed able to recognise their dreams by non-verbal associations. The judge's only guideline was the recorded utterances of someone who had just been woken up.

After twenty-four nights of tests, ESP rather than chance seemed to have been demonstrated. There were nineteen direct or partial hits and only five misses, but the sceptics said the dream lab was just having a run of good luck. And there were not that many direct hits, which perhaps indicated to the critics some lack of clear telepathic input.

But direct hits there certainly were. As with the later Ganzfeld tests, the dreamers sometimes picked up the target very clearly, and at other times the ESP seemed more oblique. An obvious direct hit was the dreamer whose target picture was a painting by Bellows of a world heavyweight boxing match at Madison Square Garden. He said, 'Something at Madison Square Garden . . . a boxing fight.'

A more subtle direct hit came from a woman writer. The target picture was a crystal Easter egg by Fabergé. This apparently caused her to dream of two huge heads, one Polynesian and one Egyptian. Next day, she had no difficulty in nominating the egg as the target for her dream. 'At the outset there were two huge heads. They were very eggish because the men were bald.'

There were some statistical failures and some subjects were better at it than others. A real star was psychologist Dr William Erwin. Until he was taken seriously ill after the seventh of a series of tests, Erwin had scored five hits with two misses. His hits were so highly ranked that the independent judges and the statistics supported the hypothesis of telepathy. The odds against lucky guessing were given at a thousand to one.

It was another two years before Erwin was well enough to participate in a further series. By then attempts to influence the dreamer were more sophisticated. Researcher Sol Feldstein made drawings and concentrated on objects as well as the picture. For instance, a boxing glove was used to reinforce the image of a prize-fight. One of Erwin's target paintings was *Downpour at Shono* by Hiroshige, and as part of his transmission, Feldstein took a shower. Erwin's guess the following morning was: 'Something to do with fountains, maybe water.'

The use of multi-sensory targets produced extraordinary results. Six of Erwin's second series of eight sessions were all direct hits and the other two were very high hits. The statistics suggested telepathy was occurring.

The experiments became more ambitious. ESP images were transmitted to dreamers from locations miles away from the sleep room, and with some success. Of course, they didn't top astronaut Ed Mitchell's ESP test in 1971 when he tried to send telepathic messages 200 000 miles across space from the Apollo 14 mission. He did not have US space agency approval for his tests and the results were said to be 'borderline and ambiguous.'

Eventually, the dream-lab at Maimonides tackled the big question. Could someone dream of a future event, which had not even been planned at the time of the dream? Is precognition a psychic reality, and does it occur in dreams?

A young man with recognised psychic ability, Malcolm Bessent, was chosen in 1969 to be the subject. His task was to dream about some unknown experience that would happen to him the following morning. For the first test, Bessent simply went to sleep and was woken up at intervals throughout the night to record his dreams in the normal way. Next morning, after transcripts of his dreams were sent to independent judges, Stanley Krippner began to plan a powerful experience for Bessent. Nothing had been decided in advance, to guard against the possibility of the dreamer getting hold of the information by telepathy.

Dr Krippner, with no idea what Bessent had dreamed, was given two numbers, selected by someone else, and these were used to produce at random a key word from a book of prose. The word was 'corridor'. Krippner then went to their large collection of art prints and selected an appropriate picture it was *Hospital Corridor at St Remy* by Van Gogh, showing a lone figure in a corridor of a mental hospital.

The task was to construct a sensory experience for Bessent so powerful it might have been reflected in his dreams the previous night. Dr Krippner decided to treat Bessent almost as if he were a patient in an asylum. When Bessent appeared he was, without explanation, called Van Gogh by everyone. To background music of Rosza's *Spellbound*, mixed with the sound of hysterical laughter, Bessent was shown paintings by mental patients and was made to taste medicine with a glass of water. He was 'disinfected' by being dabbed with acetone. Then he was led by Krippner, dressed in a white hospital coat, through a darkened corridor. He was shown Van Gogh's picture of the lone mental patient.

Details of this sensory experience were sent to the judges, along with seven other possible experiences and different key words. These were all to be ranked against Bessent's dreams the night before.

From his first dream, Bessent recorded 'an impression of green and purple – small areas of white and blue.' This was a fairly good match for the colours in Van Gogh's painting, which are predominantly orange, green, blue and white.

After his second dream, Bessent said, 'There was a large concrete building – it was architecturally designed and shaped – and there was a patient from upstairs escaping – it might have been a woman, she had a white coat on, like a doctor's coat.'

He also said, 'I felt that a negro patient had escaped – he or she had put on a doctor's white coat and got as far as the archway.'

These statements seemed to match the painting of the patient in the corridor, perhaps even with the addition of Krippner's white coat.

In this third dream, Bessent seemed to refer directly to the strange treatment he received from his colleagues at the dream lab 'Something I had done aroused hostility in people. It had to do with my work and I think all the people were medical.'

All the judges correctly picked 'corridor' and the Krippner sensory experience as the one that best matched Bessent's dreams the previous night. It was a direct hit for precognition. In all, Bessent took part in eight tests of this type and scored five direct hits and two hits in the top half of the judges' scorecards. Statistically, the odds against this happening by chance were given as five thousand to one!

Had the dream laboratory therefore shown that people can glimpse the future in their dreams? Not conclusively, said other parapyschologists. They pointed to a loophole in the argument – the interesting possibility that Dr Krippner might have telepathically picked up what Bessent was dreaming the night before. Perhaps the sensory experience had been tailor-made to match the dream, since after the word 'corridor' was randomly obtained, the experiment was entirely in Dr Krippner's hands. Some people are hard to please! The consolation, for those who believe in ESP in dreams, is that this explanation, to negate the idea of precognition, concedes the reality of telepathy!

The dream lab results were seen as strongly supportive of ESP in dreams and there was the inevitable backlash from scientific orthodoxy. Various attempts were made to replicate the Maimonides test. Some were successful, but others were not. In particular, critics pointed to tests at the University of Wyoming, which failed to reproduce the Maimonides results. These were said to have nullified the findings of Ullman's dream telepathy experiments, but the Wyoming tests were far from the straightforward scientific experiments they appeared to be on the surface.

At the centre of this controversy was the most successful telepathic dreamer in the history of the Maimonides project, Dr Robert Van de Castle, the Director of the Sleep and Dream Laboratory at the University of Virginia. Known as the King of the Dreamers, Dr Van de Castle had been strikingly successful in picking up the thoughts of others in experiments at the Institute for Dream Research in Miami. At Maimonides he was positively sensational.

From January to November, 1967, he made eight tests all of which were successful. Independent judges picked five of his tests as direct hits, and Van de Castle himself scored six direct hits. The odds for telepathy and against chance were ten thousand to one. He had a great ability to recall dreams in depth. His transcripts, recalling a night's dreaming, could fill sixty to seventy pages. An average dreamer might complete twenty to thirty.

Dr Van de Castle went to Wyoming with high hopes, as the clear champion of the cause of dream telepathy. After two weeks, the verdict was that he failed to demonstrate the phenomenon – and the scientific world generally shrugged its shoulders and turned away. But that failure in 1971 was not all it seemed.

Before the very last test at Wyoming, the result of the whole series hung in the balance. If Dr Van de Castle scored a hit with the final target picture, the series could be construed as 'supportive of telepathic influences.' If he scored a miss, it would be judged a failure and the Maimonides results would not have been replicated.

Shortly before the final dream session, the sender of the target picture, with whom Dr Van de Castle had already scored two direct hits, was taken ill and replaced. The substitute was a person with whom Van de Castle had achieved no successes at all.

After the night's dreaming, as part of the normal procedure, before he was shown any possible target pictures, Van de Castle was asked what the target picture might look like. He said, 'It would deal with a foreign culture or people from a foreign culture. Maybe something like a hippy culture within America, which would be sort of like a foreign culture – the element of exotic or foreign culture, far away places kind of thing.'

You might think it would not be too difficult to identify such a picture, if there was one within the target group of eight. Unfortunately, there were no fewer than seven pictures of that type. Choosing the right one became a lottery! He wrote afterwards that seven of the eight were 'thematically similar pictures that showed people from a foreign culture or an ethnically distinct sub-culture in America.'

Dr Van de Castle failed to place the target picture high enough, which meant that the series was adjudged a failure. From the first day of the test, he had complained to the organisers that the pictures being chosen were too similar in theme, many lacked impact and were in black and white – 'I was particularly distressed at the lack of emotionality and content differentiation in the picture pool,' he said.

In Ullman and Krippner's book *Experiments in Dream Telepathy*, Dr Van de Castle has written an illuminating appendix, *Comments on the Replication Failure by the Failing Subject*. He notes that at Maimonides, subjects for dream telepathy who had just had a night of being repeatedly woken up, were given an interval of several weeks to get over any sleep deprivation caused by the test, before doing another. At Wyoming, all eight tests were completed in two weeks, sometimes with only a single day between experiments.

Years earlier, Professor J. B. Rhine, of Duke University, North Carolina, the pioneer of modern psi research, wrote that for exceptionally high ESP scoring, it was conducive to have an atmosphere of 'contagious enthusiasm and intense audience appreciation.' Did the sceptical atmosphere of the experiments at Wyoming change and distort the test results? Dr Van de Castle writes, 'At Maimonides, the staff always gave me the feeling I was a visiting sultan and the red carpet was rolled out with a flourish. At Wyoming, not only was the weather cold but the reception also.'

None of this means Dr Van de Castle is a whingeing parapsychologist claiming he has been bushwhacked by the scientific establishment. That is made clear by Dr David Foulkes, one of the scientists who supervised the Wyoming tests.

In retrospect we may have erred too much on the side of Scientism to the exclusion of creating conditions in which telepathy, if it exists at all, might reasonably be expected to flourish. It proved hard to escape the role of protector of scientific purity or guardian of the scientific morals. Were we sympathetic and encouraging observers, or scientific detectives out to prevent a crime from being committed before our very eyes?

Particularly revealing personally was a brief moment of intrapsychic panic when it seemed as though some telepathic influence might be coming through – how could it be? Where had I failed to prevent a leakage? Our subject (Van de Castle) clearly felt himself on trial before a not entirely sympathetic jury, and we could not totally avoid the feeling that we too were on trial – with a favourable verdict for the subject raising doubts as to the scrupulosity of our judgement process.

There's no place for sloppy dream research, whether on telepathy or anything else. But being too rigorous is a different matter from insecurely flaunting one's rigor as we may have done in our first study.

Dr Foulkes was courageous enough to make his reservations public. Of course, there were other tests that failed to replicate the dream lab results, but Dr Foulkes has said something fundamental about the scientific attitude to dream research and parapsychology overall. Dr Rhine has also commented on this. 'The fear that retards the scientific acceptance of psi is a social one: the fear of losing caste in one's profession.'

Whether dream studies have added to the evidence for telepathy is difficult to evaluate. Dr Gardner Murphy in 1973, in the foreword to *Dream Telepathy*, summed up what was known about psi, and nothing seems to have changed since – even the analogy with electricity is still in use today.

What are these hidden powers at work within us? Our seventeenth century ancestors knew that blankets gave off sparks in the cold weather. But what was electricity 'good for'? Today, electricity drives our machines, lights our halls, monitors our studies of man. Dream telepathy dealing with the individual's efforts to make contact with distant reality and with the social nature of man's unconscious powers is likely to be among the sparks which will be made into a science within the next century. We cannot afford to ignore such sparks.

Whether telepathy or psi, if real, will truly advance the case for survival after death was called into question by the parapsychologist Charles Honorton. He said psi was a double edged sword. He conceded that a power of the mind capable of acting outside our five senses raised the possibility of an aspect of mind capable of surviving physical death. On the other hand, he said such a power of psi could itself explain the phenomena people regarded as evidence for survival. In other words, people are not in touch with the dead, they are simply obtaining information from elsewhere by telepathy. That's an argument we can judge only after looking at the direct evidence for life after death.

PART TWO

Visions and Voices

It is possible that there exist emanations that are still unknown to us. Do you remember how electrical currents and unseen waves were laughed at? The knowledge about man is still in its infancy.
ALBERT EINSTEIN

CHAPTER SIX

Back from the dead?

*And when he had thus spoken, Christ cried with a
loud voice 'Lazarus, come forth.' And he that was
dead came forth, bound hand and foot with grave
clothes and his face was bound about with a napkin.*
THE BIBLE (JOHN XI, 43—44)

For many people the story of Lazarus has always been a fairy tale.
But if Lazarus was raised from the dead today, he would probably
be regarded as neither a fairy tale nor a miracle – just another Near
Death Experience. There are more Lazaruses about today than in Biblical
times – thousands each year are raised from the dead by the wonders of
scientific medicine. The startling aspect is that a great many of them testify
that, when seemingly dead, they experienced an existence in another
dimension. Recent Gallup surveys have shown that millions of people
worldwide have had these Near Death Experiences (NDEs).

Until a few years ago, scientific orthodoxy treated such claims with
derision. Some medical men who published studies of these cases were
ostracised and some were penalised by the withdrawal of grants for
research. Nowadays, NDEs are so overwhelmingly widespread that they
have forced their way into the pages of the scientific journals. The explanation put forward in most cases is that these are hallucinations in a dying
brain, a defence mechanism against the trauma of death. But many serious
observers have studied the evidence and find this verdict hard to accept.
They sense a genuine mystery, even if many are reluctant to accept NDEs
at their face value – signs of a true dimension beyond death, which some
people have entered and returned from.

A typical NDE might be a person who appears to die from a heart
attack, but is revived in hospital. The patient claims to have been out-of-
body, and, while apparently deeply unconscious, to have watched nurses
and doctors at work. He or she had travelled down a black tunnel towards
a brilliant light and in an atmosphere of love and harmony, met someone,

perhaps a religious figure like Jesus Christ or Krishna, who told them to go back. In some cases, the patient was shown a complete review of his past life.

Similar death-bed visions – dreams of angels and glimpses of an afterlife – have been reported for many centuries. Were they fantasies modelled on each culture's archetypal ideas about life after death or could it be the other way around? Today, some observers believe traditional religious texts describing the next world might be based upon ancient Near Death Experiences.

Among antique writings, the Egyptian *Book of the Dead* and the Tibetan *Book of the Dead* both describe realms of existence beyond death, which more or less conform with modern NDEs.

The Tibetan *Book of the Dead* is an instruction manual to be whispered in the ear of the deceased. The texts guide him through his various encounters in the spirit world, and perhaps enable him to escape the cycle of rebirth and move to a higher plane of existence. Like someone going through a modern NDE, he meets a series of beings surrounded by brilliant light.

The Egyptian *Book of the Dead* also bears comparison to an NDE. The deceased enters the afterlife on a boat down a black tunnel heading towards a bright light. Ancient Egyptians induced NDEs to attain wisdom – followers of the cult of Osiris, the God-Pharoah, were locked into coffins and suffocated. They were then revived at the brink of death, undergoing this ordeal in order to experience the black tunnel and see the bright light – an archetypal NDE.

Not everyone who has an NDE has a good trip, although most find it a life-enhancing experience. Lazarus, whom Christ raised from the dead, was glad to be called back after a very unhappy time in the next world. He was in the realm the ancients called Purgatory, where the souls of dead sinners were cleansed.

Lazarus, after his miraculous revival, not surprisingly became a devout follower of Christ, and was either expelled from the Holy Land for his beliefs or found it expedient to leave about the time of the Crucifixion. He took ship to the island of Cyprus, and spent the rest of his days in the town of Larnaca, where the church of St Lazarus is named after him. The legend he left behind is of a man who never smiled. What he had seen and experienced in his short stay in the next world sobered him for life.

Nowadays, few people admit to NDEs that give them a foretaste of hell – perhaps it's something they want to keep to themselves. The consensus is that most NDEs are joyous experiences. Since Raymond Moody's book *Life After Life* in 1975, many thousands of cases have been reported and analysed by study groups around the world, and there is an International Association for Near Death Studies. Fascinating research into the NDEs of children has been carried out in Seattle, USA by paediatrician Dr Melvin Morse, author of *Closer to the Light – learning from the Near Death Experiences of children.*

I met Dr Morse one Sunday morning in a busy children's hospital in Seattle where he was examining babies and reassuring anxious mothers. He told me about his first NDE case in 1982 – a seven-year-old girl who nearly drowned in a local swimming pool. She was as close to death as you could get without dying, and was in a deep coma for three days. She had no pulse or respiration for nineteen minutes. Ordinarily, brain damage sets in after just six minutes without oxygen, but somehow, the child made a full recovery.

Dr Morse, with no knowledge of NDEs, asked her what she remembered about the incident in the swimming pool. He wanted to find out whether she had hit her head, or possibly had a seizure. To his surprise she replied, 'Do you mean when I met the Heavenly Father?' He was startled, and the girl became embarrassed and refused to talk further. Three weeks later, at a follow-up interview, Dr Morse learned her story.

> She could actually see me while I was resuscitating her. What was even more extraordinary, she could give me all sorts of accurate details about what we had done to her. For example, she accurately reported we had put a tube in her nose. She said, 'First you worked on me in a big room and then you took me to a little room, where you put me into a big machine.' That was, of course, a small child's description of what we had done medically. She had never seen me before while conscious and yet she claimed to recognise me and told her mother, 'That's the one with the beard who was working on me.'

The child told Dr Morse that in her NDE the world became dark and she grew frightened. Then a woman came towards her named Elizabeth, who had golden hair, and the world became light. Elizabeth told the child she was there to help, and took the girl to a place she perceived as heaven, where she met lots of other children and adults. Dr Morse continued the tale:

> Some had just died and others were waiting to be reborn. The girl was allowed to see what her family was doing and she met someone she thought was Jesus. He asked if she wanted to stay with him and the child replied that she did. But she was told it was her responsibility to help her mother and she was returned to her body.

After hearing this remarkable story, I became fascinated by these experiences. At the very least, comatose patients seemed to have extraordinary abilities which we have never properly understood. I had thought they were unconscious, when it was obvious from her description of her resuscitation that she was aware during the entire process. I determined to study these experiences further.

Over the next eight years, Dr Morse questioned hundreds of children who survived cardiac arrest. Comatose patients, eyes closed, could accurately describe their treatment and even knew what the nurses were saying at their bedsides. Many described leaving the physical body, seeing their own body below them with people attempting to revive them, and entering a world of darkness before seeing a brilliant light.

Dr Morse set up a research team, the Seattle Study, which included neurologists and psychiatrists. One question they asked was where in the brain could NDEs be generated? They found that the temporal lobe was an area genetically coded for having NDEs. Two members of the team took part in experiments to stimulate the brain electrically. When this happened, the patients said 'Oh my God, I have left my body.'

We then had to speculate why would we have such a place in our brains. What possible function could it serve? The only answer that we had come up with is that this is an area of the brain which allows the sense of 'self' or soul. It allows the soul at least to think it's leaving the body.

There's a limit to how far science can go, and I don't feel we will ever be able to prove the existence of a soul. It's not going to be weighed or measured in a laboratory. But if you don't believe in a soul, you're stuck with trying to explain why we have an area of our brain which allows us to think we leave our body at the point of death.

Some doctors feel this could be come natural defence mechanism – to ease a person through the dying process. That's not entirely satisfactory, because it's hard to think what evolutionary pressure could generate this since the person is dying anyway and there would be no survival advantage to think they were leaving their body at the point of death.

Dr Morse said science can explain all the aspects of a Near Death Experience, except for the perception of light at the end of the tunnel. The initial idea of a tunnel can be explained by the cut-off of blood to the occipital lobes at the back of the brain, causing tunnel vision. There was also the area of the brain which could allow patients to imagine they were leaving their body, possibly as a natural defence mechanism against a life-threatening situation. And it would make sense for a patient to enter a world of darkness when his brain was dying and sensory input had shut down.

> If there was nothing else to the Near Death Experience, it could be neatly explained by science. We would enter a world of darkness and simply die. And yet the children we interviewed did not say the experience ended with darkness. At the end of the darkness came a beautiful light, filled with complex emotional overtones. Clearly not caused by a dying brain, because the entire brain would have to be working, particularly the limbic system and temporal lobes. They would have to be working to generate both a vision of light and complex emotional images.
> So it is obvious this light is not coming from a dying brain. Where this light comes from at the point of death is currently unknown, but I feel comfortable in saying it is not generated by a brain that is dying.

The group's research demonstrated that NDEs were not caused by drugs, sensory deprivation or psychological stress. They studied patients who were on various medications or psychologically stressed and found these people did not have Near Death Experiences.

> I feel we have advanced our understanding to know that at death all human beings will undergo a sensation of leaving their body and travelling towards a beautiful, loving light. This obviously conflicts with a materialistic view. The simplest explanation as to why people would think they are leaving their body and travelling towards a beautiful light would be that they are doing what they say they are. If we want to apply Occam's Razor to this situation – that the simplest hypothesis to explain any data is usually the correct one – then the simplest explanation for our data is that human beings actually have a soul that leaves the body on the point of death. But I suppose other more contorted explanations could be advanced.

One explanation by some eminent scientists is that the Near Death Experience is a universal remembering of the birth experience – travelling down the dark tunnel of the birth canal and being confronted with the bright light of the outside world at the moment of delivery. Dr Morse pointed out several problems with this theory. For instance, some patients born by Caesarian section have had Near Death Experiences but clearly had never travelled down a birth canal.

This theory is a misunderstanding of the birth process itself. When an infant is born, it is not travelling down a tunnel face forward with eyes open, but is being squashed and smashed through a birth canal with head flexed and eyes closed.

Furthermore, when children have told me about their Near Death Experiences they do not describe being in a confined closed tunnel until suddenly confronted with the shock of a bright light. They are in a wide black tunnel and are having a psychic experience. And why would the bright light be loving and wonderful to someone being born? The child has left the womb, usually cries and is immediately given to strangers and washed and scrubbed. If an NDE is simply a memory of a birth experience, I do not see that the light at birth would be a wonderful loving experience.

An impressive aspect of Dr Morse's research is that he has not simply recorded what his child patients said, he asked them to draw their experience on paper. He now has a collection of large and colourful pictures of the next world, which are sometimes very poignant because the child artists have since died.

Dr Morse's first picture was by the girl who nearly drowned. It showed a world of darkness and there was Elizabeth, the woman with the golden hair. The girl had drawn a dark tunnel which became brightly lit and led to heaven, covered with flowers.

Dr Morse showed me the work of another young artist, Michelle, who was in a severe diabetic coma with the highest blood sugar level ever recorded at the Children's Hospital, Seattle. She was given only a 10 per cent chance of surviving, but recovered. Michelle drew herself floating above her body on the bed. She drew two female figures at her bedside, whom she said were women doctors she had seen when unconscious. Morse thought it unlikely that she would have been attended by two women physicians, but on checking medical records found the girl and the picture were correct.

Another small girl, a Mormon child, drew a picture of a Near Death Experience that disturbed her for some years, and posed an interesting problem for those who say an NDE is only a reflection of the subject's own values and mind.

This five-year-old girl, who nearly died of bacterial meningitis, said she floated out of her body and into heaven. There she met Jesus sitting on a stump – not the classic Jesus from the family Bible, but one she drew in a jolly red hat and a blue smock. She also drew pictures of dead people she met, who said they were waiting to be reborn. Morse said:

Many people would say such an experience is a result of the child's cultural conditioning. But this child was deeply disturbed by her experience because she had been taught you weren't supposed to see Jesus. She said to me over and over again she didn't know either that a soul went to heaven to be reborn. There is no reincarnation in her religion. Her NDE conflicted with her spiritual training, and she was deeply troubled by this experience, having nightmares for years afterwards.

A child who had a cardiac arrest during an x-ray session drew a picture of what she saw when unconscious – it was her father picking her up and running with her to an emergency room for treatment.

To Dr Morse this seemed unlikely to be true – not the kind of thing hospital staff let happen during a cardiac arrest. He thought the child being saved by her father was a Freudian embellishment. However, he looked at the medical records and talked with the nurses, and found the child was correct – father panicked when he saw his lifeless daughter and picked her up and ran to the emergency room, chased by frantic doctors and nurses.

One picture Dr Morse values highly is by Cory, a small boy who died of leukaemia. This child had visions of what would happen after he died – he would cross a rainbow bridge and enter a crystal castle which he drew tall and elegant as a Disney castle, surrounded by starbursts of light. He said he would go to live in that castle, made of crystal and bright colours, with an old man called God. The boy was already a frequent visitor to the crystal castle.

At the age of seven, after four years of painful illness, Cory and his mother decided to refuse further treatment. 'Don't worry about it,' the boy said, 'I've been to the crystal castle and talked about it with God.'

There was a poignant last birthday party for the dying boy, whose bedroom was decked with balloons and toy clowns. Dr Morse was unhappy about the decision to discontinue treatment, but everybody had learned to respect Cory's pronouncements from the crystal castle. For example, in her schooldays Cory's mother had had a boyfriend, crippled in a car accident, who had spent several painful years unsuccessfully trying to get back onto his feet. She had never spoken of this man to her son. One day Cory told of a visit to the crystal castle and said he had been approached by an old high school friend of his mother. 'Don't worry, Mom, the man said to tell you he can walk now. He is in the crystal castle,' said the child. A telephone call to a friend confirmed that the man had died on the day Cory had his vision.

During Cory's years of treatment, nine of his friends died from cancer. Dr Morse says the boy said he saw them all in the crystal castle. Cory himself died within a few days of the date he said God had told him he would go and live in the crystal castle forever.

Dr Morse told me, 'There's no question that Near Death Experiences are going to challenge our religious thinkers, our philosophers and our scientists to come up with new concepts of mind and body. We are not some sort of soulless machine – obviously it's far more complex than that.'

CHAPTER SEVEN

A shoe on a ledge

Nowadays a miracle or paranormal phenomenon not only runs counter to all our everyday experiences, more importantly it appears to threaten the entire closely woven fabric of modern science. For it presents us with a new class of phenomena which science has not only never led us to expect but appears powerless to assimilate. DR JOHN BELOFF

A middle-aged woman, apparently dead from a heart attack, found herself floating out-of-body near the ceiling of the ward and watched doctors and nurses working frantically to save her. She drifted out of a window and around the back of the hospital, where something odd caught her eye – a tennis shoe on a window ledge.

Almost as soon as she had revived, she told hospital staff – and the shoe was recovered! The patient was a stranger to the city, seriously ill in bed, wired up to various machines for the whole of her stay in hospital. She could hardly have put the shoe on the ledge herself even if she had wanted to.

For our television series this was a Near Death Experience that offered some verification for NDEs as an extra dimension of personal reality, a form of consciousness existing outside the brain of the dying person.

On the face of it, this patient showed that going out-of-body at the hour of death was not a fantasy but a 'sighted' experience, remote from her physical body. Can there be perception independent of our five senses? At death when our physical body, the seat of human intelligence, is reduced to ashes and a puff of smoke at the crematorium, will we find ourselves still in existence – floating about in space or on our way down a dark tunnel towards a sanctuary of light?

Many people claim their NDEs are corroborated out-of-body experiences. Unconscious, even seemingly dead patients, have eavesdropped on relatives making telephone calls in another part of the hospital, sometimes to the embarrassment of the caller. People with no medical background have described in elaborate detail doctors fighting to save their life, even to the precise order in which different scalpels were used.

Such claims may not be properly verified until somebody records on camera the statements of a newly resuscitated patient and then corroborates his or her story. Some scientists suggest an answer might be to place a motif or secret message, out of sight, near the ceiling of an emergency treatment room. Anyone claiming to have risen out-of-body would be invited to repeat the hidden message or describe the motif. The shoe on the ledge was as near as we managed to get to such a test.

Another NDE we tried to record had offered an unusual verification. An eminent American researcher said an elderly woman, blind since she was a young girl, was able to see again when out-of-body during an NDE. In this 'sighted' state she correctly described the goings-on about her. Unfortunately, she was not interested in taking part in our television programme.

For some critics an NDE seems such a fantastical event, so different to any observable reality, that it is impossible to take it seriously, no matter what supporting evidence is put forward. An out-of-body patient who remembered a Muslim text pasted to the ceiling of the emergency treatment room might have got the information somehow from the man who pasted it up there! Sceptics about NDEs are hard to convince, but perhaps that is understandable – claims for NDEs relate to a dimension the scientist cannot find in his laboratory.

But if you compare the NDE experiences of a wide variety of people, a few things become clear. There are so many reported cases and all are unreservedly convinced their outlandish experience was 'real'. Their eyes shine as they recall a life-enhancing event, and many have been motivated towards a more virtuous and truthful life. Are such people likely to be interested in exaggeration or deception?

Others found their experience difficult to accept and remained silent, often for years, for fear of being ridiculed. Would they fabricate the source of their own potential embarrassment? Would they ever have spoken out unless they were sure the experience was 'real'?

Some insisted on telling their stories in the face of even greater odds. Some patients told their NDEs to doctors and relatives, and were immediately assumed to have become mentally unbalanced. 'The doctor told my parents I was delirious and hallucinating. They thought I'd lost my mind and I was sent to a mental hospital,' was a comment by one patient.

An alternative to disbelieving every far-fetched NDE you hear, is the idea that some dying people, by a process we don't yet understand, possibly akin to telepathy or clairvoyance, may know what is going on around them, which they perceive as an out-of-body experience. That cannot explain everything about NDEs, as Dr Melvin Morse has already pointed out, but slightly prises open the closed mind to the possibility of dimensions of mind not found in medical textbooks.

The shoe-on-the-ledge case happened in Seattle, a seaboard city in Washington State, famous as the home of the Boeing aircraft company, and as the coronary-care capital of America. They say in the States, if you're going to have a heart attack, have it in Seattle, where the standard of coronary care is so high that a greater percentage of patients recover than in most parts of the world. Consequently, Seattle is rich in Near Death Experiences.

The main cause of Seattle's reputation is an efficient emergency ambulance service, Medic One, a fleet of critical-care units, fitted with the latest life-support systems and crewed by skilled paramedics. They treat heart-attack patients within seconds of reaching the scene. Most coronary cases used to die before they got to hospital, but not any more. Medic One say they can treat a patient, anywhere in the city, within three minutes of the distress call, and they took us on a demonstration run, racing through the streets, lights flashing and sirens blaring, to prove the point.

The shoe-on-the-ledge case began in April 1976, when a Medic One ambulance rushed a heart-attack victim into the Harborview Medical Center. Maria, a woman of Mexican descent, aged about 50, had collapsed on a visit to the city from the Cascade Mountains, Washington State, where she worked as a crop-picker.

In the hospital, a young social worker, Kim Clark Sharp, who later became an assistant clinical professor, helped Maria and contacted her relatives who were not on the telephone.

Three days after Maria was admitted, Kim Clark Sharp saw the emergency team rush past her office to the patient's beside. From the doorway, she saw the 'crash' team go into action – Maria's heart had stopped beating.

Air was squeezed from a bag and down the patient's throat. Doctors and nurses pounded her chest, while an electro-cardiograph machine spilled printouts of Maria's condition onto the floor. Electric shock treatment was tried, 'live' paddles applied to either side of her body, and the flat line of her heart rhythm on the display monitor changed to a blip. There was a flickering of her pulse and Maria was resuscitated.

Some hours later, Kim Clark Sharp was paged to return to the coronary care unit. Medical staff asked her to calm the patient who was so agitated that they feared another cardiac arrest.

In a flurry of words, Maria told the social worker, 'I saw it. I saw it all. The doctors and nurses were running around and shouting. They punched my chest. Paper was running out of a machine and made a big pile on the floor. A man pushed something over my face.'

Maria said that during the resuscitation, she found herself up at ceiling level, looking down on what was happening around her bed. Kim Clark Sharp told us Maria's story.

Maria didn't remember seeing me in the doorway, but I was at a distance from her bed. She had everything else completely right, she knew who was in the room, what the equipment was doing. I didn't believe her. This was at a time when the phrase Near Death Experience had not been coined and literature about the subject was not widely available as it is today.

I had never heard of such a thing. I knew hearing was the last sense to go, so perhaps Maria had heard something of what went on. She had been told what would happen in the event of a cardiac arrest, and she knew who would be tending her, because they'd been about all day. There's a psychological term for what people do when they don't know how to get from point A to B – they sort of fill in the blanks. That's what I thought Maria was doing.

She then told me she was distracted by something outside the window, and just by thinking of a place she was there. It was like her mind had travelled to that point in an instant, rather than finding herself as a body floating about the room like a ghost, which wasn't the case at all.

She found herself hovering above the emergency room of the hospital. She described it exactly. How the doors automatically opened, how vehicles came in from one direction and left by another. All of this I knew to be true.

So I thought, maybe somebody in housekeeping pushed her bed over by the window, which was above the emergency room, in order to clean the floor. This was a dumb idea because someone in housekeeping would have to disconnect a critically ill patient from all this machinery to move her bed. It just wouldn't happen. Plus there's a roof that separated the line of vision from the active area of the emergency room that she was describing.

I didn't take any of that into account. I was desperately searching for a way to explain what she was telling me. Then, she said she was further distracted by an object on the third floor of the building, but in a different part of the hospital. That was the real reason she was upset –

she wanted me to go find this object – it was a tennis shoe and she wanted me to get it. I only wanted to go home. This was weird. Because she was so sincere, I wanted to believe her, but there was my rational academic medical side that said, 'This can't be happening.' I couldn't believe it.

To calm the patient, Kim went outside and looked up at the hospital from the car park. She could see nothing on any window ledge. She almost gave up, but decided to walk around the third floor on the off-chance.

I went from room to room. The windows were narrow and so I had to really press my face against the glass to look down and see the ledge at all. I was thinking I wasn't going to find the shoe, then I looked down and found the shoe. It was an incredible, jarring experience.

I had some choices to make. I could at this point believe Maria was a hummingbird – I ruled that out. I could believe Maria had somehow gone into a tall, downtown building half a mile away, gained access to an upper office, had high-powered binoculars or a telescope, and had spotted this tennis shoe on the ledge. All this, in case she had a heart attack and was admitted to that particular hospital. That didn't make any sense either – I was right back to thinking Maria was a hummingbird.

Or I could believe that Maria, when I witnessed her 'death', was out of her body and travelled clear around the corner of the building and up a floor and was able to describe to me an object as small as this shoe. She had given me details – the shoe was scruffy and the lace was under the heel. I knew that was true. But she didn't tell me at the time what colour the shoe was.

Well, after I got over my shock, I reached out of the window and pulled the shoe up. I hightailed it back to the coronary care unit, but I put the shoe behind my back. I walked into the room more calmly than I was really feeling and I asked Maria to describe the shoe again. For the first time I asked what colour it was.

She said 'Blue.' I was holding a blue tennis shoe and I asked her again about the appearance and she said, 'The lace was tucked under the heel and the side of the shoe was scruffed up.'

And then, rather dramatically, I pulled the shoe from behind my back. She was elated and so grateful. We were just swept away by the emotion of it and embraced in sheer joy. I had no choice but to believe that this woman, by all accounts dead, had been out of her body that was no longer functioning. Right then my whole perspective about life and death shifted. Maria was really my great teacher.

Maria returned to her life as a migrant crop-picker and for four years wrote to Kim at regular intervals. Suddenly, the letters stopped and Kim Clark Sharp believes Maria is dead. 'I had no way of reaching her because of her lifestyle, but she would find me and then it stopped. My sense is that she is deceased because she was very good about keeping in touch.'

Kim's life was altered by meeting Maria. She became a member of Dr Morse's Seattle Study research team and now leads the Seattle Chapter of the International Association for Near Death Studies. Every month about seventy people meet to talk about their NDEs. These will mostly be first-hand brushes with death but I doubt if any will be such a challenge to orthodox explanations of NDEs as Kim's story of the shoe on the ledge, which strongly suggests a sighted out-of-body experience and not an hallucination.

One aspect bothered me: what was a tennis shoe doing out on a window ledge in the first place? I went to see the actual window where the shoe was found, now part of office accommodation but then a hospital ward. The sun was warm on the side of the building and the answer seemed clear. If your canvas shoe was wet, if it had fallen into a bath or bowl of water, that window ledge was a perfect place to dry it in the sun. Only an old shoe, it was forgotten or abandoned, until it was found by a woman having an NDE and became an enigma of modern medicine.

CHAPTER EIGHT

The Vietnam veteran

Truth sits upon the lips of dying men.
MATTHEW ARNOLD

An American soldier, severely wounded in a Viet Cong attack on a United States forward base in the Vietnam war in 1965, had a dramatic and classic Near Death Experience. Tough and down-to-earth Dave Cook lost his left leg in a surprise night raid and was on the brink of death. It changed his outlook on life.

Listening to Dave's compelling narrative in August 1990 was an almost surreal experience. His story of a hail of mortar shells was told against the backdrop of the charred ruins of his burned-out home, which had caught fire a few days earlier due to a fault in a heating system.

An hour's drive from Seattle, we seemed almost back in the rubble of Vietnam in 1965 – behind us was the blackened shell of Dave's house and over our heads, the Stars and Stripes flew from his personal flag-pole. In this bizarre but appropriate setting, he told his story as if it had happened yesterday.

The tale began with a precognitive dream he had in October 1965, a month before he lost his leg. Asleep in South Vietnam, he imagined he was back in America, at the Oakland Army Terminal, confronting a crowd of anti-war demonstrators. He was gripping a Colt .45 revolver in his left hand, and then he noticed there were crutches under his arms – his left leg was missing! He didn't take the dream seriously and a month later was at a front-line base.

The next day, 21 November, was my birthday, so me and two other guys went downtown for a party and we had a ball. Anyway, I was tired so I went to bed. I was sound asleep when I heard a round being dropped down the tube of a mortar. It was clanking as it went down the barrel and I heard when it hit the firing mechanism. I heard the round come back up out of the tube, a faster trajectory, and I sat straight up in bed, sober as a judge. I sat there and I heard where the round exploded.

I recalled the old man telling me, 'Dave, if you ever get under a fire-fight like this, run for the closest fortified bunker.' That flashed right in front of me. I waited for the next round that was in the same area, so I knew which way to run, and I took off. The third round hit in the same area so I said, 'Well you're doing good, you're safe.'

Then I was running down the long crushed gravel walkway, and the fourth round came over the top of my head. It was in a position where you feel you could reach up and grab it, it was that close. I heard the sound of the clicking of the fins in the back. They say, as long as you can hear that, you're safe. But when you don't hear it, you have to look out because it's coming down. Well, that round went past me, but for some unknown reason I passed it when I ran around the corner. I could see the fortified bunker about twelve feet in front of me, just the silhouette of it. I heard no more sound and I turned and looked and six feet away the round hit. And everything at that point seemed to go into slow motion.

I could see the rocks, the colours of them and then a hole just started to open up in the ground and things were just lazily going through the air. The next I remember is I hit the top of the bunker, right here on my buttocks, and I fell over onto the bunker, 'Wow, what's going on here?' and I threw myself forward, slid down and hit the ground.

Another round came in and hit just a few feet from the other one. I seen my friend, he took off, and went sailing into the darkness. So I said, 'Gee Whizz, he needs medical aid.' So I started to crawl over there, but at the same time I seen what had happened to me – the whole ground in front of me was red, my knee section from here to here was gone, except for four tendons and one nerve. Other guys came running in, and they'd kick the leg I'd lost into my lap. I'd throw it off. They kicked me in the face accidentally and this whole side was bruised from them getting into the bunker.

The next thing I remember I was lying down and the exec officer said, 'Give me a belt for a tourniquet.' I'd lost so much blood I was in convulsions and I lost my eyesight from bleeding to death.

At that point in time, I began having this Near Death Experience. I could see my life, from when I was born, I could see it in vivid technicolour, the purest colours that you could ever possibly imagine. It just went right in front of my eyes, until the present day.

After I went through my life, there was a long black tunnel, which I presumed was square or a rectangle because the light at the end was in a square. It was way down at the other end and it was pure white. As I proceeded down this tunnel the rays at the end started projecting out, beautiful rays and everything was peaceful and quiet. As I entered this chamber I felt you'd have to squint because of the brightness of the light, but it wasn't in that fashion. It was so pure of a white, you just look all around you and it was 360 degrees around me.

And there was no spoken words or anything at this point in time, but my answer to what I perceived was a question to me – did I want to stay there? – was that I screamed, 'No I want to see my son.' And that's when I was back, when the company exec officer yelled to the sergeant to give him a belt for a tourniquet. Then they took me to the field hospital.

There was one happy sequel to Dave's NDE. A few weeks later, on 8 December 1965, the baby Dave and his wife had been expecting was born. It was a boy, as he'd anticipated in his NDE. Dave spoke about the effect the experience had on him.

What the experience tells me is there is life after death and that it is peaceful. To tell you the truth I'm no longer fearful of it. It changed my way of thinking of life too. I'm now a supervisor in a shipyard so I have ninety employees working for me, and I pay attention to their personal problems. I used to be a hot-head. I'm no longer that way. I reason things out. Rather than hit someone, I think about it first. I respect life very much. It has made a better person out of me.

CHAPTER NINE

Sea changes

A drowning man's life flashes before his eyes.
FOLKLORE OF THE SEA

A New York artist, whose studio overlooks the waterfront, paradoxically found only self-awareness and inspiration when she nearly drowned at sea in the aftermath of a hurricane. Anne Sharp, a talented painter, was a sixteen-year-old schoolgirl when she disappeared under the waves. Her brief life flashed before her eyes as the prelude to a classic Near Death Experience – a black tunnel leading to a beautiful garden, angels and a voice that told her to go back. There was even a presence which seemed to guide the drowning girl to the shore.

It was a religious experience that changed the schoolgirl's life. She became an art student, then a dedicated painter, consciously drawing upon a new inner harmony, a dimension of meaning she felt was revealed in her mystical near-death encounter.

Only occasionally do the actual images of her drowning experience find their way onto canvas. Her NDE made her aware of dimensions of space and time. For appropriate images, she looks not into the sea, but to space travel. The fascination is so real that Anne Sharp applied to become an astronaut, but was turned down. Her paintings indicate she managed in a sense to get there anyway – the most exciting journeys take place in the mind and she paints planets and stars, juxtaposed with perceptions about people.

Anne's NDE began near her home on the New Jersey shore. It was the season for hurricanes, the sea was running high and the beach was closed. Not surprisingly the girl who wanted to become an astronaut was not deterred.

> I had just got my senior lifeguard badge so I really thought I was a great swimmer, and I looked at this incredible surf coming in and I thought it must be like California. I said to three of the boys at the beach, 'Let's go in and go surfing.'

I started going under the waves and coming up. I thought this was just great. There is a certain point usually where you can get beyond the waves but somehow that point never quite came. I was getting a little tired and I looked back to see where the boys were and, of course, they weren't there. Even then I really wasn't afraid, I said, 'Oh well, they're not a lifeguard.' So I kept going under the waves and I was getting breathless. I really got tired and I was thrown under the water and disoriented. I didn't know which way was up. There were rocks and sand and my bathing cap was torn off. I didn't know how far I could keep going under these enormous waves.

Then all of a sudden I noticed a flash, like my whole little life was being shown to me. I was only fifteen but I saw this sort of film, but it was somehow in a circle. I heard noises and didn't know what was happening. I heard church bells, crickets and a whoosh – like the wind. I didn't feel any pain.

The next thing I know, it's real dark, and I'm afraid of the darkness. Just black, velvety black, and then there was this long tunnel. Not all black, with little lights like galaxies, and then it was very bright, like honey colour, clear but not sticky. It was like a bright, warm feeling and I looked and saw very calm water going into this beautiful garden. There were two angels and some people I didn't know. It was wonderful, I'd never seen anything like it and I forgot where I was and everything. Then a voice said, 'Go back.' I was always an indecisive person and the voice said, 'Go back, you have a wonderful life, you have to tell people things.'

I didn't have any choice, and then there was a blinding flash of bright, white light, not like the yellow, golden light. All of a sudden, like putting a jacket on, I felt myself back in the ocean. I looked up and it was still foggy. I turned toward shore and it was as though someone was helping me, I just swam very easily all the way. I've never been that calm before or since. It was so warm and loving. At the end, one of the boys reached out to grab me, screaming that I'd been gone so long. I backed away and then he grabbed me and kind of slapped my face.

When I came out of the water, I just was so overwhelmed by the experience that I didn't really want to tell anyone. I felt something really different had happened to me. I didn't dare tell my parents either, although I told my father I had a close call in the water. I was afraid that under the water maybe something happened to my brain. I did tell someone I had a wonderful experience and they looked at me like I was crazy. 'It was a terrible thing, you almost drowned!'

My whole personality really changed, because from being aimless, just drifting, I really became focused on going away to New York and becoming an artist. I knew this was what I had to do and it would all come out all right. It also made me much more tolerant of all types of people. Before I was a very difficult child. I always had to have my own way. Now I became a bit more mellow and tolerant, and just wanting to see the whole world. I had a feeling of harmony that I never had, which is the most important thing.

In relation to time and space I began to see everything existing at once. I also found I believed in Jung's Theory of Synchronicity, when certain things and events come together. My belief is that it's always happening. The part of the experience that really got to me was this feeling of space and time being one in a whole other dimension.

I don't care what the scientists say. I may have other fears, might be neurotic, but I have never questioned there's life after death. I don't mean life as we know it, but a whole different existence, and I got as far as being in this wonderful light. Now I know, the more I read, that this will happen to everybody, no matter how bad the illness or how sudden. I read some Eastern quote that death is just like changing your jacket. And that's one fear I actually don't have, the fear of death.

One time I almost got caught out when I heard somebody had this Near Death Experience and I said, 'How lucky he is to get to die twice,' and I laughed. People were shocked and that's why I felt it was best to hold back on saying some of these things in public. I laughed because it was a joyous experience, the happiest I've frankly ever had, except in maybe trying to do my work. Sometimes in life and death situations where I've been around someone who is near death, I can find this light again, which gives me this feeling of warmth and harmony, and it takes away the fear of losing someone.

❖   ❖   ❖   ❖   ❖

A New York man, whose apparently lifeless body was dragged from the sea after a scuba-diving mishap, witnessed his own despairing efforts to reach the shore from a strange vantage point – high up in the air, hovering out-of-body, above the drama.

Today, years after the incident, John Migliaccio is convinced his Near Death Experience was much more than an hallucination in a dying brain. He is sure he was truly out-of-body because, from above the shore-line, he saw parts of the coast he had never seen before. His narrow escape from death in the sea off New Jersey was in many ways a typical NDE, although he describes travelling 'through blackness at great speed,' instead of journeying down a black tunnel. He feels his life has been changed by this experience.

I don't even care if people believe me or not. I know it was as real as anything else, and no other experience has made so much impact. People are right to question these experiences and I spent ten years myself trying to be sceptical about it. But I couldn't come up with any conclusion other than that it happened and was real.

He was eighteen years old when his ordeal began – he was scuba-diving on his own and ran out of air. In his wet suit, oxygen cylinder strapped to his back, he decided to swim towards a jetty on the shore. He soon recognised a problem – a strong ebb tide was pushing him away from the shore.

After swimming for quite a long time I looked to some sight-points I had made on the jetty and found I hadn't gotten very far, which didn't faze me. I just keep swimming and swimming. I just kept trying to go against the current until I realised I was exhausted. My arms felt like lead weights.

As I was swimming I suddenly found myself looking down at my body from a few hundred feet up. I could see myself in my wet suit, the scuba equipment on my back. The first thought was, how can this be happening? It was the strangest thing I had ever experienced, because not only did I see myself swimming but I realised in my body that I was looking down at myself. It was like being in two places at once. I thought, 'This is impossible,' like having a separate set of eyes, a separate thinking apparatus and being in two places at once.

When that thought occurred I saw myself close up, as vivid as day. Then I popped back up high. My body was about the size of my thumb, a little black thing down in the water swimming. It was a very enjoyable peace. I recall silly things. The blue of the sky still makes my mouth water, it was so blue. The fluffiness of the clouds, like cotton up in the sky.

I had a view up and down the coast and a view inland to trees and other areas. The thing that convinced me this was really happening was that I could see both sides of the jetty. I had only seen one side of it as I was walking down to the beach but from in the sky I could see the other side, I could see the beach. It was extremely pleasant to be able to experience it all without a body, as if one brain was in two places. This lasted a few minutes and then I was back down in my body swimming.

For the first time I became very afraid for my physical safety, because I heard myself breathing and what was coming out of me was grunting. It was just scary and I thought to stop swimming and try and make an emergency signal – but I decided if I stopped swimming I would drown right there. So I began to tell myself, 'Keep swimming, don't panic.' I was probably fifty to sixty yards at least from the shore and I just completely blacked out. I have no recollection of any physical movement.

The next thing I recall is the flipper of my left foot touched something solid, just brushed the sands, and I kind of woke up, and lifted my head up out of the water to see where I was. I apparently had swum all the way up to the beach, and as I lifted my head up, with my mouth open, a wave just caught me right in the face and I was breathing sea water. Everything went black, but I still knew what was going on. I had a sense of a voice, simply something that communicated to me – 'It's OK, don't worry, everything's going to be all right,' which I consciously resisted.

The second time that that happened I simply stopped resisting this information and then I started travelling, it's the only way I can put it. Going at 20 zillion miles an hour, straight up through dense blackness. It was completely black and different from the blackout prior to that, because I knew what was going on, I was aware of travelling so fast, and I had a sense there was a boundary out there somewhere, although I couldn't see it, couldn't feel it, couldn't touch it. I just knew out on the horizon there was a boundary through this blackness.

I reached one point, and the only way I can describe it is that I felt I was a firework going off, and connecting with everything that there was in terms of information. Everything made sense. The whole universe made sense, I felt the connection between myself and everything else that ever existed. The old saying about the entire universe is contained in a grain of sand, it was like the grain of sand and the universe both shared the same consciousness. It's like knowing about everything that's out there, feeling extremely at peace, not excited, and accepting all that was happening.

I remember kind of looking back and not really looking back, but just becoming aware of being outside earth and seeing a pinpoint of light, very, very far away in this blackness. I heard a voice say, 'He must have panicked,' as if you overhear a comment about you as you're walking very quickly down the street, and they're passing the other way.

It was like I was turning round saying, 'No I didn't panic.' As soon as I said that – bam! I was back down in my body. I felt like a rugby ball in the middle of a scrum with all these people and voices. I didn't see anything, I just heard a bunch of people around me, looking down, and then heard somebody say, 'He made a noise, he's going to be all right.'

About two days after the experience, a doctor came in who actually had taken care of me in the emergency room. He sat down and said, 'You know you're very lucky. You were dead. They couldn't find any pulse and you weren't breathing when they got you out of the water.'

I tried to tell him that very strange things had happened and he said, 'Don't worry about it, you're OK now.' So I treated the experience almost as if it was an hallucination or something, but it would never let me go. Finally, ten years after I had the experience, I talked to someone else who had had one. His experience was even more unbelievable.

What does it mean and why me? Why did I come back? A lot of people die and never come back and a lot of people die, are revived and don't have an NDE. The important changes in me did not come in any dramatic way. I haven't become a saint, I have not gone out and devoted myself to good works. It comes in very small decisions you make every day. A difference is there's no fear of being dead. And if you're really not afraid of that, there's not much else to be afraid of in your life. It gives you a frame of reference, the absolute love that's out there makes you much more concerned about everything else in the universe. It makes you concerned about trying to be the best person you can possibly be.

CHAPTER TEN

Seattle Studies

Death opens unknown doors. JOHN MASEFIELD

In Seattle, a middle-aged woman told us she'd been out-of-body three times, the first when she was struck by a heavy piece of furniture at the age of two. But a young man went one better – he had an NDE and found himself crawling up a black tunnel towards a bright light, when he was only nine months old!

There was corroboration for this teenager's remarkable story from his parents, who were both convinced he had had this experience at the age of nine months. Medical records confirmed he was desperately ill in a coma at that time.

Mark's NDE has been studied by Dr Melvin Morse who said, 'At first, most people are sceptical about this story of a nine-month-old child apparently crawling to heaven. They ask if it is possible for a child that young to remember a Near Death Experience. The answer is "yes".'

Dr Morse said research showed that learning and memory begin earlier than had been thought. Seven-month-old infants were shown a video demonstrating how a toy was fitted together, and afterwards they were able to put it together themselves. Another group of seven-month-olds were not shown the video and they found it impossible to assemble the toy.

Our television team met Mark and his parents as part of a day visiting people who had experienced NDEs in the Seattle area. Our guide was Shannon Greer, researcher with the Seattle Study, the group set up by Dr Morse which analysed data about NDEs in children. In 1986 Dr Morse published the group's findings in the *American Journal of Diseases of Children*, and came to several important conclusions. NDEs didn't seem to happen to children who were simply seriously ill, they had to be close to death. In 121 seriously ill children, no NDEs were reported, but of twelve children who had been close to death, eight said they had left their bodies and travelled to another realm. These NDEs were not caused by drugs or hallucinations due to lack of oxygen.

To Dr Morse's irritation, as a result of this study he was turned down for a grant to make a similar study with children of Asian parents, a chance to compare the results for different cultures. Although taking part in Morse's programme was entirely voluntary, the committee decided his research would 'intrude on patients' rights.'

Dr Morse's verdict was, 'I feel that intruding on patients' rights had nothing to do with the decision. The real reason is that doctors don't like to research death. Although most people die in hospital, the subject of death is almost taboo there.'

The first NDE we talked to was Helen, a woman close to fifty, whose memory of what happened when she was eight was as fresh as if it was yesterday. She had been in the local swimming pool:

> I was in the deep water and I couldn't get back because I was extremely tired. I started to go down and after the second time, my body was so heavy I couldn't get back up. The third time I went down I blacked out. Then I saw myself at the bottom of the pool, and I was going up in the air, and heard the life-guard yell, 'Everybody out.'
>
> The next thing I knew, I was on a road and it was a black road. I don't know why, but there was a little deer with me and I was walking on this road. Then I was in this beautiful garden with a gigantic tree and a river. There were children by the tree playing. They wore outfits that reminded me of togas – what they used to wear in Roman times. They saw me and asked me to come in. I tried to go in and I was halfway when I felt a sort of wall or force, I can't explain quite what it was, but the next thing I was being pushed like I was in a vacuum. I was back in my body.
>
> Just before I heard the lifeguard ask me if I was all right, an angel said something to me. Since I was only eight, I didn't understand what it meant. But as I got older, it made sense to me. He told me if I led a good life, I had nothing to fear from death. Ever since then, I've tried to do that – but no one's perfect.
>
> I said nothing for years, because I was afraid of what people would think, especially my family. I kept it quiet until I heard that other people had had this experience. I think it's the reason I'm not afraid of death, because I know that when I die there's nothing to be afraid of. My parents are both gone now, but I'll probably see them and it will be a joyous occasion.

Another middle-aged woman in a suburb of Seattle sat in the lounge of her home and told of three out-of-body experiences as a child. She has a reputation for being psychic, which fits in with a survey which showed people who have had an NDE are likelier than the rest of us to display psychic ability. This is her story:

It was the first thing I recall in my whole life. It was very vivid. I was just two years old and I was trying to climb on top of a very large piece of furniture, a very old-fashioned radio which was twice as tall as I was, and I pulled it down on top of myself.

The next thing I knew I was across the room watching myself being repaired in the lap of a man with a dark uniform and a matching dark hat. I was in the same room, but they were sat on the sofa and I was watching the whole proceedings. There was a lot of bright light around me.

Next thing, I was awake again. It wasn't a classic situation where I was pronounced dead, but I'm absolutely certain I was out of my body. I confirmed with my mother years later that the man in the uniform was a fire and rescue man. I never told her until I was thirty years old. She was astonished. What happened was I had a blow on the head and I carry the scar to this day.

The next time it happened I was eight years old. I had scarlet fever and was ill for about six weeks. One night in the dark of my bedroom I floated right out of my body. I was aware of myself on the bed, but I floated outside the house through the roof.

I suddenly began experiencing an alternating presence of a brilliant light that was enormous, expansive, just filled horizon to horizon and alternated with a feeling of darkness and being closed in. This would go back and forth and I believe was connected with going in and out of my body. That was extremely vivid and I didn't tell anyone about it.

I had been extremely ill for several weeks, getting progressively worse. I had a high temperature and I carried this within myself – I knew I had died at that time.

My third experience happened some years later when I was fifteen. I was at the dentist's. We were quite poor, I hadn't been there for years, and it was discovered I had thirteen cavities. To help myself feel better about all these fillings, I wore my favourite dress, with hieroglyphics all over it. I was sitting in the chair reading magazines, and the dentist came out, gave me an injection and left the room.

I felt my heart completely flip over. It was totally unexpected. It just almost leaped out of my chest and stopped. It was astonishing, like being hit in the chest. The next thing I knew I was on the ceiling looking straight down upon myself. I saw a chair, a body with long, blonde hair parted in the middle and I saw the dress, and it clicked – that's mine, how can that be? I'm up here.

All there was from my level up was that bright expanse of light. I looked down, starting to wonder what to do next, when I woke up in the chair.

I discovered later that I was sensitive to that anaesthetic, which can create an allergic reaction, causing adrenalin rush to the heart. Several people die every year not knowing they are allergic to it. To this day, I have to tell the dentist about it in advance or I start going into shock. I'm not afraid of the dentist, but I tell them ahead of time or I might be up there again, looking down.

It may seem grotesque, but to me the experience is totally peaceful, a feeling of perfection and completion. There's no struggle. I'm not afraid of dying. There are people who don't want to go, but I feel it's part of the whole living process.

Mark, the teenager who nearly died as a baby, was the most startling case we met that day. To claim memories from the age of nine months is very unusual, even accepting that a Near Death Experience is something few people seem to forget.

We met Mark on a netball court, being coached by his father and shooting baskets with great ease. A well-built youth, Mark hopes to make a career in sport. He shows no sign of his years of ill health as a child. Dr Morse told me Mark was born with a tracheomalachia or floppy wind-pipe. A tube was inserted into his throat as a temporary measure. At the age of nine months, he was rushed into hospital. This is Mark's story:

I was a tummy sleeper and I was rolled onto my back and my implant in the throat fell out. I had a cardiac arrest. I died and I was gone for about forty minutes. I went out of body. I remember seeing doctors and nurses and my bed with me in it. There was like a wall that divided my grandfather and my mother from me. They were hugging each other and crying. I could see them but I couldn't get through to go to them.

I just remember floating out and I could see my body down below and there was nowhere to go except up into a dark tunnel and I started crawling into the tunnel. It's endless, it's dark and I couldn't see any light. Time had no meaning. I didn't know how long I crawled in the tunnel but after a little while I could see light and I just kept on going.

There was like a helping hand as I went up the tunnel. I'd go a little way and I'd fall back a little bit. Eventually, I made it to the top and it got really super-bright. I wasn't crawling any more. I wasn't floating, I wasn't walking – it was like gliding in a way.

The first thing I saw was white figures of crowds of people. They didn't have a scarey face. I didn't have anybody dead at the time so I didn't know anybody up there. Then I remember seeing golden roads, and I was wandering around and God appeared and he kind of just telepathically talked to me. All of a sudden we were gliding down the golden roads and I felt better.

Then we stopped and somehow he said to me 'Would you like to go back home?' I said 'No,' and he goes, 'Well, you have a purpose in life and you need to go back.' Then I was back in the hospital and I was in a coma for about three months.

Today I feel kind of special in a way. Not special compared to anybody else but special because it happened to me. I experienced something a lot of people never experience and I'm not afraid of dying because I know what will happen. I don't want to be stabbed or anything – that kind of scares me – but dying doesn't scare me at all.

I first told my parents about this when I was about five. We were eating lunch. My parents were getting ready to tell me what might happen in hospital where I was going for an operation. They didn't have a chance, because I asked my dad, 'Did you know I died?'

He said, 'Oh really?' and I said, 'Yeah, and did you know I ran up and down the golden roads up there?' My dad pointed down the road outside the house, and I said, 'No, silly. I ran up there with God in heaven.' Eventually, they started believing me.

Mark's mother confirmed that singular lunch-time conversation.

He was eating his lunch when he told his father he had died and he'd run and run. His dad thought he meant out on the street, but he said 'No, I was up there with God and I didn't hurt.'

We were shocked because this child had never been told the extent of what happened to him when he was a baby. He continued to tell us what he saw up there and what had happened to him. The shock was so real because he said to me, 'You were down the hall and Grandpa was holding you and you were crying. I wanted to come to you but I couldn't.'

I thought: this child was in a hospital room, way down a hallway from me. I was around a corner and yet he knew what I was doing and who was with me. He had no idea his grandfather was there because his grandparents arrived after he'd gone into surgery and he was in a coma. So it's like he is really telling me the truth because he has seen things he doesn't know happened, things that we had not talked about as a family.

He also remembered a time when he had a short cardiac arrest when both of his lungs deflated. He told me later he was out-of-body. I didn't think he could say those words but he said, 'Mom, there was a mobile in my room. They were aeroplanes and they went round and round and you and Daddy used to blow them and look at them.'

And he had never seen the mobile. He was in a coma all that time. No one talked about the mobile to him afterwards, it was something that just wasn't important.

An intravenous bottle was connected to his arm because his veins were very bad and they invented this system with paper medicine cups and every nurse had to be very careful. We never told him about this, but when he was telling us his experiences, he told us all about the I.V. He didn't know about it because he was unconscious and yet he's telling us what he sees and exactly what happened.

He also told us about a little girl in the room beside him when he was in a coma and had an out-of-body experience. We never knew her or met her, but we found she was brought into his room to have her hair washed, and yet he could tell us all about this little girl.

Mark's father, listening to this conversation, chimed in.

It was spooky. At first I couldn't accept it. He must be making it up or somebody told him a story. Then after he told us a few more things, what could I say except, 'Maybe you're telling the truth.' Now, I know too that when I die I can look forward to something in the end. I'm not afraid to die, just like Mark, who doesn't want to die violently but would like to go peacefully. That's just how I feel now.

CHAPTER ELEVEN

Vision of the future?

**They that dwell in the land of the shadow of death,
upon them hath the light shined.**
THE BIBLE (ISAIAH IX, 2)

The spirit of an American G.I. was taken on a conducted tour of the next world by Jesus Christ. After a review of his own past life, the soldier saw apocalyptic visions of this world's past and future. Trying to return to this life, he began searching an army hospital for his body, which he found when he recognised his fraternity ring on a hand sticking out from a sheet covering an apparently dead man.

This was just a part of the most incredible Near Death Experience I heard in America. Today, the G.I. is a psychiatrist, Dr George Ritchie. He told his story, for our benefit, to the eminent parapsychologist Professor Ian Stevenson of the University of Virginia, as they sat together at the rear of Ritchie's handsome home on the banks of historic Chesapeake Bay. The full version of Private Ritchie's amazing NDE is related in his book *Return from Tomorrow*.

Ritchie regained consciousness on Christmas Eve 1943, and his NDE was clearly a religious experience. His visions and the underlying message of love and hope would not be out of place in the Bible. Like so many who have an NDE, he glimpsed an idyllic afterworld which changed his life. Like the others we met, he spoke of his experience with passion, even half a century later.

George Ritchie's experience began in late December 1943. He was twenty years old and had just finished his basic training at an American army camp, when he collapsed with double pneumonia. Within twenty-four hours Ritchie had no pulse, respiration or blood pressure and an army doctor certified he was dead. Later, a ward orderly thought he saw the body move and persuaded a doctor to inject adrenalin into Ritchie's heart, which technically saved his life.

> Probably at the time I was pronounced dead, I sat up on the side of the bed, not liking to acknowledge that I saw something that looked like

me lying in the bed. I looked around the room for my uniform. I knew I had missed the train and had to get back to Richmond, Virginia. I couldn't find my uniform so I went out of the double doors into a connecting corridor. There was a ward boy coming down the corridor and I turned to tell him to watch where he was going because he was about to bump into me – I either went through him or he went through me.

As I got outside the door, I suddenly found myself about 500 feet above the ground, going at an incredible speed, heading for what I hoped was Richmond. From up in the air I could see the topography changing. From the trees of Western Texas, I crossed various frozen rivers.

Then came this city and I saw a civilian walking along the street getting ready to go into this all-night café. I thought I'd ask him if I was going in the right direction. When I stopped in front of him, he acted as if he could neither hear nor see me. When I went to tap him lightly on the cheek, I found my hand went right through him. I went to lean against a telegraph post and went through that. Then it suddenly hit me that some radical changes had taken place. I had better consider going back to that hospital in Texas. What could I do in Richmond if nobody could see me?

Let me say here that two months later, having recovered, I was in a group going from Richmond to see New Orleans, by car, when we crossed the bridge at Vicksburg. I saw there this white all-night café that I had seen two months earlier, and I had never been to Vicksburg in human form before. I think that's important because it takes this out of the realm of being a possible dream or delusion.

Anyway, I made a great discovery about that form of travelling I was doing that night – the moment I thought about going back to this station hospital – zoom – I'm going back at a terrific speed. I had no trouble in going back but I did not know which ward I had been in. I was going from room to room, I could see the nurses, the doctors, the soldiers lying on the bed, but I could not communicate with them because they could neither see nor hear me. Finally, lying there on a bed with a sheet pulled over its head was this body. I recognised it as me by my fraternity ring. I also saw my pale, emaciated hand, the same colour as my grandfather's, who I had seen die three years before. I was absolutely horrified.

My religious background was strict orthodox Southern Baptist, so my idea of life after death was that when you died you immediately went to either heaven or hell. Nobody told me about this state of suspended animation where you weren't anywhere. And I'm sitting there looking at this body with all the hopes, all the dreams I'd ever had dashed.

So I'm sitting there in this state of fear and frustration, when the light at the head of the room kept getting greater and greater in intensity. I found myself virtually propelled up off the bed and the hospital walls disappeared and I saw an entire panoramic view of my life. Seeing my own Caesarian section birth, being brought home from the hospital in a shoe box, and everything that had happened to me up to my twentieth year.

Suddenly out of this light stepped the most amazing being I have ever met, totally different from any of the stained glass pictures of Jesus I have ever seen. One of the most powerfully built beings I have ever seen and yet he wasn't in human form. He was in a form that emulated from that terrific, brilliant light, and I could feel the most total love I have ever experienced. We didn't talk as you and I have to, it was pure mental telepathy. The first question he threw at me was, 'What have you done with your life?' He meant had I been able to love and accept my fellow human beings, the way he loved and accepted me, and quite obviously the answer was 'No.' So I thought, 'I'm too young to die,' and the thought came back, 'No one is too young to die.' I realised he wasn't asking the questions for his information but to give me the chance to really see my life.

Soon after that he told me to stay close to him and the next thing we were again travelling out of the hospital at a terrific speed. We came down in this large city beside a large body of water. Whether it was New York, Chicago, San Francisco, I have no idea. I could see all the bright lights, as when you come down at night in a 'plane. I could see everything that you and I normally see, but it seemed to me I also saw another realm. On a downtown street, I could see physical beings but I could also see other beings. I could see soldiers, sailors and civilians getting intoxicated, they had an electrical field around them that would open at the top, and these other beings would try to influence them.

In another scene, war factories worked three shifts around the clock and I could see the physical beings at the assembly lines and the other beings standing beside them, trying to tell them how to run the factory. But, of course, they could no more hear or see them than the guy in Vicksburg had been able to see me.

Suddenly I find myself in a section where they are having people who are dying from all over the place. Some were deciding what's going to happen to them. What impressed me most was seeing the beings who had attempted suicide, trying to make them see how their act had hurt the people who loved them.

Then he changed realms again and we were where I wouldn't want to be under any circumstances. I have never been in a room with so much hate, so much animosity, such self-righteousness, such know-it-all. These beings were still trying to bludgeon each other to death or trying to commit some lewd sex act, not out of sexual enjoyment, just out of hate or anger. Even in this room beings of a higher order were trying to express love and trying to get these beings to change their minds.

The next room I call the mental or intellectual room, centre of higher learning. I heard some of the most beautiful music I ever heard in my life.

I was conducted through a building of laboratories. Now I had majored in chemistry and biology in pre-med school, but I simply could not understand the instruments with which these beings were working. You know, ten years later, about 1953, I felt the hairs go up on the back of my neck when *Life* magazine carried a picture of the first atomic lab in 1943, prior to Hiroshima, and there was one of the instruments I saw these beings working with.

After that I was taken to a library, bigger than all the downtown buildings of Richmond put together. This I gathered housed all the holy books of the universe. The Christ wasn't at all upset that they were studying the different religions. Now, you can imagine what that did with my background, where if you were Baptist, Methodist or Presbyterian you were saved, Catholics were just about beyond redemption and if you were Jewish you were hopelessly lost.

By that time, I really think I have seen everything. Next thing we're travelling out into space itself. I'm not sure to a planet, almost a realm of sheer light. The beings there were more likened to the Christ who was conducting me. This was the first room where the beings could actually see us. These beings were very evolved souls that had learned to love the way Christ had taught us.

I was shown natural disasters getting worse and worse, earthquakes and hurricanes. I saw explosions I couldn't comprehend – this was 1943 before Hiroshima and Nagasaki. I saw a time when great peace came to the planet. And then he let me know I had to return.

I found myself losing consciousness and next thing I remember was opening my physical eyes and seeing the ring on my finger and passing out again, until the morning of 24 December.

PART THREE

Intruders from the Psychic World

All that we see or seem is but a dream within a dream. EDGAR ALLAN POE

CHAPTER TWELVE

Echoes of the dead

Ghost stories are always listened to and well received in private, but pitilessly disavowed in public. For my own part, ignorant as I am of the way in which the human spirit enters the world and the way in which it goes out of it, I dare not deny the truth of many such narratives. IMMANUEL KANT

Hospital doctors and nurses in the United States and India said dying patients frequently saw apparitions of dead relatives and friends who had come to 'take them away to the next world.' Mostly, these were not NDEs but death-bed experiences of patients who died within twenty-four hours of telling staff about their unearthly visitors.

This testimony, covering almost 1000 patients in the two countries, is part of the research that goes into thanatology, a new branch of science, named after the Greek word for death, and devoted to the study of death and dying. Apparitions, says the evidence, are seen by healthy people as well as the dying, and much more frequently than we generally imagine.

In autumn 1990, a Gallup Poll reported that about half the population of Europe, and considerably more in America, believe in some form of life after death, and a large proportion claimed some personal paranormal experience, such as an encounter with an apparition or a ghost.

At his company headquarters in Princeton, USA, Dr George Gallup Jr gave his view. 'Incredible things are happening to people's lives. Large numbers not only believe in the paranormal, but many have experienced something themselves. The data is really quite stunning and comparable in the different countries. It's a phenomenon that hasn't been properly explored. If this century has been devoted to the exploration of outer space, then the next will be devoted to the exploration of inner space.'

Other surveys, aside from Gallup, have shown that apparitions in the West are very different to the traditional ghost-story images of clanking chains, a chill presence, and grey ladies flitting about in ivy-covered mansions. Ghosts aren't the prerogative of the aristocracy any more, a status symbol to go with the castle. Nowadays, apparitions are frequently seen by ordinary people in everyday surroundings.

For instance, widows and widowers in a country parish in mid-Wales were asked in 1971 if they had been contacted by their dead partners – astonishingly almost half said they had. Dr W. Dewi Rees published his findings in the *British Medical Journal*. For 'The hallucinations of widowhood' he questioned almost 300 people or 81 per cent of all widows and widowers in the parish. He was concerned only with waking experiences – he did not include dreams or anyone who had seen an apparition 'in their mind's eye.' Anyone uncertain if they had been contacted was also left out. The survey showed widows who had been happily married were most likely to have had encounters with their dead husbands. There were even fifteen people who felt their dead spouse was always with them. Rees said these hallucinations should be regarded as a normal part of widowhood – this means half of all widows can expect a visit from their dead husbands!

He also discovered why most of us never realised widows and widowers lead such an active spiritual life – it's because they don't talk about it. None of the widows interviewed had ever told her doctor, and only one had told a clergyman. The reasons for their secrecy were almost unanimous – a fear of being ridiculed, which seems an indictment of the attitude of physicians and priests, and perhaps of the rest of us too.

Three other surveys since 1971, using large national samples, confirmed Rees's statistic that one widow in two believes she has been contacted by her dead husband. Most will 'feel his presence,' one in seven will actually see him, a good many will hear his voice, and a few will even have a conversation. Some will feel themselves physically touched.

But did these contacts really happen or were they imagined by lonely and bereaved people projecting their need to be comforted? The answer could vary from case to case, but a caution for those who assume these are hallucinations caused by grief, is that those widows apparently grieving the most, the ones being treated for depression, were least troubled by apparitions.

Similar doubts were raised about the apparitions appearing to the dying in hospitals. As with NDEs, the question was whether these are the fantasies of a stressed and dying mind or some sign of a dimension beyond death.

Parapsychologists Dr Karlis Osis and Professor Erlendur Haraldsson published their findings *At the Hour of Death* in 1979, after fifteen years of research. Their parallel surveys in hospitals in India and the United

States found the same phenomena in each country – apparitions of human figures, usually a dead near relative, came to take away the dying patients. This happened to 591 of a total of 877 patients, divided almost equally between American and Indian hospitals. Drugs were ruled out as a possible cause of hallucinations.

Compared to known statistics for apparitions seen by the ordinary British public, the dying seem three times more likely than the rest of us to see an apparition.

In the hospital survey, there were some differences between the United States and India. Dying Americans were much more likely to have a woman come to collect them, perhaps a deceased mother. In India, a male-dominated society, men usually came to take away dying patients. Minor religious figures were sometimes seen, but a person's religious beliefs did not seem the cause of these apparitions – in fact, a dozen patients who did not believe in life after death saw apparitions which came to take them away.

Patients who saw apparitions changed visibly. Dying is a gloomy and sometimes painful experience, but the vast majority, 72 per cent of those visited by an apparition, became elated and were very willing to go. Naturally, not everyone wanted to make the trip and a few screamed for help. More Indian patients than American were reluctant to accompany their spectral visitors – only one American said he was not ready to go to the next world.

It was this overall acceptance that Dr Osis found so remarkable. He told me, 'Doctors and nurses said the patients were mostly not disturbed by the apparitions, but would light up with expectation. Imagine if a terrorist with a gun came in here, with the power to take you away. How would you feel? I would have very cold feet. But here, the will to live, the strongest instinct in life, is overturned by something transcendental. That impressed me.'

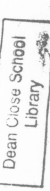

In evaluating this survey, it's worth remembering that doctors and nurses are trained scientific observers of the sick – not people one would imagine giving easy credence to claims of paranormal activity in hospital wards. Osis and Haraldsson find evidence for life after death in this survey. In their final paragraph, they say the central tendencies of the data support the 'after-life hypothesis,' which they define as 'the transition to another mode of existence.'

When the researchers were asking Indian medical staff about apparitions, they met a doctor who was not an onlooker but a patient in a remarkable experience. Dr Bhanu Iyengar is a hospital pathologist and this is the story she told me in Delhi.

I was very ill in hospital and I wasn't conscious of much going on around me at the time. I had a temperature of about 106. I was being visited by my mother and a student named Kirti.

While I was lying there, I suddenly saw Kirti's grandfather coming in. He was not a very tall person, he had on very thick spectacles and was wearing his usual dhoti – I recognised him because he was dressed as he was when he used to come to pick up Kirti. He stood at the foot of the bed and kept saying, 'Please send my grand-daughter back. Send my child home.'

He was very persistent and I got a little irritable. I turned over onto my other side, but he still stood there and said, 'Please send the child home.'

When he persisted, I decided to tell Kirti to go home – I didn't mention that her grandfather was waiting, because I obviously thought she had seen him too. She told me she wouldn't go home because I was too unwell and she would like to stay with me. There was some argument, and I told her she should at least telephone. She made a call and came running back into the ward, very upset – she had been told that about five minutes before her call, her grandfather had died. So she went rushing home.

I was so ill I didn't say anything to her about her grandfather. Later, I realised he had actually come to call her, perhaps as he was about to die. At the time, I really thought he was standing there.

On thinking it over, there seemed two or three possibilities. As a doctor, one doesn't really think that apparitions happen, so one imagines maybe it was due to my high temperature, or perhaps I had a delirium or an hallucination.

It was a very strange coincidence that just at his point of death, I should see the apparition of him standing by my bedside. It's very difficult to explain – there is no scientific explanation for it.

Dr Iyengar's mother was there that day at the hospital with Kirti. She told us what she remembered.

I was sitting on the bed when she asked Kirti to go home and she was quite strict about it. When the girl refused, she asked her to telephone the house. When the girl came back, she told my daughter her grandfather had died a few minutes before. I told my daughter it was a very good thing she was very strict. She told me she had seen the grandfather by her bedside and that was why she had wanted Kirti to go home.

Kirti's grandfather was very fond of her. Sometimes you can see people just before this kind of thing – I believe she saw him because I believe that people, just after death, sometimes have the power to reach and convey a message. The grandmother was all alone at home, so naturally, the grandfather might have appeared to summon the grand-daughter.

※   ※   ※   ※   ※

According to the surveys, if you see an apparition it is likely to be in broad daylight and will be someone you know, probably a man, who has just died a violent or sudden death. It's possible that you may already have seen a ghost and never realised it – the vast majority of sightings are by people who have no idea the 'person' they saw was dead. About one in four of us can expect knowingly to see an apparition, or at least have some contact with a dead person, according to the 1990 Gallup Poll on the subject.

Nowadays, scientific research into apparitions is concerned more with statistics than sensational, individual cases. Parapsychologists look for a pattern, something to provide a theory to link with other branches of science. A recent survey, *Encounters with the Dead*, written by Professor Haraldsson in 1989, dented a few myths, with its analysis of 450 appar-itions in Iceland.

More than half the apparitions were seen in daylight or under full electric light – contradicting traditional ghost story sightings at dead of night. About a third were seen at twilight and only one apparition in ten appeared in darkness. The spirits of the dead don't seem as afraid of the light as many mediums, who work in darkness, have claimed!

Most people recognised the apparition they saw. Usually it was a dead relative – only one person in six saw a total stranger. Eight out of ten who saw apparitions had no idea the person was dead or dying. Haraldsson told me of an example which impressed him: a woman who worked in a sanatorium knew a patient named Jacob who was sometimes depressed. They became friends and she suggested, to cheer him up, that he should visit her and her husband for dinner. Jacob agreed and promised to come next day.

During the night, I wake up and all strength is taken away from me. I am unable to move. Suddenly I see the bedroom door open and on the threshold stands Jacob with his face all covered with blood. I am unable to speak or move. Then he disappears and it felt as if he had closed the door behind him. I became my normal self and told my husband about the incident. I said, 'I can swear that something has happened at the sanatorium.'

The woman telephoned first thing in the morning and was told Jacob had committed suicide in the night.

But what is an apparition, what causes it? Scientific analysis of apparitions is not new. Modern research started in 1886 with two large volumes of *Phantasms of the Living* by Edmund Gurney, Frederick W. H. Myers and Frank Podmore. These founders of the Society for Psychical Research investigated hundreds of cases and launched a debate about their cause that continues to this day.

Gurney believed apparitions were due to telepathy by the person who sees the spectre. It is psi power by a living mind, able to access information from a distance. Podmore too believed the best explanation was telepathy. On the other hand, Myers felt the person *seen* as the apparition was the key player – a person, perhaps dying or even dead, who was somehow able to project a message in the shape of an apparition. Myers' view supported the possibility of survival, after death, whereas Gurney and Podmore explained it all by telepathy in a living mind.

The same debate goes on today. Dr Charles Honorton, pioneer of Ganzfeld, told me that psi powers might explain all the phenomena which people take as evidence for Survival – the same idea as Gurney but a hundred years afterwards.

A different view was taken by Professor Ian Stevenson of the University of Virginia. He says motivation is the key factor in deciding who might be the cause of an apparition. Does the person who sees it have overwhelming cause to seek information about someone else by psychic means? Or does the person who is seen as an apparition have outstanding cause to try to pass a message about himself? The evidence seems to support the second idea in many cases.

Dr Stevenson analysed more than 300 apparitions from Gurney and Myers' *Phantasms of the Living* and found that violence and sudden death had ended the lives of more than half the people seen as apparitions.

He concluded, 'I suggest that the feature of suddenness increases motivation on the part of the agents to communicate the desperate situation in which they find themselves, to persons they think likely to be interested. Persons who die more slowly have adequate time in which to communicate normally.'

Dr Stevenson cited some well known apparitions who clearly had a strong desire to pass on information. The poet Dante, for example, is supposed to have appeared after death to his son, and beckoned him to where Dante had hidden the final Cantos of the Divine Comedy. Dante's son, it was said, did not know his father had written the Cantos. Stevenson said some apparitions could be caused by the person who saw the spectre, whereas others, at least in part, resulted from 'the activity of deceased or dying persons who may be regarded in some sense as "present" where they are seen.'

Dr Haraldsson also entered the long-running Gurney – Myers debate about the motivational force behind apparitions. In his survey, a third of people who were seen as apparitions had died violently or suddenly. And those apparitions who suffered a violent death were 'strong communicators.' Haraldsson said, 'This finding gives considerable support to Myers' theory and the popular belief that the apparition of the dead person plays an active role in the encounter. As a step further, one might ask if suffering a violent death makes contact with the living more desirable or easier?'

Sometimes the motivation for an apparition seemed to be to prevent the death of others by giving a warning. Icelandic fishermen, who took part in the survey, provided good examples.

A teenager out fishing in a small boat heard a voice say, 'Leave the fishing line and row ashore!' Just as he got back to harbour, a storm blew up and the young man barely managed to reach the dock. He associated the voice with a recently drowned brother.

In another case, the crew of a fishing boat were sleeping at night when they were woken early by an urgent voice telling them to get up. This happened twice. Some members of the crew were roused and found a dynamo in the engine room beginning to catch fire. A possible fatal explosion at sea had been averted.

Dr Haraldsson's survey asked more than eighty questions and came to a clear conclusion.

Our new large collection of cases strongly indicates that the prevailing academic attitude that experiences of this kind are 'just hallucinations,' appears unsatisfactory. Many of the cases revealed to us dramatic intrusions of meaningful imagery into consciousness.

The crucial question is where do these intrusions come from? Who initiates these echoes of the dead? Many of our cases point to an active role of the agent, particularly cases involving persons who have suffered violent death. The best cases have some features that may best be explained by accepting some form of a survivalist theory.

Many non-scientists may find statistical evidence less convincing than individual cases. There are many stories of apparitions attested by good witnesses. At the end of the nineteenth century, one of the most stringent fraud hunters in the history of psychical research investigated a classic case – a murder trial dominated by evidence about an apparition of the victim.

Dr Richard Hodgson of the ASPR first read about it in the *Chicago Evening Journal* of 3 July 1897, under the headline 'Queer Evidence Convicts.' The report said that a coroner's jury had recorded a verdict of death by heart disease of a woman found dead in her home. But after the funeral, the dead woman's mother saw visions of her daughter, a Mrs Shue, who insisted she had been strangled by her husband. The mother was given such convincing details of the murder by the apparitions that she persuaded the authorities to exhume the body. The husband was tried for first-degree murder, convicted and sentenced to life imprisonment.

To verify this story, Hodgson got written statements from the mother, a Mrs Heaster, and seven witnesses who said they were told all about the visions before the crime was ever proved. Hodgson also corresponded with the prosecuting assistant district attorney and secured transcripts of official trial records.

In court, Mrs Heaster said it all began after the daughter's funeral when 'I prayed for her to come back to tell me all about her death.' The dead woman then appeared four times to her mother and described how Mr Shue arrived home for his evening meal on the day she died. 'He was mad. I had not cooked any meat. But I had butter, apples, cherries and three kinds of jellies and plenty on the table...'

There was a quarrel and the apparition of Mrs Shue said her husband took her pictures from the wall and piled them and ornaments and clothes into a basket where wool was kept. One of the jurors wrote to Hodgson that this was where the items were eventually discovered.

Mrs Heaster, an elderly lady, told the court how her daughter described the murder. 'Ma, he just took his hands and squeezed my neck off.' The old lady was asked if she might have been dreaming. She replied she was going to bed when she first saw her daughter by fire-light. 'I felt her arm to see if it was real. It was flesh and blood.'

Cross-examined, Mrs Heaster added, 'When she came, I got up on my elbows and reached out a little further as I wanted to see if people came in their coffins ... I wanted to see if there was a coffin and there was not. She was just like she was when she left this world. I wanted her to come to talk to me and she did.'

For weeks Mrs Heaster tried to persuade the authorities to open her daughter's grave. Two things made them take her seriously. The clothes she said her daughter wore when she saw her were those she had worn on the day of her death. And Mrs Heaster, who had never visited her daughter's home, gave a description of the crime which matched the layout of the house. Eventually, the old lady was allowed to take the sheriff's men to the house.

A juror wrote, 'Mrs Heaster went with them to the house and showed the way through the doors as directed (by Mrs Shue). She stopped at the last door and pointed out to the men with her the exact spot as directed, and there they found blood and signs of a scuffle on the floor, although she had never seen the house before.'

Mrs Heaster told the court, 'I saw the place just exactly as she told me and I saw blood right there, where she told me. I never laid eyes on that house until since her death. She told me all this before I knew anything of those buildings at all.'

Witnesses testified that before the body was exhumed, Mrs Heaster gave more details about the cause of death. Mrs Heaster reported that her daughter had said, 'It was the last joint and he squeezed it until it was all bloody.'

When Mrs Shue's body was examined, the first joint of the neck was found to be broken, between the atlas and axis vertebrae. A juror who attended the exhumation and postmortem wrote, 'Upon examination, we found every iota just as Mrs Heaster told several others and myself beforehand.'

The apparition of Mrs Shue seemed motivated by a desire for justice and revenge – she was also more than a little annoyed about the unfair accusation that she gave her husband a poor meal on the night of the murder. Mrs Heaster said, 'She told me something about that meal every night she came. She came four times, four nights – but the second night she told me that her neck was squeezed off at the first joint, and it was just as she told me.'

The assistant district attorney admitted to Hodgson that the 'vision, dream or whatever it was' was responsible for the trial because it had prompted the exhumation of the body and the postmortem examination.

Did the husband get a fair trial? An apparition's version of events was heard in court almost as if it was Mrs Shue herself giving evidence. The prosecutor admitted, 'The court instructed the jury of its own motion that the vision was not evidence to be considered. But I have ever thought it made an impression on the jury unfavourable to the prisoner.'

CHAPTER THIRTEEN

The ghost of Operation Stone Age

We are both onlookers and actors in the great drama of existence. NIELS BOHR

A phantom warning of imminent danger that triggered a naval action in the Second World War was the most powerful story to emerge from a simple experiment. I asked a few friends and acquaintances if they had ever had a supernatural experience. It was a way of testing the claim, implicit in Gallup and other surveys, that many more people experience the paranormal than is generally realised.

I expected to hear one or two run-of-the-mill stories of strange happenings – instead there was a flood of testimony about apparitions, precognitive dreams and Near Death Experiences, a few of which I was able partially to verify. None of these anecdotes prove the paranormal, but they confirm that people's lives are spiritually and psychically richer and more complicated than I had imagined.

A close friend, Tegwyn Hughes, told me the story of an incident aboard HMS *Orion*, a British warship in the Second World War. Tegwyn died on Easter Monday 1991, six months after writing this account.

The November 1942 convoy from Alexandria to Malta had 'secured' from the usual precautionary, sunset 'action-stations', and darkness was closing in. Our guns were on standby for another night at sea. Aboard HMS *Orion*, one of the escort cruisers, the Petty Officer who did the post action-station rounds left the cramped space of our transmitting station (T.S.), again assaulting our eardrums with the change of pressure as he lifted, slammed down and clipped shut the counterweighted four-hundredweight hatch above us. Our nine-man crew shuffled around like dogs, each one settling down on his bit of deck space for another night of waiting for the dawn. On that ship, no one left his action-station for more than a few seconds at a time – between alarms we only 'relaxed.'

Soon each vanished behind his section of the T. S. table, a seven feet long, three feet high compact mass of electrical and mechanical instruments for passing information, from several sources, to the port and starboard four-inch gun-batteries on deck. The chatter died out and we all settled down to read, write letters, or doze in the narrow space between table and bulkhead. Everyone did a 'trick' in turn on one or another of the headphones.

As 'number one' on the table, I sat at the end, under the hatch, with my left shoulder jammed against the side of the vertical ladder, my upper back to the bulkhead and my right elbow on the deck. On that particular night, I hadn't bothered to pass the headphones around the side of the table to able seaman Taff James. I half lay back and relaxed to read, aware that the chat on the phones had stopped. All was silent, except for the creaking of the ship as she zig-zagged towards Grand Harbour, Malta. The night dragged on.

Some time later, came a rush of noise, as the heat of our transmitting station met the cool air up top and I heard the hatch slam open. Then the hurried scraping of boots on the vertical steel ladder, and the ear hurting thump as whoever it was swung the hatch cover down after him, and clipped it shut. I didn't bother to look up – all visitors were a nuisance.

The footsteps drew level with my shoulders and I glanced left as the last two rungs to the deck were negotiated. There were no feet, no legs. A quick upward look confirmed – nobody was there!

Taff James' face peered around the table at deck level, mouthing the words 'Who's that?' Another face from behind the large deflector screen at the far end of the table asked the same question. I didn't reply. I was already upright, reacting instinctively, calling out over the headphones the order 'All guns close up.' Our T. S. crew was now 'closed up,' waiting, alert, listening for something and hearing only the equipment and the sound of clothes rustling. The seconds stretched out towards a hoped for tomorrow.

Into that strange silence, came a muffled shout over my headphones. Could that be the masthead lookout, I thought incredulously? He was more than seven decks above me, high up in the crow's nest. He shouldn't be able to contact me – but who else could it be?

I held back my shout of 'Repeat' as the words filtered through, hovering on the edge of audibility. 'Aircraft on the starboard bow' – pause – 'Bearing green, four-zero.'

The T. S. crew watched me calmly, hearing nothing. I responded with the order. 'Starboard battery, red barrage, red-load, load, load!'

The Lieutenant, high above the bridge, wondered how all his starboard 'gun-ready' lamps were burning, showing the guns loaded – no alarms had sounded and no orders had gone from the director or the bridge to the T. S. or the guns. But he had heard the clatter from the gun-deck, so he asked no questions – he fired the salvo!

On short fuses, the exploding shells lit up and shook the attacking Italian torpedo bombers – they lifted with the blast, and the first 'fish' or torpedoes, went deep before levelling out.

From the opening of the hatch to the first salvo had taken only a few seconds! Now, over the noise of the guns as we swung to starboard and increased speed, came a high-pitched hum which climbed steadily.

'Torpedoes!' whispered Taff James.

'Shut up!' I said, looking around the tensed crew. The sweat dripped from the end of my nose onto the plot, a chart moving slowly from one roller to the other, forecasting the enemy's course.

Time went into the standing still routine again – long seconds crawling by. The snarl of the torpedo became a scream as it came in under the hull immediately below us. Then the sound dropped to a loud hum, fading rapidly, as the Doppler-effect confirmed that the fish had missed its target, passing under the ship. Someone on the guns called out that another torpedo had crossed the bow, missing by a few yards. A minute later, we heard and felt the shock of an explosion. We thought we'd been hit astern, but it was the cruiser *Arethusa* that had been torpedoed. She survived, badly damaged, with the loss of many of her ship's company.

A few days later, the *Orion* arrived safely back at Alexandria and moored up. As we crawled out through the T. S. hatch, I reached down under the deck head and turned off the light. I looked down into the silent darkness, and thought about the crew which had manned that T. S. before us.

We had known all along that on a previous voyage, the ship had been hit several times. Bombs and fire had fused the metal of the hatch and the deck, and cracked the fuel tanks. The sealed up T. S. had slowly filled with oil and fumes. No one could get through the wreckage to rescue the men of the T. S. They controlled the shoot as long as they could – but gradually all suffocated.

Looking into that darkness, I wondered . . . did someone? Did they . . . ? If that strange warning hadn't come . . . if the guns hadn't fired and the enemy aircraft hadn't lifted, would that torpedo have passed under us? As seafarers, we didn't look too closely at the workings of fate. The look might be taken as a challenge!

A fascinating story of an apparition whose timely warning saved the nine-man crew of the T. S. from the fate of their predecessors, all killed in the Battle of Crete. An apparition, never seen, but whose presence was felt by at least three members of the T. S. crew. The phenomena included a warning voice, heard by Tegwyn alone over his headphones.

Stories of apparitions telling of imminent danger are not unknown amongst seafarers, but what about straightforward, historical facts? The war records of the cruisers *Orion* and *Arethusa* confirm the basic outline of Tegwyn's compelling narrative, as I discovered from the naval section of the Ministry of Defence and the Public Record Office at Kew, London.

Simply stated, Tegwyn's account says that sometime after *Orion* went to sunset action stations, she was attacked by enemy torpedo bombers but emerged unscathed. Her sister ship *Arethusa* was badly damaged and suffered casualties.

The story of Wednesday 18 November, 1942 is told in the dog-eared pages of the ship's log of HMS *Orion*. She joined the convoy at sea early that morning and at 17.25 hours that winter's evening, took up her station in the 'night screen' of warships guarding the convoy. A naval spokesman confirmed that the ship would certainly have been on 'sunset action stations' at that time.

A handwritten entry told what happened forty minutes later. '18.05 hours. Enemy aircraft. Attacked by torpedoes. *Arethusa* hit and hauled out of screen. Courses as requisite to take avoiding action.'

Other documents from the Ministry of Defence painted the full picture of this assault upon a historic convoy, codename Operation Stone Age, which was attempting to break the German and Italian blockade of the British-held island of Malta. North of Benghazi on the coast of Libya, *Orion*, a 7000-ton cruiser with four and six-inch guns, had been the first in the convoy to come under attack from Italian torpedo bombers. *Orion* escaped, but another cruiser, *Arethusa*, was hit and there were 155 casualties from a massive explosion. HMS *Pethard* towed the crippled *Arethusa* back to Alexandria for repairs.

Despite these losses, Operation Stone Age was a success. The rest of the convoy ran the gauntlet of aircraft and submarines and brought badly needed supplies to the beleaguered garrison, which held out throughout the war, against everything the German and Italian air forces could throw at them. The British awarded Malta the George Cross Medal, to mark the collective bravery of its inhabitants.

A vital postscript to Tegwyn's narrative is his knowledge that the previous crew of the four-inch transmitting station aboard *Orion* had been killed in the Battle of Crete. This was confirmed by Admiralty documents and the ship's log for Thursday May 29, 1941, when the British Navy were desperately trying to evacuate thousands of troops from the Cretan port of Heraklion, during the Allied withdrawal from the island.

Under constant attack from German dive-bombers, British ships were sitting targets as they ferried off the soldiers. The destroyer *Imperial*, flagship of Rear Admiral Henry Rawlings, was sunk and so was the destroyer *Hereward*. The cruisers *Dido* and *Decoy* were crippled. Rawlings transferred his flag to the *Orion*, whose decks were crowded with over a thousand exhausted troops, many wounded.

Later that May morning, German dive-bombers scored two direct hits on *Orion* within two hours – there were explosions, fire and flooding. Over a hundred crewmen died, including almost certainly all the men of the four-inch T. S. *Orion*'s captain was killed and Rear Admiral Rawlings seriously wounded. Of the evacuated troops, who may have thought they had reached safety aboard the cruiser, 260 were killed and another 280 wounded.

The Admiralty's detailed report of the attack says that after several near misses, causing damage to fuel lines, *Orion* took its first direct hit from a heavy bomb just after nine o'clock in the morning. But most damage was done nearly two hours later, when a second heavy bomb, with a delayed action fuse, passed through the upper bridge and exploded within the ship. 'Blast effect severe. All personnel in the Lower Steering Position and in the vicinity, over 200 in all, were killed ... engine room telegraphs and steering gear were out of action, and the ship began to turn in circles and took a list of eleven degrees to starboard.'

A seven-page official report on bomb damage does not detail precisely what happened to the handful of men in the four-inch transmitting station, nor any other section of the crew, but it speaks of flooding by water and ruptured fuel-oil tanks. The fate of the four-inch T. S. is indicated in a paragraph on gunnery. 'Damage due to the second bomb was mostly confined to flooding of the four-inch and six-inch transmitting stations.'

So the T. S. flooded, but could the crew have escaped through the hatch cover? Tegwyn was told that their only escape route was cut when the hatch cover jammed as the deck buckled under the force of the explosion. Other survivors of *Orion*'s crew from the Battle of Crete were on the Malta run and the fate of the previous T. S. crew was well known aboard ship.

The official report describes the damage. 'The blast effect from the second bomb was severe. The explosion occurred well down within the ship within a closely confined space ... the plating of the lower deck was bulged upwards about three feet, and beams were blown upwards with the plating and were distorted ... the four-inch magazine, the Transmitting Stations etc., were flooded by damage to Platform Deck and bulkheads.'

Orion limped her way to Alexandria, many of those aboard either dead or dying. For part of that journey, she crossed the same stretch of sea as she did the following year, when, with Tegwyn aboard, she again came under attack from the air. On that occasion she was outward bound from Alexandria.

Orion was so badly damaged in the battle of Crete that she was taken for repair to Simonstown, South Africa, and then to dockyards in California. A year later, restored to fighting trim, she reappeared in the Mediter-ranean just a few months before setting out to run the Malta blockade.

Historically, Tegwyn's outline of events aboard *Orion* was true. But had there really been phantom footsteps on the ladder and a ghostly voice on the headphones? I asked him how he remembered everything so clearly after fifty years.

Some experiences are so powerful, so meaningful, you never forget. I've not talked about it much because it may be too unusual an experi-ence for people to accept. But it's as vivid in my mind today as the day it happened, and it hasn't changed over the years.

Could the steps on the ladder have been part of a dream or group hallucination? In a situation of danger and aware of the fate of the previous T. S. crew, had Tegwyn in the stress of that moment hallucinated and imagined the voice on the headphones? That seems unlikely since it is surely an extreme coincidence for an imaginary voice to sound a warning at precisely the moment when enemy aircraft were about to attack.

Ignoring the aspect of the footsteps, is it possible that someone topside on the ship saw the aircraft and gave Tegwyn a warning down the headphones? This too seems unlikely. Look-out type information was not available down that vital circuit which was for the officer directing the guns to talk to the man who transmitted his orders. If the voice had been the officer in charge of the guns, he would not have warned Tegwyn but would have rapped out his orders to the T. S. as to what action to take. Tegwyn knew the officer's voice and is certain he did not give the warning.

For a moment, Tegwyn had wondered if it had been the masthead lookout speaking, but his voice was relayed by a separate telephone circuit, never over those headphones. A salient point is that Tegwyn told me no one ever stepped forward on that ship to say, 'I saw those planes. I gave the warning that saved the ship.'

The source of the warning remains a mystery, and half a century later, we have not been able to trace other crew members of the T. S., who might recall how the hatch appeared to open and someone climbed down the ladder. Somehow, in that charged atmosphere of a sealed room, whose previous incumbents had all died, a warning was given just as history seemed about to repeat itself. Knowledge of what was happening remotely on the outside of the ship was somehow passed to a man inside the T. S., in time for action to be taken. There are two possible explanations of a paranormal nature. Could Tegwyn have received his warning by ESP? In that room, so recently a tomb, when everyone's future was precariously balanced, perhaps Tegwyn's mind generated some psi ability. Did he clairvoyantly detect the danger and manifest it as a warning voice in his head?

The other alternative is that this was an apparational warning, that somehow a force associated with the dead in the Battle of Crete gave a warning to the living. It seems certain we will never know.

✳　　　✳　　　✳　　　✳　　　✳

A cluster of other strange stories came from another friend, Pearl, a senior staff member of the BBC in Cardiff. One summer afternoon in 1989, Pearl looked out of her office window and saw an old colleague striding purposefully across the grass towards the department he used to work for.

'I said to myself, "Good heavens, look who's there. I haven't seen him for ages." He was walking briskly but he didn't look well. He seemed troubled and was frowning.'

Next day Pearl was told by telephone this friend was dead. She remarked 'Well that was sudden. I only saw him yesterday.' Later, she learned he had died some hours before her sighting of him. He had been in hospital for a couple of days, and it was quite impossible for her to have seen him. I asked if she could have mistaken someone else for our mutual friend, but Pearl described his distinctive walk, and the way he was dressed – typically in navy trousers and blue shirt, under a roll-top sweater. She'd seen his face close enough to register his expression.

Was she mistaken about time and date? She was telling me all this five weeks after the event.

'It made such an impact on me, I wrote it all down in my diary, as soon as I heard he was dead.'

I suggested it could still be a case of mistaken identity, for no one else had seen our friend that afternoon. 'Right,' she said, 'I'll give you an example you can check. This sort of thing has happened to me before.'

Twenty years ago, Pearl and her then husband lived in a block of flats in the town of Merthyr Tydfil, in South Wales. The next-door neighbour had died and his body was taken to an undertaker. 'Through the wall we heard what at first sounded like someone playing hymns on his piano – something he often did. We thought some kids had broken in and one of them was playing. We went outside to make sure, but the flat was quiet and totally secure. No one was there. Eventually, I came to the conclusion the person we heard playing the piano had to be the man who had died.'

A few days later, in September 1989, I spoke to Pearl's former husband. I said I was gathering stories of strange experiences – had he ever had one when he and Pearl lived at Merthyr?

'I can certainly remember something frightening that happened once,' he said. 'It was years ago and the man from the next-door flat was dead and waiting to be buried. We both heard someone playing hymns on his piano. We went around to see what was happening, but everything was locked up tight. It was bizarre.'

Pearl was a fund of such stories. Some years ago, working late in Broadcasting House, Cardiff, she saw a man in tail-coat, breeches and stockings walk past the open doorway. On the way out of the building, she told a security guard there was an actor walking about on the third floor. There was no drama in production, so a search was made but no one was found. The guard told Pearl she was the latest person to see 'the ghost of Baynton House,' an old mansion demolished years before to make way for Broadcasting House.

The security men I spoke to about Pearl's sighting of an actor told their own stories of unexplained sightings and noises. While checking empty rooms, a security guard opened a door and saw a middle-aged man in a grey suit sitting in a chair, looking straight ahead. The guard was startled and apologised for barging in, and left.

Outside the room, he had second thoughts. What was a stranger doing in that office at night? 'I re-opened the door to ask him, but the room was empty. I couldn't believe it. There were no connecting doors, the windows were secure, so where had he gone? I even looked in the cupboards to see if he was hiding.'

Once people learned I was interested, I was told stories of ghostly knockings, haunted rooms, strange messages from spirits on home-made ouija boards. A BBC Wales production assistant had a story about a dream.

At the age of eight, Susan had a nightmare she has never forgotten. It was about a favourite aunt who used to take the child clambering amongst the rock pools along the shore. One night, the child dreamed they were looking into a dark rock pool when her aunt screamed and fell in. She went spinning down into the blackness, arms and legs spreadeagled like a starfish. Susan was very upset and was comforted by her mother, whom she told of her dream.

The following morning, Susan's uncle called at the house. His wife had been knocked down and killed by a motor-cycle. She ended up spread-eagled on the black tarmac of the road – very much as in Susan's pre-cognitive dream, which happened some hours before her aunt was killed.

It was beginning to seem that almost everyone I knew had some strange tale to tell – all I had to do was ask. A senior designer told me his story.

Julian lived in a small, friendly, South Wales village. His neighbour, a Mr Welshman, suffered from multiple sclerosis and spent much of his time doing woodwork in a shed at the bottom of his garden.

A few years ago, Julian returned from a holiday, and opened a window to let in some fresh air. Mr Welshman was in his garden and smiled warmly and waved. He then walked in his typically faltering way to his shed and Julian heard the lathe being started.

Later, in a corner shop, Julian was told, 'Bit of excitement while you were away. Mr Welshman died suddenly. You missed the funeral.' Julian became annoyed. Stories like that could cause a lot of distress, and there was an angry scene, with Julian insisting his neighbour was still alive. On the way home, he began to wonder. He called at another house, and was told the story was true – Mr Welshman dropped dead soon after Julian went on holiday. The funeral had already been held.

'But I saw him this morning. Does that mean I've seen a ghost?' said Julian.

'Yes, of course,' said the lady, who Julian says was the type of person who believed in that sort of thing. 'The whole street turned out to see him off and you were the only friend who wasn't there. So naturally Mr Welshman had to say goodbye to you as well.'

Next a friend of mine for thirty years sent me details and a drawing of a Near Death Experience I knew nothing about. Years ago, young Jim Lynch of Macclesfield, Cheshire, was knocked unconscious with multiple skull fractures when his bicycle hit a lorry.

I became aware I was looking down on myself from about eight feet up in the air. I had been placed on a footpath and I saw myself and two men kneeling beside my prostrate body. I knew one of the men, the village policeman P. C. Twigg, who was wearing a flat cap, dark jacket and trousers which did not match. I noticed he wore black boots and cycle clips. The other man was similarly dressed but my body obstructed my view of his boots. I should mention that I am extremely myopic and in normal circumstances would not be able to see a face let alone details at that distance.

These anecdotes are not verifiable but they add to the weight of evidence that a very large number of people have had experience of the paranormal in some form or other, and, like the widows in the Welsh survey, are willing to talk about it once they are sure they will not be ridiculed.

CHAPTER FOURTEEN

The Age of mediums

Physical phenomena (movements of matter without contact, lights, hands and faces materialised etc.) have been one of the most baffling regions of the general field, or perhaps one of the least baffling prima facie – so certain and great has been the part played by fraud in their production.
PROFESSOR WILLIAM JAMES

A hundred years ago, Europe and America were gripped by a fever, a public obsession with psychics and mediums who claimed to speak to the dead. To some Christians it seemed as if the spirits themselves were protesting, from the next world, at the post-Darwin claims of science that human kind were mere animals and the notion of an after-life was superstitious nonsense.

The psychic display was brilliant and widespread – the dead spoke and materialised, sat amongst the living at seances, and mediums levitated, walking on air held up by ghostly hands. It seemed a new age of miracles had come. Or was it fakery and foolishness, as the sceptics said?

In 1882, some leading scientists and intellectuals decided to test the truth of these claims. Academics, psychologists, physicists, lawyers and others formed the Society for Psychical Research in London, and a few years later along came the American Society for Psychical Research. There has been nothing quite like the early days of the SPR and the ASPR before or since. Lecturers and chemists went fraud-hunting amongst the mediums, who were strip-searched, weighed, bound hand and foot and sometimes even nailed to the floor by their clothing. These amateur sleuths published massive amounts of remarkable research into the paranormal. Some fakes were exposed, some claims made for supernatural activity. It was all part of a huge and acrimonious public debate about religion and whether there was life after death.

Today's mediums and the general level of public interest in them are only a shadow of those days. The scientists have mostly returned to their laboratories and even the spirits, so profuse a century ago, seem largely to have quit the scene. But the SPR and the ASPR are still with us and their records of the pioneers of parapsychology allow for us to glimpse those turbulent years in the nineteenth century.

Charles Darwin's *Origin of Species* had been published in 1859, and by the 1870s it seemed to religiously minded folk that two thousand years of belief were being put to the sword of materialism. The spiritualist counter-attack had its origins back in 1848, when the young Fox sisters heard paranormal rappings at their home in Hydesville, USA. They knocked back and opened a dialogue with the supernatural that led to spiritualism, which became the fastest growing religion in the world.

To the God-fearing it seemed the spirits themselves had come to the rescue, asserting the value of religious beliefs and saying 'Look, we are here, we are real.' To the sceptics, it was self-delusion on a grand scale. Frauds and tricksters were trading on the fears of the gullible and spiritual-ism was the hysterical reaction of people, raised in the belief that Man was the Son of God, who felt abandoned and insulted on being told man was a distant cousin to an ape with no prospect of an after-life.

Everywhere, people queued to enter the tents and halls of mediums, ordinary families rapped out messages to the dead on kitchen tables, while the crowned heads of Europe, Prime Ministers and American Supreme Court judges held seances in exclusive drawing rooms. The planchette for recording spirit messages was invented in France, and the ouija board, a similar device dating back to Pythagoras, came into its own. Everyone was caught up in the great psychic debate. Mediums became celebrities – the public avidly read of their exploits in newspapers and special magazines. Occasionally, one crashed to earth as a fake, but they mostly brazened it out, accusing the investigators of lying. By the time they had read the following morning's newspapers, the public hardly knew whom to believe.

The superstars of spiritualism were the materialising mediums, who could call spirits back in human form. These seances were the Grand Opera of mediumship. The great name amongst nineteenth-century ma-terialising mediums was Daniel Dunglas Home, a Scotsman who claimed to be an illegitimate relative of the Earls of Home. He was taken to America at the age of nine and brought up by an aunt in New York State, but she turned him out of the family home in his teens – she had put up with his visions, but when strange rappings and bangings continued to follow him about the house, despite the efforts of a Congregational Minister to exorcise evil spirits, her patience was exhausted.

Fortunately, a Harvard professor investigated the rappings, which occurred without warning in the vicinity of this delicate youth, and pronounced them 'paranormal.' The young man's career was launched and he never looked back. In a few years, D. D. Home was a celebrity. He could produce most of the classic phenomena: he could float up in the air and cause people and furniture to do the same, and the spirits who accompanied him sometimes showed themselves as apparent flesh and blood; disembodied hands were a speciality. There were 15 000 mediums in the USA, but Home's reputation soared above all. A Supreme Court judge became a spiritualist through witnessing Home's seances.

But how real were all these alleged phenomena? In a long career he was never caught cheating and was one of the rare mediums who preferred to hold seances in good light. On the other hand, he was never formally tested by the SPR, which was not founded until 1882, when Home's career was virtually over.

But that was not the position in 1855 when Home, a young man of 22, already famous, set sail for his native Britain, where he was taken up by high society and became the superstar of the drawing room seance.

The poets Robert Browning and Elizabeth Barrett Browning entertained Home and so did various peers of the realm. At the Browning house, Home levitated flowers which settled on Mrs Browning's hair. He paid her some attention, and incurred the jealous dislike of Robert Browning who attacked him with a satirical poem *Mr Sludge the Medium*.

The novelist William Thackeray was more generous. He witnessed Home's mediumship in America and Europe and endorsed someone else's comment, 'I have seen what I would not have believed on your testimony, and what I cannot, therefore, expect you to accept on mine.'

In the autumn of that year, Home moved to the warmer climes of Florence, Italy, where his reputation got him into trouble with some followers of Roman Catholicism. His spirit voices and manifestations were believed by some to be an effort to raise the dead by necromancy. Home was stabbed three times by an unknown assailant.

During this crisis, his spirit guides announced his powers would leave him for a year. In his hour of darkness, the young man turned to religion, and was granted an audience with Pope Pius IX.

He became a convert to Catholicism, and promised to enter a monastery.

It never happened. Home's powers returned a year to the day, as predicted, and he re-embraced spiritualism, setting off on a tour of the courts of Europe. He performed for the Emperor Napoleon III of France, whose wife the Empress recognised a materialised hand as her father's

1 *Above left* Tessa Cordle during a Ganzfeld ESP experiment. Her eyes are covered by half ping-pong balls and 'white' sound is played through headphones (see page 3).

2 *Above* A bronze angel 'Peace' by Greg Wyatt is the centrepiece of the park near the Cathedral of St John the Divine, New York. It is turning green, exactly as Tessa said.

3 *Above* Tessa's drawing of 'a large statue of a man with wings ... turning green ... in a small peaceful park.' For the Remote Viewing test, she could have visualised any location in New York City, but the target, quite unknown to her, was a small park dominated by a large statue.

4   *Above* The Canadian psychic Terry Marmoreo used psychometry to try to find the killer known as 'Son of Sam.' With a map of New York in front of her, and holding a blood-stained scrap of a victim's purse, she came close to pinpointing where the killer worked. She gave her information over the telephone from Canada to New York, to parapsychologist Dr Karlis Osis and New York Police Department detective Rodney Roncoglio (see page 12).

5   *Left* Dr Osis and detective Roncoglio outside the New York post office where Son of Sam worked. Two psychics had said he was a postman and one said she saw a big bird towering over him, probably the postal service logo.

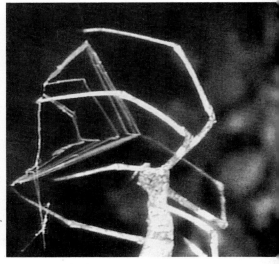

6 *Top* At the Dream Laboratory, New York, where experiments in dream telepathy were made in the 1970s, Charles Honorton (right) saw the possibility of a simplified test which became the Ganzfeld remote viewing test (see page 35).

7 *Above left* Sometimes a remote viewer in a Ganzfeld test gets an impression of a picture's meaning or associations, rather than seeing it with pinpoint accuracy. This picture of George Washington was 'seen' as Abraham Lincoln sitting at the Lincoln Memorial, the Fourth of July and fireworks, and the 'viewer' quoted a line from the US National Anthem.

8 *Above right* Remote viewing results improved when Charles Honorton used moving pictures as targets. This spider spinning a web was seen as basket weaving and the vanes on a windmill before being correctly identified as a spider (see page 39)

9 *Above* The cruiser *Orion* (see page 104).

10 *Left* Royal Navy seaman Tegwyn Hughes was aboard the British cruiser *Orion* in 1942 when there was a 'phantom' warning of an attack by enemy aircraft.

11 *Above right* The medium D. D. Home's accordion is inside the cage under the table, a device built by the investigator Sir William Crookes, a scientist, who reported that it played without the medium touching it. Crookes also saw it float freely in the air, playing *Home, Sweet Home* (see page 118).

12 *Right* D. D. Home's accordion is now held at the Society for Psychical Research headquarters in London.

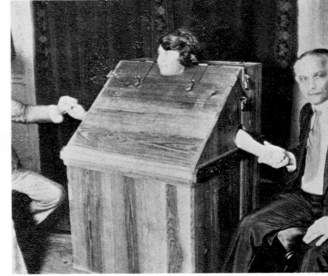

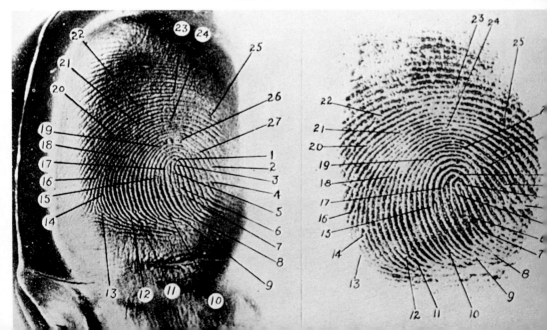

13   *Far left* Mrs Leonore E. Piper of Boston, the 'queen of psychics,' whose reputation was unequalled among trance mediums (see page 120).

14   *Above left* The American medium Margery, real name Mrs Mina Stinson Crandon, who produced spectacular phenomena in the 1920s and 1930s (see page 134).

15   *Left* This 'fraud-proof' wooden box was created for Margery by the escapologist Houdini.

16   *Below left* The thumb-print (left) of Walter, Margery's spirit guide, was made on a wax pad at a seance, but turned out to be virtually identical to the thumb-print of Margery's dentist (right), and the reputation of the medium was badly affected. The similarities are clear.

17   *Above* Father Giuseppe Riccardi, who was shot dead at the altar of a church in Canton, Ohio, USA in 1929. He is said to have appeared at a seance in Italy almost twenty years later (see page 136).

18　*Right* A table-turning experiment in London. With hands on the table-top it moved dramatically but never lifted right off the floor when we filmed it. However, the group sent us a video they had made which appeared to show that 'William,' the name they have for the 'force,' had lifted the table clear of the floor – the sitters' hands were still in contact with the table (see page 139).

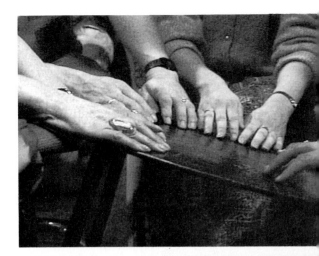

19　*Centre right* Gordon Higginson, President of the Spiritualists' National Union in Britain, at work as a medium, conveying messages from spirits to friends and relatives at a public meeting (see page 138).

20　*Below right* A spirit-hand is supposed to have caused this plaster cast, which belongs to the Society for Psychical Research, London. The spirit guide of a Polish medium is said to have immersed its hand in a bowl of warm paraffin wax from which a cast was taken. If it was a human hand that was immersed and then withdrawn, how can the hand be narrower at the wrist than across the palm? Sceptics have suggested that such hands might have been made by blown-up rubber gloves, which would be deflated in the wax and then withdrawn.

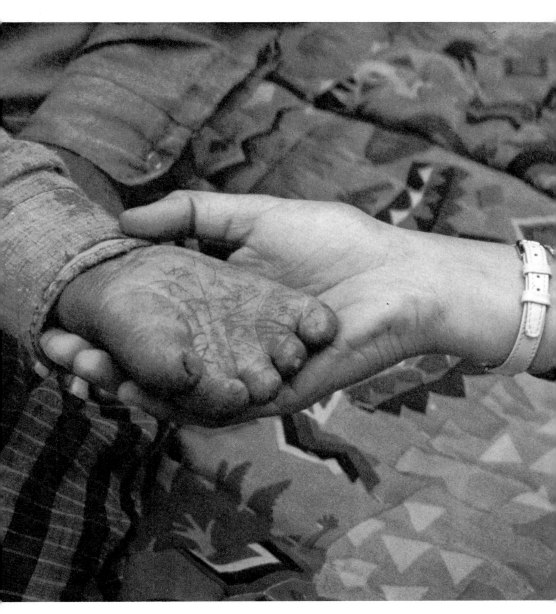

21 *Above* A boy in India, born without fingers on his right hand, remembered a previous life as a child whose fingers were amputated in an accident with a fodder-chopping machine (see page 150).

22 *Above* Twenty-year-old Manju Sharma and her two young children in an unusual family group in India. Manju remembers drowning in a well in another life and has spent half of this life living with the dead girl's parents (shown here) as their daughter. The two little girls are accepted by the elderly couple as their grandchildren (see page 160).

23 *Above right* Eighty-one-year-old Ling Rinpoche died on 25 December 1984. The Tibetans believe he has been reborn (see page 162).

24 *Right* This five-year-old boy was in a Tibetan orphanage until he was recognised as the reincarnation of a high Lama, Ling Rinpoche, senior tutor to the Dalai Lama.

25 *Above* Seated on her father's lap is nine-year-old Shanti Devi in Delhi, India, in 1935, when she led a committee of inquiry on a guided tour of the town of Mathura, where she remembered living in a previous life (see page 167).

26 *Above right* Mrs Emma Michell of the Wet'suwet'en Indians in British Columbia, Canada, sings the Beaver song, accompanying herself on a drum. Emma knew of several cases of reincarnation within her family (see page 176).

27 *Right* Emma Michell (left) as a little girl almost eighty years ago with her family. Standing behind her is her brother Jimmy who was found dead in the Bulkeley River in British Columbia, and who, when reborn, told Emma how he had been murdered.

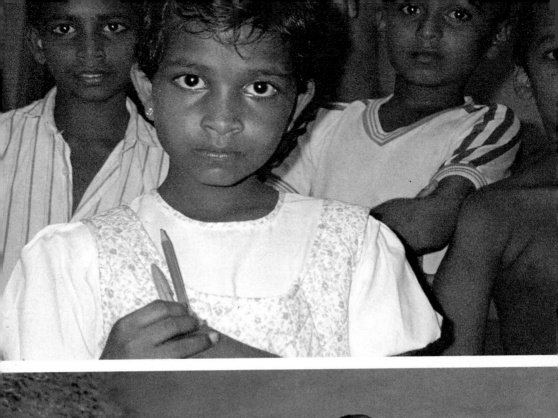

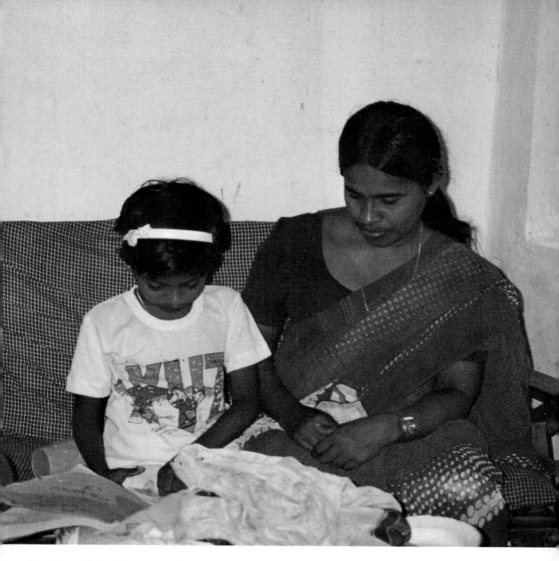

28 *Above left* Nine-year-old Thusitha, a tailor's daughter in Sri Lanka, who recalled drowning in another life, when she was pushed into a river by a dumb boy (see page 185).

29 *Left* Flower seller Mrs Dharmadasa stands by a river where her small daughter drowned. She believes her child has been reborn as Thusitha, who lives in a village in another part of Sri Lanka.

30 *Above* A Sri Lankan child, Dilukshi, looks through clothes and books belonging to a dead girl whose life she claims to remember. The girl's parents say that Dilukshi appeared to recognise some of the items (see page 187).

31 **Above** Duminda, by pointing
to a monk in a group photograph,
shows Professor Haraldsson (left)
and Godwin Samararatne the
person he believes he was in a
previous life.

32 **Right** At a monastery in
Kandy, Sri Lanka, six-year-old
Duminda chants Buddhist texts in
Pali, a language used in religious
services. Duminda is thought to
be a reincarnated abbot (see
page 189).

because of a defect to a finger. Home appeared before the King of Naples, the Emperor of Germany, the Queen of Holland, the Tsar of Russia, and so on. He was an international celebrity.

Part of the Home legend is that he never charged a fee, but he presumably received many expensive gifts from his royal friends, on whom he was certainly making a good impression. Then, at the age of 25 in St Petersburg, Russia, Home married a Russian aristocrat. It was a society wedding, and one of the witnesses was the novelist Alexandre Dumas. Some of Dumas' stories have supernatural ingredients said to be derived from the seances of D. D. Home.

Throughout his personal life, Home was involved in various scandals and notoriety. He was expelled from Rome accused of sorcery, his wife died after bearing him a child and there were legal wrangles over money. But in an often hostile world, D. D. Home the medium was never caught cheating, although many observers were convinced he had to be a fraud, because his phenomena could not be explained.

The celebrated pioneer of electricity, Michael Faraday, announced he was prepared to investigate and expose Home. The medium agreed to Faraday's tests, but the sittings never took place, because Faraday tried to impose an extra and unacceptable condition – Home should acknowledge in advance that his phenomena, however produced, were contemptible and ridiculous!

Home gave sittings to other scientific critics. Dr Ashburner, a royal physician and Dr John Elliotson, one time President of the Royal Medical Society, both attacked Home's mediumship and independently set out to test him. Both were won over and became public converts to spiritualist beliefs. Frank Podmore, a stringent SPR investigator wrote, 'Home was never publicly exposed as an impostor. There is no evidence of any weight that he was ever privately detected in trickery.'

The best account of Home's mediumship came in 1871 from Sir William Crookes, an eminent physicist and inventor, who picked up the Faraday challenge. Crookes told the eager Press he would investigate spiritualism with no preconceived ideas. There was a clear expectation that the great man of science would soon debunk the Scottish psychic and his ilk. Crookes said 'The increased employment of scientific methods will produce a race of observers who will drive the worthless residuum of spiritualism hence into the unknown limbo of magic and necromancy.'

Of course, it didn't turn out like that. Some scientific journals would not publish Crookes' findings, which were favourable to spiritualism, once they had read them. Crookes explained his change of heart. 'A medium walking into my dining-room cannot, while seated in one part of the room with a number of persons keenly watching him, by trickery make an accordion play in my own hand when I hold it keys downwards, or cause the same accordion to float about the room playing all the time.'

Crookes was converted. It was salt in the wound for the sceptics when he named the tune the accordion played – *Home, Sweet Home*!

Crookes used elaborate electrical and mechanical devices to test Home. He had the accordion put in a wooden drum-like cage which fitted tightly under a table. The cage was insulated with copper wire carrying an electrical current to detect any interference. Home sat at the table, hands firmly held on either side, and the accordion still played and floated freely about inside the cage.

Today, the accordion is an exhibit at the headquarters of the SPR in Adam & Eve Mews, London, where we filmed it, along with a fine bust of D. D. Home. The accordion still plays and we were allowed to record another version of *Home, Sweet Home*, but this time the player was clearly to be seen.

Back in 1871, Crookes and others witnessed more apparent wonders. Home went to the fire-place and picked up a glowing coal, the size of an orange, cupped his other hand over the top and blew on the coal until the flames licked out between his fingers. Crookes and Lord Adare saw Home lie down in front of an open fire and put his head amongst the burning coals.

Crookes was so intrigued he hired a man who claimed to handle fire with impunity. He was able to hold a red-hot iron for a short time, but after he left Crookes said 'the house smelled of roast negro.' He had detected no smell of burning when Home handled fire and Crookes inspected the medium's hands, which were unmarked. Sometimes, Home used a sitter's handkerchief to pick up burning coal, and the handkerchief was returned unsinged. Crookes analysed the material and found no traces of any heat-resistant substance.

Home was famous for his rappings and his levitations. In London, heavy tables, chairs, sometimes with sceptical witnesses seated in them, were said to rise high up in the air. Home too floated upwards to the height of the ceiling. Sometimes, said Crookes, he had onlookers holding onto his legs while this happened. Crookes estimated that a hundred people had seen Home floating about in the air.

Lord Adare wrote that he and two other witnesses saw Home step out of a third floor window and re-enter the room from a window on the far side of the building. Apparently, he had walked around the outside. It is not surprising that some critics have found the testimony about Home's manifestations hard to accept.

The medium himself always said he had no control over his phenomena – the power came and went and sometimes nothing happened at a seance. Most of Home's manifestations – hands and limbs – were produced in good or half light. Home even publicly denounced 'fraudulent mediums' and those who insisted on performing only in the dark.

If Home was a cheat, how did he do it? One suggestion is he was a master hypnotist, able to create any illusion he chose in the minds of entranced subjects. But people were very familiar with hypnotism or Mesmerism last century, and if Home was simply a hypnotist, it would have been observed. Not everyone is suggestible and there is no record of anyone claiming that Home tried to hypnotise him. Another possibility is that he was a conjuror. If so, he was a remarkable one – able to levitate heavy dining-room tables in houses he had never visited before.

Of course, most of his seances were private and some say his phenomena were not adequately investigated by scientists. As to whether they were genuine manifestations, perhaps it is fair to record an open verdict for lack of evidence, but to note that D. D. Home in his day was not afraid to be scientifically tested. He told Crookes, 'Now William, I want you to act as if I was a recognised conjuror, and I was going to cheat you and play all the tricks I could. Don't consider my feelings, I shall not be offended.'

D. D. Home was a devout spiritualist and possibly the greatest medium ever. But there was one who came after him, whose abilities were more stringently tested and who therefore provided greater evidence for the possibility of life after death. If Home was the king of mediums, then Leonore E. Piper was certainly the queen of psychics.

CHAPTER FIFTEEN

The queen of psychics

I should be willing now to stake as much money on Mrs Piper's honesty as on that of anyone I know, and am quite satisfied to leave my reputation for wisdom or folly, so far as human nature is concerned, to stand or fall by this declaration.
PROFESSOR WILLIAM JAMES

In all the clamour of psychic visions and voices from the nineteenth century, one medium stands out – the American Mrs Leonore E. Piper whose long career is perhaps the best evidence for survival after death from the age of mediums.

She was subjected to the most rigorous tests imaginable and her phenomena were pronounced twenty-four carat genuine by some of the sternest judges of the age. After years of research, the great American psychologist William James had no doubt about Mrs Piper's paranormal abilities, and the toughest psychic investigator of them all, Richard Hodgson, went a step further – he became convinced Mrs Piper was truly in touch with the spirits of the dead. No other medium achieved such endorsements.

Mrs Piper turned her back on the fortune she could have earned as a professional medium, and devoted her career to assisting psychical research. Her sittings were controlled firstly by James, on behalf of the ASPR, and then by Hodgson and other researchers. She received £200 a year from the society.

First signs of psychic ability had come in 1867, when little Leonore E. Simonds, eight years old, was playing in the garden of her home. She felt a sharp blow on her ear and heard a voice say, 'Aunt Sara is not dead but with you still.' The child ran to her mother sobbing. Several days later a letter arrived saying Aunt Sara had died on the day of the incident. Later, the child complained of bright lights in her bedroom and of being unable to sleep because her four-poster bed was rocking about. Otherwise she grew up normally and at the age of twenty-two married William Piper, who worked in a Boston store.

Three years later she went with her father-in-law to a seance conducted by a blind clairvoyant, J. R. Cocks, and her life was changed. Mrs Piper went spontaneously into a trance when Cocks put his hand on her head.

She walked to a table and wrote a note which she handed to a stranger. When she came to, she thought she had fainted and was surprised when approached by Judge Frost from Cambridge, Massachusetts, who said her note had given him the proof he was seeking that his only son, who had died some years earlier, was alive in the next world.

Within a short while her reputation was known throughout Boston and William James, Professor of Psychology at Harvard University, anonymously went to a sitting out of curiosity. He was told numerous facts about his family – and assumed the medium had somehow recognised him.

He began to pay serious attention when his mother-in-law, Mrs Gibbins, produced an unopened letter from Italy. Mrs Piper held it to her forehead and spoke at some length about the writer who was known to only two people in America. Professor James was further impressed when Mrs Gibbins said she had lost her cheque-book and Mrs Piper told her where to find it. Mrs Piper also told James and his brother that their Aunt Kate in New York had passed away in the early hours of the morning, and James would learn of it when he returned home. Reaching his house an hour later, James opened a telegram containing news of his aunt's death.

The psychologist wrote about the medium to his friend F. W. H. Myers at the SPR in London. 'Insignificant as these things sound when read, the accumulation of a large number of them has an irresistible effect. And I repeat what I have said before – taking everything that I know of Mrs Piper into account, the result makes me feel as absolutely certain as I am of any personal fact in the world, that she knows things in her trances which she cannot possibly have heard in her waking state, and that the definite philosophy of her trance is yet to be found.'

✳   ✳   ✳   ✳   ✳

Mrs Piper's other famous assessor, Richard Hodgson, at this time was making his reputation in England, not as a skilled student of human personality, but as a debunker of fakes. Hodgson was an Australian-born lawyer, who studied at Cambridge University, England, and was a founder member of the SPR in London in 1882. Two years later, he was sent by the society to India to investigate claims of fraud against Madame Helena

Petrovna Blavatsky, a 53-year-old Russian exile, founder of the Theosophical Society, and the best known mystic in the world.

Blavatsky's new religion, based in India, aimed to bring esoteric Buddhist teachings to the West, and the public was agog for reports of astonishing psychic phenomena. Blavatsky and her associates testified to the SPR in London that they were guided by two Mahatmas from a mystic brotherhood in Tibet, and that these Mahatmas regularly teleported written messages to the society, and sometimes appeared in person by materialising themselves.

Witnesses gave evidence that on several occasions they had seen the Mahatmas appear, and that they had witnessed the arrival of letters from Tibet, which materialised in a puff of dust and floated down to the floor. Sometimes these letters appeared in a locked cupboard in the shrine room at the Theosophical Society headquarters in Adyar, India.

The SPR had already made a preliminary finding, accepting much of these alleged phenomena, but disturbing reports of fraud were coming out of India and Richard Hodgson was sent to investigate.

When Hodgson returned months later, his report was a sensation. The phenomena were faked and Blavatsky was behind it all. The Mahatmas were Blavatsky accomplices wearing dummy heads and shoulders. The messages had all been written by Blavatsky herself, as hand-writing experts testified, and Hodgson demonstrated how they materialised in mid-air – usually they were hidden in crevices in the ceiling and released by an accomplice pulling on a string. In the shrine room at Adyar, there had been a false back to the cupboard where messages and apports (objects supposedly brought there by spirits) appeared. The back of the cupboard was connected by a secret passage to Blavatsky's bedroom.

The evidence was overwhelming and Blavatsky was forced out of the leadership of the Theosophical Society, which nevertheless survived. Madame Blavatsky was paid a wry compliment by Hodgson, 'Madame Blavatsky is a most remarkable person, nearly as rare as a Mahatma!'

There were more sensations to come. The foremost materialising medium in Britain, William Eglinton, was caught up in the furore. His spirit guides had authenticated the Mahatmas and there had been an exchange of materialised messages with Blavatsky. Hodgson demonstrated that these messages were faked and Eglinton, whose seance phenomena had converted the Prime Minister, W. E. Gladstone, to spiritualism, was also denounced as a fraud.

There was a furious backlash within the SPR with eminent members such as Alfred Russel Wallace supporting Eglinton's mediumship. The accused medium was famous for slate writing amongst other things, and it was pointed out by his supporters that a new medium S. T. Davey, who was accepted as genuine, was able to perform the same psychic feats as Eglinton.

Davey demonstrated his slate writing and various Eglinton-type phenomena and then publicly revealed them to be conjuring tricks. Davey's manager and collaborator in the exposure of the Eglinton mediumship was Richard Hodgson, a skilled conjuror himself. Eglinton gradually made alternative career arrangements, and for a time was editor of the society magazine *The Tatler*.

Hodgson's third controversial debunking of a celebrated psychic was some years later in 1895. His target was the Italian materialising medium, Eusapia Palladino, a colourful figure with flashing eyes and a fiery temper, who sometimes physically attacked her critics. Eusapia had had a tragic childhood. Her mother died when she was born and her father was murdered by bandits when the girl was twelve years old. Eusapia, hardly educated, became a nurse-maid in Naples.

A few years later at a seance in London, a spirit guide known as 'John King,' who appeared at many seances for different mediums, announced that a powerful medium was living in Naples and gave Eusapia's name and address. John King said the new medium was his own reincarnated daughter. Eusapia had been discovered and a famous career was under way. She could make objects move and float in the air, bells ring and tambourines play without touching them. Spectres of people, sometimes in full form, appeared at her seances. Eusapia's seances were held in the dark, but she made herself available for scientific investigation for twenty years and was highly thought of by researchers in Europe. Impulsive, generous and neurotic, she had strange phobias – she was afraid of staining her hands and frequently believed she could see her own ghost.

Her willingness to cheat on occasions was also quite well known. One Continental researcher watched her gathering flowers in a garden, which later turned up as apports at a seance.

Eusapia received a glowing write-up in the SPR journal after a series of seances in France at the home of Professor Charles Richet, a leading international parapsychologist. There was a published exchange of letters between Richet and Richard Hodgson who suggested that the observers had not taken adequate precautions and he doubted if Eusapia's phenomena were genuine. Richet observed testily that after three months' practice with Eusapia, he was perfectly capable of knowing whether he was holding the medium's hand securely or not.

Hodgson's response took the form of a practical demonstration in Cambridge, England. Hodgson quietly allowed Eusapia to slip her left hand free of restraint and it became clear to all that the phenomena were being produced in the dark by Eusapia herself.

Myers, who had been so impressed in France, wrote, 'I cannot doubt that we observed much conscious and deliberate fraud of a kind which must have required long practice to bring it to its present level of skill ... the fraud occurred both in the medium's waking state and during her real or alleged trance. I do not think there is adequate reason to suppose that any of the phenomena at Cambridge were genuine.'

The Continentals closed ranks around Eusapia. Hodgson was criticised for unsportingly allowing Eusapia to cheat. One expert, Professor Camille Flammarion of France wrote, 'One can readily conceive that when she is able to perform certain wonders without any expenditure of force, merely by a more or less skilful piece of deception, she prefers the second procedure to the first. It does not exhaust her at all and may even amuse her ... her fixed idea is to produce phenomena and she produces them no matter what.'

Hodgson took a very different view, which had been expressed by William James, 'Once a cheat, always a cheat.'

÷ ÷ ÷ ÷ ÷

In 1887, this much feared investigator, Richard Hodgson, turned his attention to Mrs Piper when he took over as secretary of the ASPR in Boston. He had no doubt what he expected to find. 'Nearly all professional mediums form a gang of vulgar tricksters, who are more or less in league with one another.'

Despite all the assurances to the SPR by Professor William James that Mrs Piper and her trance were genuine, Hodgson arrived in Boston knowing what he had to do. 'During the first few years, I absolutely disbelieved in her power. I had but one objective, to discover fraud and trickery, and I had had plenty of experience with those. I went to Mrs Piper with the object of unmasking her.'

Hodgson saw that Mrs Piper in her trance seemed to find her sitters an open book, knew all their secrets as if she had some prior knowledge of them. Hodgson made life difficult – he introduced every sitter as 'Mr Smith', and invited passing strangers in from the street to be sitters at the last moment. People were taken into a sitting after Mrs Piper had gone into a trance, and were seated behind her, so she could not see them, even had her eyes been open.

Could she be getting information from agents or correspondents? Hodgson hired private detectives to find out. They intercepted the mail and read Mrs Piper's letters.

Could members of the Piper family be secretly meeting with strangers or compiling notes on Boston families, perhaps making lists from tombstones in cemeteries? More detectives were hired to follow members of the Piper household.

But the surveillance did not pass unnoticed. Mrs Piper was furious and threatened to have nothing more to do with Hodgson, who said he was acting in the interests of science. Professor James, called in as peacemaker, pointed out that if Hodgson did not rule out trickery, some people would say trickery was behind the Piper phenomena. James urged Mrs Piper. 'I hope neither you nor your husband will take this thing seriously. It has its comic side and you are the ones who can best afford to laugh at it. Above all, keep good friends with Hodgson, who is perhaps the most high-minded and truthful man I know.'

The detectives reported that neither Mrs Piper nor any of her household had made any suspicious journeys, questioned anyone indiscreetly, employed agents to act for them or visited any cemeteries to obtain lists of names and dates from tombstones. The quarrel was patched up. The detectives were called off, but Hodgson insisted on retaining the right to scrutinise letters that came for Mrs Piper. He also forbade her to have newspapers for the days immediately before a sitting, and called at the newsagents to make sure his instructions were carried out.

The sittings were unaffected. Mrs Piper and her spirit guide, a Dr Phinuit, continued as before. Hodgson turned his attention to the Piper trance. To see if Mrs Piper's trance was real and not feigned, Hodgson held a lighted match against her forearm. Mrs Piper did not flinch, but Phinuit complained of a slight feeling of cold. Hodgson pulled back the medium's eyelids and noted her eyeballs were rolled up into her head. He held perfume under her nose, which Phinuit could not smell, and he tested her with strong ammonia, which also produced no reaction. Mrs Piper seemed not to detect a spoonful of salt put on her tongue. The most drastic experiment was undertaken by Professor James, a qualified surgeon, who made a small incision on Mrs Piper's left wrist. During the trance, the wound did not bleed, but bled freely when Mrs Piper woke up. She had a small scar for the rest of her life.

All the while, Phinuit carried on as if nothing was happening. A succession of Smiths came and went. They were told many intimate details about their lives and frequently talked with dead friends.

A new challenge came from Dr James Hyslop, Professor of Logic at the

University of Columbia, who secretly arranged with Hodgson to be a sitter. Hyslop arrived unannounced one night and entered the sitting wearing a black mask covering his entire face. He spoke in a disguised voice and uttered very few words. Hyslop was regarded as America's foremost cynic and materialist. It was therefore a Press sensation when he announced, after a series of sittings, 'I believe I have been speaking with my dead relatives, it's simpler.'

At the sittings, despite his disbelief, Hyslop had found himself apparently talking to his father Robert Hyslop, his uncles Carruthers and James, a cousin Robert and sister Annie. Hyslop's father, an obscure invalid, talked about his Calvinistic religious beliefs, remembered all the members of the Hyslop family and asked after 'Tom' – a horse on a farm in the mid-west!

After fifteen sittings, Hyslop abandoned his policy of asking few questions and decided to speak to his father as if it were a real conversation. 'The result was we talked with as much ease as if we had been talking down the telephone.'

After two years of tests, a baffled Hodgson decided to give the research a new dimension. Somehow, despite every precaution, Mrs Piper continued to give a flood of information about her sitters. But in the United States she was on home ground – how would she cope in a foreign land where she knew no-one? Mrs Piper was persuaded to visit England as the guest of the SPR. Accompanied only by her small daughters, she was met by Frederick Myers and Sir Oliver Lodge and was tested by them at sittings in various parts of the country.

Everywhere Mrs Piper went, even shopping, she was accompanied by someone from the SPR. Just as in America, the investigators did not stand on ceremony. To test the reality of Mrs Piper's trance, Lodge moved quickly up to her and plunged a needle into her arm. Mrs Piper did not even blink.

Sir Oliver Lodge invited the medium to his home at Liverpool. As soon as she arrived, he insisted on searching her luggage to see if she had any research material. He had taken the additional precaution of bringing in fresh servants, so there was no-one around that Mrs Piper could question about the family. He also hid all family photographs and documents, including the family Bible.

At the seance, Lodge gave Mrs Piper a pocket watch to hold, which had been specially delivered that morning from a relative far away. The medium correctly identified the watch as belonging to Lodge's long-dead uncle Jerry, who said, 'This is my watch and Robert was my brother and I am here – uncle Jerry, my watch.'

Lodge was intrigued to be told about Jerry's boyhood exploits with his brothers, involving a rifle, a snake-skin, killing a cat and swimming a mill race – all events of which Lodge knew nothing, and which had taken place over seventy years before. Eventually, by writing to a few elderly relatives, scattered around the country, Lodge established that these strange stories of long ago were true, but how could Mrs Piper have known about them?

Lodge took a leaf from Hodgson's book – he called in the private detectives. Could they, by normal information-gathering techniques, learn what Mrs Piper had known about those incidents in far-off days that seemed to exist only in the memory of a few elderly relatives? The detective agency eventually reported, 'Mrs Piper has certainly beaten me. My inquiries in modern Barking yield less information than she gave. Yet the most skilful agent could have done no more than secure the assistance of the local research keepers and the oldest inhabitants living.'

As with every medium, there were sittings when Mrs Piper's spirit voices gave wrong information or seemed unaware of facts they might have been expected to know. Nevertheless, on that first visit to England, Mrs Piper made a huge impression on Sir Oliver Lodge, an outstanding scientist, who acknowledged that the sittings had convinced him of survival. 'The hypothesis of surviving intelligence and personality – not only surviving but anxious and able with difficulty to communicate – is the simplest and the most straightforward and the only one that fits the facts.'

Mrs Piper returned to America in some triumph. The President of the SPR had been convinced but what of Richard Hodgson? The Secretary of the ASPR delivered his eagerly awaited verdict in 1892, after four years of research.

Hodgson was satisfied that Mrs Piper was not a fraud, her trance was genuine and she seemed able to obtain information by paranormal means, only partially explained by telepathy from the minds of sitters. But he said the evidence did not justify a conclusion that Mrs Piper was in touch with the spirits of the dead. He suggested that Mrs Piper's subconscious mind was somehow impersonating dead people, based upon information she was getting telepathically. Hodgson did not believe Mrs Piper's spirit guide, Dr Phinuit, to be genuine – he was perhaps a secondary personality produced by Mrs Piper. Hodgson had researched the details Phinuit gave of where and when he lived, and had concluded no such person ever existed.

The report pleased no one. The Spiritualists complained that the ASPR man had not confirmed that Mrs Piper's spirit voices were real. The materialists felt he had not exposed the medium as a fake.

Mrs Piper said Hodgson's conclusions seemed fair. She did not know what happened during a trance, so she was prepared to accept the theories of the experts. But Dr Phinuit, on his next appearance at a sitting, was furious. 'I am real. I once lived in a body and if those cranks weren't so stupid they could find me.'

There was an intriguing postscript in Hodgson's first report – new evidence was emerging which he had not yet had time to evaluate. Fate had taken a hand.

In February 1892, a young Bostonian lawyer, George Pelham, a friend of Hodgson and a noted sceptic about mediums, was thrown from his horse in New York and killed. Pelham had once attended a Piper sitting and told Hodgson afterwards that if he should die and find himself surviving, he would try to contact Hodgson and 'make things a bit lively.'

Within a few weeks of his death, Mrs Piper in trance spoke with a new voice. A sitter, the usual 'Mr Smith,' was surprised when George Pelham introduced himself as an old friend. The sitter asked Pelham if he could produce any proof that would show beyond doubt he was really Pelham. Mrs Piper's seemingly lifeless hand moved towards a nearby pad and pencil and wrote a message which convinced the sitter he had really been in touch with George Pelham.

Pelham's father and stepmother attended a sitting in a sceptical mood and were greeted by, 'Hello father and mother, I am George.' They left convinced.

Amongst the next 140 sitters, Hodgson introduced more than thirty of Pelham's old friends, all under the name of Smith. Pelham recognised each one and spoke to them exactly as he had in the days of their friendships. There was only some hesitation with one sitter – a young woman who had been a child when Pelham had last seen her.

There were numerous sittings, all minutely recorded by a notetaker, where Mrs Piper's voices showed knowledge that could not be explained by normal means. As with Sir Oliver Lodge, events were described that were unknown to the sitters, so telepathy seemed an unlikely explanation. Illnesses were correctly diagnosed by Dr Phinuit, prophecies were made which came true, sitters were given news of the death of friends and relatives, or were sometimes given messages to relay to others, which were of real significance.

In 1897, fifteen years after he had begun his investigations about Mrs Piper, Hodgson produced his second report for the SPR. The unthinkable had happened and Hodgson wrote, 'I cannot profess to have any doubt that the chief communicators are veritably the personages they claim to be, and that they have survived the change we call death, and that they have directly communicated with us, whom we call the living, through Mrs Piper's entranced organism.'

In an article published later, Hodgson said, 'I entered the house profoundly materialistic, not believing in the continuance of life after death, and today I simply say, I believe. The proof has been given to me in such a way as to remove from me the possibility of a doubt.'

Professor William James never committed himself to say Mrs Piper talked with the dead, but he maintained she had genuine paranormal powers. That she was very special amongst mediums, most of whom were regarded as fakes, he made clear in a celebrated speech. 'To upset the conclusion that all crows are black, it is sufficient to produce one white crow, a single one is sufficient.' Mrs Piper was James' white crow.

CHAPTER SIXTEEN

Riddles of the dead

*There is no such a thing as chance. What we regard
as blind circumstance actually stems from the
deepest source of all.* FRIEDRICH VON SCHILLER

I n the early years of this century, mediums in different parts of the world began to receive spirit messages which made little sense in isolation – but when put together like pieces in a jigsaw puzzle, an overall meaning emerged. It seemed the minds of individual mediums were being influenced by an intelligence outside themselves.

Did these messages, fragmented amongst mediums thousand of miles apart, dispose of the idea that each medium somehow invented her own phenomena – hallucinations in a state of self-hypnosis with some facts perhaps taken telepathically from the minds of the sitters opposite? Today, some observers say these cross-correspondences are the most convincing evidence for Survival from a century of psychical research.

Some of the cross-correspondences took years to communicate and the mediums were in the separate continents of America, Europe and India. The cross-correspondences were highly intelligent riddles often quoting Latin and Greek classics, and showing a scholarship beyond the knowledge of most of the mediums concerned.

The messages purported to come from a small group of psychical investigators, founders of the SPR, who had all died around the turn of the century. It was an effort to demonstrate Survival, and the ringleader seemed to be Frederick W. H. Myers, a poet and classical scholar of Cambridge, England, who died in 1901, just five years before the cross-correspondences started.

The mediums were mostly automatists, who in trance used pencil and paper to write down messages from the dead. As examples of deceased academics dictating to psychic secretaries, the scripts are sometimes human as well as learned. Giving a Latin quotation to the medium Mrs Holland in India, the scholarly Myers observed, 'How could I make it any clearer without giving her a clue?' The quotation was *'Ave Roma Immortalis'* or 'Hail Immortal Rome,' which fitted into a cross-correspondence amongst various mediums describing how Pope Leo persuaded Attila the Hun to spare the city of Rome.

A fine example of a cross-correspondence which unfolds with all the twists and turns of a detective story is 'Sevens.' In November, 1908, Mrs Margaret Verrall, a Cambridge lecturer, psychical researcher and celebrated automatist, told SPR secretary Miss Alice Johnson that she had identified a profusion of references to the number seven in the work of four automatic writers.

These were herself, her daughter Miss Helen Verrall, Mrs Piper of America and a Mrs Frith of England.

Miss Johnson already knew of two other automatists where sevens featured strongly in recent scripts – Mrs R. Home in England and 'Mrs Holland' whose messages came in mid-ocean, aboard ship between England and India. 'Mrs Holland' was the name used by Mrs Alice Kipling Fleming, wife of an army officer and sister of the novelist and poet Rudyard Kipling.

Alice Johnson had now identified six pieces of a jigsaw about sevens, but knew there was one piece missing. Some of the messages were explicit – Mrs Piper, under the control of the late Richard Hodgson, had written, 'We are seven,' and later, 'There are seven of us.' Miss Helen Verrall in Cambridge, on behalf of Myers, had also written, 'We are seven.'

Within a few days, Miss Johnson had, quite inadvertently, identified the seventh player. He was J. G. Piddington, member of the SPR Council and an expert on cross-correspondences, whom Miss Johnson consulted about the sevens case. But 'Sevens' had a significance for Piddington of which Miss Johnson was unaware. At first, Piddington was taken aback, but he returned to the SPR offices in London a few days later to explain his position. He asked Johnson for a sealed letter he had left with her four years earlier with the written instruction 'To be opened only after my death.' Piddington had intended the letter to be part of an experiment – if he survived death, he intended to try to convey the contents of his sealed letter to a medium. Since 1904, the letter had remained locked away at the SPR and only Piddington knew its contents.

Now, in November 1908, Piddington, very much alive, asked Miss Johnson to open his 'posthumous' letter. The reason became obvious in the first paragraph. 'If I am ever in spirit and if I can communicate, I shall endeavour to transmit in some form or other the number SEVEN.' Piddington wrote that he would try to use the word in various phrases and gave four examples. One was 'We are seven,' which had turned up in the automatic writings of both Mrs Piper and Mrs Verrall.

Piddington and Miss Johnson decided to keep quiet about the letter until they were ready to publish their Sevens report. Piddington felt none of the automatists should know of the letter in case it prejudiced any further messages about Sevens. It was a wise precaution. Exactly two months later, Mrs Verrall in Cambridge, receiving automatic writing from Myers, wrote, 'Has Piddington found the bits of his sentence scattered among you all?'

Writing in the SPR *Journal*, Miss Johnson said Mrs Verrall had known nothing of the Piddington letter. When she was told about it, Mrs Verrall was able to give further evidence. Piddington's letter had been written and sealed at midday on 13 July, 1904, in London. At 11.15 am that day in Cambridge, Mrs Verrall, doing automatic writing for Myers, wrote, 'Note the hour. In London, half the message has come.' Did Myers mean that Piddington's references to Seven had just been sealed in his letter at the SPR? It could be so, since Mrs Verrall also wrote, 'Let Piddington choose a sentence and send part to each.'

The key events in this typically complicated cross-correspondence are:

13 July 1904, Piddington's Sevens letter written in London.
13 July 1904, Mrs Verrall in Cambridge – 'In London half the message has come.'
28 August 1907, Mrs Verrall – 'Let Piddington choose a sentence and send part to each.'
August 1907 to 24 July 1908, Six mediums receive communications about Seven.
27 November 1908, Piddington's letter opened, unknown to Mrs Verrall.
27 January 1909, Mrs Verrall writes – 'Has Piddington found the bits of his sentence scattered among you all?'

Whose mind was responsible for setting this quite complex riddle? Piddington's letter about Sevens was the starting point, but the key statements are by Myers or Mrs Verrall. Could the Cambridge automatist, a classical scholar in her own right, have somehow known the content of Piddington's letter and telepathically influenced the minds of other mediums, some thousands of miles distant? Or was the spirit of Frederick W. H. Myers responsible?

A fascinating aspect of Sevens is that Myers, in automatic writing through Mrs Verrall, discussed these very possibilities. 'And what has been the success of Piddington's last experiment? Has he found the bits of his famous sentence scattered among you all? And does he think it is accident or started by one of you? . . . But even if the source is human, who carries the thought to the receivers? Ask him that.'

His idea is clear –no matter whose mind has set the Sevens riddle, the information is carried across oceans and put in the minds of mediums by spirits of the dead. It sounds reminiscent of Dr George Ritchie watching the spirits who whispered messages in the ears of the living – is that what telepathy is?

The best cross-correspondences have a sting in the tail. The jottings of different mediums are put together, but are they a pattern or a string of coincidences? Then, a new discovery leads the researchers straight to the front-door of one of those dead investigators from the SPR.

Such a cross-correspondence was 'Hope-Star-Browning,' which began in 1907 with Mrs Piper in Boston. She told Piddington of the SPR to 'Look out for Hope, Star and Browning' in the writings of Mrs Verrall. They were indeed there – Hope was mentioned conspicuously, there were quotes from Browning's poetry and intriguing references to Star, such as 'Anagram would be better, tell him that – rats, star, tars and so on. It has been tried before.'

Miss Helen Verrall in Cambridge, quite separately, wrote, 'No arts avail and a star above it all, rats everywhere in Hamlin Town. Now do you understand?'

The sting in the tail was that Piddington's memory was stirred. He recalled some notes he had seen amongst the private papers of Dr Richard Hodgson, who had died in Boston in 1905. He wrote to Hodgson's executors and they sent him Hodgson's hand-written notes about anagrams, including 'rats, arts and star.'

There was a similar end to another scholarly jigsaw known as 'The Ear of Dionysius.' The principal medium here was Mrs Willet, real name Mrs Winifred Coombe-Tennant, who received messages about a stone quarry at Syracuse, Sicily, famous for its echo-chamber effect. Today, visitors stand in this rocky cleft and listen to their voices reverberating around the walls. In the fifth century, Dionysius, the tyrant of Syracuse, put political prisoners to work in this quarry and stationed his spies at the top, where they heard every word the prisoners said – this was the 'Ear of Dionysius.'

Clear references were made by several mediums to the cave and to Dionysius over four or five years. But researchers were confused by other references to the one-eyed Cyclops from Homer's stories of the Ancient Greek hero Odysseus, dating from several centuries before. The two legends seemed muddled until Mrs Verrall, in automatic writing, gave the key word 'Philox.'

Philoxenus was a poet sentenced by Dionysius to work in the quarry. He revenged himself by writing a little-known satire about the partially blind tyrant, whom he depicted as the Cyclops of earlier Greek legend.

The sting in the tail is that the story of Philoxenus is told in a book *Greek Melic Poets* by Dr H. W. Smythe of Pennsylvania. He had sent a presentation copy to the late Dr A. W. Verrall, the Cambridge classical scholar and pioneer of psychical research who died a few years earlier. The book was still there on a shelf in Dr Verrall's library and had been a favourite volume which he used in his lectures. Dr Verrall was said to be one of the spirit authors of this cross-correspondence, in which his wife, Margaret Verrall, was one of the automatists.

Mrs Verrall who was a central player in many of these cross-correspondences, gave her own verdict on these apparent contacts between the living and the dead. 'The boundary between the two states, the known and the unknown, is still substantial but is wearing thin in places. Like excavators boring a tunnel from opposite ends, amid the roar of water and other noises, we are beginning to hear now and again the strokes of the pickaxes of our comrades on the other side of the partition.'

Perhaps the most startling cross-correspondences were by the American medium Margery, whose real name was Mina Stinson Crandon, in the 1920s. Messages from Margery's spirit guide were divided into several parts and delivered simultaneously to mediums standing ready in New York, Maine and Niagara Falls. Some messages were in Chinese which some of the mediums claimed to know nothing about. In the SPR cross-correspondences, the messages had been spread about amongst different mediums over years – in America, it all happened at the same time. In a well known example, Margery in Boston went into a trance and wrote automatically '11 × 2 = to kick a dead.' A telephone call was immediately made to Judge Cannon in New York, supervising the trance of medium George Valiantine. He said they had received '2 – no-one ever stops.' Next morning, a telegram from Dr Henry Hardwicke in Niagara Falls said their portion was '2 – horse.' Together the fragments read '11 × 2 = 22; No-one ever stops to kick a dead horse.' It was claimed this fragmented message demonstrated that the mediums were not using telepathy between the living, but were receiving parts of a spirit message from the late Walter Stinson. The problem with the Margery mediumship is that it was bedevilled by accusations of fraud. The illusionist and escapologist, Houdini, said she was a fake, although other investigators believed she was genuine.

Margery was the wife of a Boston surgeon, and her seances were dominated by the spirit of her brother Walter, who had been killed in a rail accident. Walter swore, whistled, dictated poetry and was a hugely entertaining spirit guide. But his reputation never quite recovered from a scandal about fake finger-prints. From 1926, Walter, in the dark, made more than 150 thumb-prints in wax pads, of the sort used for dental impressions – an idea suggested by Margery's dentist.

It seemed great good fortune for Margery, when Walter's mother found an old razor on which was a partial print, apparently matching his seance thumb-prints. But the triumph turned to disaster when a finger-print expert said all Walter's thumb-prints were made by the thumb of Margery's dentist!

The ASPR was split asunder. Some accepted there had been cheating, others accused the finger-print expert of tampering with Walter's prints. The medium's reputation was badly clouded, and remains so to this day.

I was given a fascinating insight into Margery's mediumship by a retired official of the ASPR, Mrs Marion L. Nester, daughter of Dr Mark W. Richardson who supervised many scientific tests on Margery. Mrs Nester, as a teenage girl, remembers Walter's whistling and his humour. She saw him make a ball run up an incline and he could tip down an empty pan on a pair of weighing scales. There were trumpets, ghostly music and psychic lights around a glass cabinet, like a telephone booth, in which Margery was sealed.

There was levitation and Walter's voice spoke from different parts of the room. Dr Richardson designed a voice machine whereby everybody held a tube between their teeth and sustained a constant water pressure which demonstrated that they could not be producing Walter's voice.

There were apports: Mrs Nester's sister was given a precious stone, and Walter observed, 'I have been robbing graves.' Solid wooden rings of different woods were psychically joined – Mrs Nester has a pair, but they became ruined as evidence when a researcher borrowed them and dropped them on the floor. One broke and was repaired with glue.

Mrs Nester is preparing a book on Margery. I asked if her father had remained convinced of Margery's genuineness, and she told me a story.

It was the day Margery died in 1941, and my father was alone in his Boston apartment. He was in bed, when there was a terrific knocking at the front door. It happened twice and there was no-one there. Then there was a metallic sound near the back door. As he said, it's one thing to hear all these sounds when there are other people about, but it's another when you're alone. He became a bit nervous and when he went back to bed, he left the light on.

Later he had a sitting with a medium at which Margery purportedly communicated and said, 'I scared you, didn't I?' Father played it down, and then she said, 'Well, why did you leave the light on all night?'

CHAPTER SEVENTEEN

Message from a murdered priest

At some future day it will be proved, I cannot say when and where, that the human soul is, while in earth life, already in an uninterrupted communication with those living in another world.
IMMANUEL KANT

A t a seance in a remote Italian village in 1948, a strange voice spoke from various parts of the room and claimed to be an American priest who had been shot to death by a woman twenty years earlier at the altar of a church. Notes were made, but this melodramatic incident meant nothing to those present. Then, thirty years later, it was found that the voice had described a real murder, just as it happened.

The shooting of Father Riccardi was one of the cases we reconstructed for our television series. Finding modern pictures of seances was difficult because the great age of spectacular mediumship has passed as surely as crinoline petticoats and sailing ships. The phenomena of the past cannot be judged by the muted phenomena of today. But we managed to film a modern medium at work and see some table-turning, and a close-up conjuror showed us how some of the 'psychic feats' of the nineteenth century were achieved – in those days when the fake and the psychic flourished.

In 1948, a seance was held at the home of Italian parapsychologist Silvio Ravaldini in a small village in Tuscany. About ten family members and friends watched a local medium in deep trance produce a direct voice, which seemed to speak from various parts of the room. Suddenly, there was a 'drop-in communicator,' a person no-one in the room had heard of. These were his words:

> I cannot see you but I feel that you exist, just as I once existed. I was a priest, I was happy. I am glad that you finally know the truth. I was killed with a revolver. I bear no grudge. I was a priest in Canton, Ohio, Giuseppe Riccardi. I do not know who you are – I only know that we are brothers – we are not against one another; we are brothers.

A woman shot me after I had celebrated Mass. The priest doesn't matter; what matters is brother Giuseppe Riccardi. When shot, I felt very warm. I raised myself up and wanted to ask this woman why she had shot me with a pistol. She was in a sort of hysterical state, and she paid no attention to me. She did not seem aware that I had asked her to lift me up. But that does not matter anymore.

We are all brothers, I wish for you light and the beautiful flowers of Ohio.

There were two other brief communications from Riccardi and then silence. Without a date for the priest's death, researchers feared he would be difficult to trace. Ravaldini wrote to America, but it was only when he met Dr Ian Stevenson, of the University of Virginia, in 1986 in Italy, that real progress was made.

The facts of Riccardi's death were soon uncovered by Stevenson. On 10 March 1929, the priest had finished saying Mass at St Anthony's Church in Canton, Ohio, when he was approached by Mrs Mamie Guerrieri, who was there with her five-year-old daughter. After a few words, she shot the priest. She fired five times and two of the bullets struck Riccardi who died in hospital later that day. Mrs Guerrieri accused Riccardi of molesting her daughter, which the priest strenuously denied. It was also suggested that the mother was mentally disturbed. After shooting the priest, she waited quietly on the steps of the church for the police to arrive. She was put on trial for the priest's death but acquitted.

In the best tradition of the early parapsychologists, Ravaldini and Stevenson looked for the answer to a simple question: How could a village medium in Tuscany know about the murder of a priest in the United States nineteen years previously? They could find no link between the medium and the dead priest. Riccardi and his family had been born in Sicily, a distant island, and emigrated to America in the early years of the century, when Giuseppe was a small boy. In 1923, Riccardi was in Rome for a year, studying the language and being ordained, but there seemed to have been no contact with Tuscany. The medium, a local man in his thirties, had been educated at elementary school and had worked as a barber and as a secretary. As a young man he saw visions and became a non-professional trance medium for fifteen years. He took no newspapers at home, and was sixteen years old when the priest was murdered. He said he had never heard of Riccardi – one of at least a hundred drop-in communicatiors at his seances.

Could he have read about the murder when he was sixteen and con- sciously forgotten about it – a case of cryptomnesia?

The researchers were satisfied that no report had been carried on the local radio station, but one of the daily newspapers delivered to the village in 1929 carried a story about Riccardi's murder – newspapers were delivered to a few houses in the village. *Il Telegrafo* had printed:

A TRAGIC EVENT IN THE CATHOLIC CHURCH IN CANTON.
(Canton, Chio)

A tragic event occurred in a Catholic church. Father Giuseppe Riccardi had just finished celebrating Mass and was just getting ready to leave the altar when a woman, who was apparently suffering from a mental illness, suddenly confronted the priest and at point-blank range, shot him with a revolver. Hit by five bullets, Father Riccardi fell to the ground and was taken to the hospital, where he died soon afterwards.

Was this newspaper story the basis for Riccardi's version at the seance? There was an important error – a misprint in the newspaper located the murder in 'Canton, Chio' instead of Canton, Ohio. The researchers conducted a small survey in the village and everyone, without exception, thought Canton referred to the Chinese city of two million inhabitants and not to Canton, Ohio, population 120 000, which most of the villagers had not heard of. The assumption that Canton was in China probably accounted for the printing error in the first place. At the seance, the voice of Riccardi had been specific – 'Canton, Ohio.' So perhaps *Il Telegrafo* was not the source.

It took almost sixty years, from the original murder, for the parapsychologists to unravel this case. At the end, the three main researchers were divided. Massimo Biondi of Rome suspended judgement and felt cryptomnesia had not been ruled out. Stevenson acknowledged that all other explanations had not been absolutely excluded, but agreed with Ravaldini. 'We favour the spiritist hypothesis, that is that the communication derived from a discarnate Giuseppe Riccardi who had survived death.'

    *   *   *   *   *

To get some television pictures of a medium in action, we filmed a demonstration by Mr Gordon Higginson, President of the Spiritualist National Union in the UK for the past twenty years. In his younger days he was said to have produced full-form materialisations of spirits who walked amongst his audience shaking people by the hand.

For our camera, Gordon Higginson, now seventy years old, stood on the platform and passed on messages from dead friends and relatives to people gathered for a conference on astrology at Stansted Hall, near London. Some wept as Higginson revived memories of people they used to know. Much of the information he gave was purely factual – names and addresses and references to relatives, usually identified by first name only – once he gave the name of someone's dog! Advice was offered about a quarrel that afternoon between two people who were both present. Afterwards, I asked them if they had ever been to a spiritualist meeting before, or had ever met Gordon Higginson – they assured me they had not.

Later, Higginson, the son of another famous medium, Fanny Higginson, told me about his mother's dramatic introduction into mediumship. An aunt took the child to a seance where the medium said there was a message from Fanny's mother saying the child would become a medium herself and hold meetings in that very hall. Fanny was perplexed by the message, since her mother was still alive. On returning home, the child and her aunt found that Fanny's mother had died.

At Stansted Hall, an accountant who is now a spiritualist and healer, told me of an experience some years ago with a spirit guide produced by a Welsh medium. 'This guide was standing in front of me, full-form, and I asked if I could touch his hands. I took hold of his wrists and he was flesh and blood. When he said he had to leave, I decided to hold on. Then I noticed he was disappearing from the floor up and I was left holding onto air.'

There are so many quite incredible stories of physical mediumship over the years, some demonstrably fraudulent, that overall scepticism is clearly in order.

Some mediums, on investigation, have turned out to be unwitting frauds, deceiving themselves as much as anyone else. Dr James Hyslop, who succeeded Richard Hodgson as Secretary of the ASPR, was once invited to test a woman medium. 'The medium sat in complete darkness, but agreed that flashlight photographs should be taken of the physical phenomena. Tambourines played and bells were ringing. On a given signal by the medium a picture was taken. When developed this showed the medium was herself playing the tambourines and ringing the bells with her own hands! She was dumb-founded and later investigation showed that her hands and arms were completely anaesthetised during the sessions, and she had no conscious knowledge that she herself was producing the phenomena.'

Some mediums felt compelled to cheat because they were faced with a public performance, for which people paid good money, and they could not always produce phenomena by genuine means. The investigators of Eusapia Palladino, for example, acknowledged she would cheat if given the chance, as it was easier for her than the exhausting business of struggling to produce real phenomena. Their advice was: make sure her hands and feet are securely held, and you may get genuine manifestations.

The stock-in-trade of many materialising mediums has been ectoplasm, variously described as a filmy or rubbery white substance that oozes from the orifices of the medium or rises like a vapour from the pores. It eventually forms hands or faces or even full length manifestations. Some old Victorian photographs of mediums with ectoplasm look very faked – figures draped in cheesecloth with facsimiles of human heads stuck in for effect. There are records of a medium's trial where evidence was given of the purchase of cheesecloth just prior to a seance and many glaring fakes were publicly exposed.

On the other hand, the writer Sir Arthur Conan Doyle, a spiritualist and a man not easily deceived, judged by his creation Sherlock Holmes, wrote that at a seance of the medium Eva C., he saw ectoplasm in a good light. He was allowed to squeeze a piece between his fingers – it gave him the impression it was a living substance 'thrilling and shrinking under the touch' – that doesn't sound very much like cheesecloth.

How seriously can we take such reports? The President of the SPR, Dr Alan Gauld, who lectures in psychology at the University of Nottingham, is an experienced investigator. He told me, 'The full-form materialisations that were produced in those days seem to me to smack very strongly of fraud and conjuring, as do the ones I have seen myself. The only difference is that whereas it was cheesecloth in those days, it's nylon or net curtain nowadays. But when it comes to less pronounced physical happenings, like raps and object movements, I do think there is some striking evidence, including that produced with D. D. Home. And these things go right down to the present day.'

Dr Gauld said that he had never encountered a materialisation he thought was genuine. He speculated that one reason such phenomena are minimal today, compared to the nineteenth century, is that advances in photography and various other devices enable investigators to see in the dark. This makes it much more difficult for mediums to get away with it.

Nevertheless, Dr Gauld says he has seen some strange things. Once a heavy table rose up under his nose, apparently unaided, whilst the medium sat alongside laughing at him. He said a friend had a table that could move without being touched.

To give television viewers an idea of such manifestations, we filmed a group of young people in a London flat. They meet regularly and have made a video of a table moving violently and apparently levitating, right off the ground. We filmed them in low light, using an image intensifier. With all five pairs of hands touching the top of the table, it certainly rocked about, but did not lift completely off the floor. The sitters were disappointed – they said normally 'William' was more demonstrative – William is their name for whatever moves the table and sends them messages.

William makes contact by writing with a pen on paper in the dark. Nobody has seen him, but he can be heard scratching away with the answers to questions. Asked who William was, the reply came – William is a name and not an individual. When he has finished writing, William gives loud raps on the table and they switch on the light. The sitters assured us that none was playing a joke on the others – picking up the pen and pretending to be William in the dark. Unfortunately, when we were there William was not in a writing mood, and the only phenomenon we filmed was the table moving about.

In the nineteenth century Michael Faraday, pioneer of electricity, put forward his explanation for the routine phenomenon of table-turning – unconscious muscle pressure by the sitters. A glass moves across a polished table-top, in a variation of the ouija board, for the same reason.

The William experiment reminded me of 'Philip,' an experimental ghost created by the Toronto Society for Psychical Research, Canada, some years ago. Philip communicated by rapping on a table which he sometimes levitated. The significance of Philip was that his personality had been collectively invented by members of the group. Once they sat down as 'believers in Philip,' the phenomena began and the information given paranormally confirmed the identity of Philip, the ghost they invented. Does this mean psychic phenomena at seances can be produced by the combined mental power or psi of the sitters?

Our London group told us William had performed other feats. A conical speaking trumpet once floated in the air, and other objects were moved around – a cassette player moved to the far side of the room. There were also apports: 15 carnations which appeared in the centre of the table, and a small crystal, given to one of the sitters. Apports are traditional phenomena whereby objects suddenly appear as gifts from the spirits. The late John Butler, author of *Exploring the Psychic World* once showed me a small white sapphire he carried with him. It was an apport that appeared inside his closed hand at a seance. He had no idea how it got there, but the other sitters each received a similar gift.

I learned more about the possibility of apports at the Department of Psychology at the University of Edinburgh. Here, a small number of students are being trained by the Koestler Professor of Parapsychology, the American, Professor Bob Morris. The course has been going a few years, with monies bequested by the late Arthur Koestler. Initial projects include some remote viewing and a psycho-kinetic (PK) experiment, reminiscent of the tests of Dr Bob Jahn at Princeton, USA: a human mind tries to influence a display generated randomly by a machine i.e. mind over matter. Another student at Edinburgh was testing people's response time to barely perceived threatening images, for cross-checking against their scores in ESP or PK tests. The emphasis is upon psychological states conducive to psi.

Parapsychologists are also taught how to spot fakes. One talented young man at Edinburgh is a close-up conjuror, Richard Wiseman, who makes cards and objects appear and disappear under your nose. He demonstrated a typical feature of Victorian mediumship – slate writing. A sitter asks a question of the spirits, and the medium takes a blank slate and a piece of chalk and holds them with one hand under the table for a few minutes. Sometimes the spirit can be heard writing on the slate, which reappears bearing a message from the next world.

From a few feet away, we filmed the close-up conjuror faking this process in two different ways. I couldn't immediately see how he was doing it. In one instance, a slate was prepared beforehand with a suitably bland message, such as, 'Yes, you will certainly be given your answer but later in the session,' and was substituted under the table.

By the other method, the writing was done by the medium under the table, using a device like a fingerstall with a piece of chalk on the end which fits over the index finger like part of a glove.

The assumption at Edinburgh is not that if a conjuror can do what a medium does, then the medium must be a cheat. Dr Morris said, 'If we know how people can cheat to produce a materialisation, then we can set up test conditions that reduce the possibilities for fraud. We have a chance to separate the real from the fake.'

The Edinburgh conjuror held out a seemingly empty hand to the camera, made a fist, and from it pulled a brightly coloured handkerchief. He waved it about and made it vanish with equal ease. By some similar means, we were told, a close-up conjuror could make a flower or some other object appear as an apport in the seance room, where in fact it had been present all the time.

A relevant experience happened last century to Alfred Russel Wallace, co-discoverer with Darwin of the Law of the Survival of the Fittest, and a scientific sceptic turned spiritualist. He and others attended a seance by a Mrs Samuel Guppy, a medium famous for apports. Flowers duly materialised and the medium asked if anyone had a special request.

A friend of Wallace said he'd like a sunflower – there was an almighty crash and a six-feet-tall sunflower with clods of earth still stuck to the roots landed on the table. Now that would be a real challenge for a close-up conjuror!

PART FOUR

Remembered Lives

I don't know what I may seem to the world, but as to myself, I seem to have been only like a boy playing on the sea shore and diverting myself in now and then finding a smoother pebble or prettier shell than ordinary, whilst the great ocean of truth lay all undiscovered before me.

SIR ISAAC NEWTON

CHAPTER EIGHTEEN

The Galileo of the twentieth century

With a free and open mind I listen attentively to the Indian doctrine of rebirth and look around in the world of my own experience to see whether somewhere and somehow there is some authentic sign pointing towards reincarnation. CARL JUNG

The claims of small children to remember previous lives have been scientifically investigated for the past thirty years. This evidence for reincarnation, one of man's oldest religious beliefs, has even found its way into scientific journals, due largely to the efforts of one man, Professor Ian Stevenson of the University of Virginia, USA.

A Canadian-born psychiatrist, Dr Stevenson has files on 2500 children with such memories. Notebook in hand, he has travelled hundreds of thousands of miles to remote areas of the world to record the recollections of children for cross-checking against medical records, police files, state records and eye-witness accounts. He has a compelling dossier of children who recall the life and death of someone else – sometimes they have the mannerisms and habits of the dead person, and some even bear physical marks that correspond with aspects of that person's life.

Dr Stevenson considers fraud, hallucination and telepathy as options in every investigation. But the kernel of his work is the twenty-five cases he believes are so strong that reincarnation is the most logical explanation.

He made scientific history in May 1977, when he wrote the first article on reincarnation to appear in a serious scientific publication, *The Journal of Nervous and Mental Disease*. In that same journal, a colleague, Dr Harold Lief, wrote, 'Either he is making a colossal mistake . . . or he will be known as the Galileo of the twentieth century.' Stevenson will soon be publishing a major work in four volumes about birthmarks and birth defects in children with memories of other lives, which should give a new dimension to the scientific debate about his research.

There is nothing new about children who remember previous lives. The ancient Greek philosopher Pythagoras, known to generations of school children for his geometrical theorems, claimed he could remember living before as Euphorbus, who was killed at the siege of Troy. Many other famous men have claimed to be reincarnated – the Emperor Napoleon, the industrialist Henry Ford, the inventor and statesman Benjamin Franklin, the poet Walt Whitman, etc.

But before Stevenson there was little evidence for reincarnation, only belief and some quirks of nature. Child prodigies were claimed as likely examples of reincarnation, displaying skills they could have learned in a previous life. The composer Mozart, as a small boy, wrote music superior to mature composers of his time, but he was from a musical family and his brilliance might have been genetically inspired. Yehudi Menuhin, the violinist, packed the Royal Albert Hall for a recital when little more than an infant. Another small child in Havana, Cuba, who had not been taught the moves of chess, watched his father's game with a local doctor and explained where they had gone wrong – later, José Capablanca effortlessly became world champion.

Children who display a special apititude for music or painting or anything seemingly at odds with their parents or home background, have been cited as evidence. So has the feeling of déja-vu, which most of us have had sometimes, perhaps when visiting a place for the first time and feeling we've been here before. Today, a large part of the world's population believes in reincarnation: Hindus, Buddhists and one in four Americans and Western Europeans, according to a 1990 Gallup Poll.

Talking to Ian Stevenson in his office in Charlottesville, I asked for his conclusions about reincarnation after thirty years' research.

'What I believe is irrelevant. My work has been to assemble the evidence and produce alternative interpretations for it. Each person must make up his or her own mind and not worry about what I might believe.'

Stevenson told me that of his 2500 authentic cases, there were a hundred he considered strong. But at the core of his archive were twenty-five cases, where a key factor was that somebody had made a written record of the child's memories, before there was any contact with the family of the person whose life the child remembered.

A typical child, aged from two to four years, might begin talking about another home almost with the first spoken words. The researcher's problem was getting to the case before the memories began to fade and before the child met the other family, which could lead to confusion and embellishment. That was the main rational criticism of his cases, said Stevenson, but it did not apply to his twenty-five strong cases.

Those cases are only one per cent of the total, but at least there are that many. Formerly, belief in reincarnation depended on religious tradition, now at least one can point to hard evidence. The evidence is not flawless, but for the strongest cases reincarnation is certainly plausible and I would say for me it's the most compelling interpretation in some cases, even though it's not the only one.

Dr Stevenson sees great advantages in working with children. They are less likely than adults to have access to information through reading or overhearing of a death in another family, sometimes a long distance away. But how do those memories come to the surface and what are the problems Dr Stevenson has in interpreting them? He explained in some detail:

The first words may vary a lot but frequently there is a longing to go to the other home. An accusation to the mother, 'You're not my mother. I want to go to my real mother.'

There may be a comparison between how things are now and how they used to be, as the child remembers it. 'We just have a greasy lamp, but where I lived we just went to the wall and made a movement like that and the room got lit up. Why don't you have that here?'

Sometimes the child would say, 'You don't need to walk to the market, send for my car – we have a car where I live and the driver can take you to the market.' The parent would say, 'What are you talking about? You don't have a car. We're in the jungle here and I'm your mother.'

In addition to statements about a previous life the child often showed some unusual behaviour, characteristic of the person whose life the child remembers. If the death was from drowning, the child is afraid of water. If the death is from shooting, then the child is afraid of loud noises and firearms. If the death is from snakebite, the child has a phobia of snakes.

On the positive side, the child may want special foods or special clothing. Vivid examples occur in some of the Burmese children who claim to remember the lives of Japanese soldiers killed in the Second World War. The Burmese have very weak tea, but the Japanese characteristically want strong tea and a lot of sugar in it. These children will ask for this strong tea and for raw fish and they grumble about the spice in the Burmese food.

The cases of children who remember previous lives as members of the opposite sex can pose a great problem for some of the parents. The girl who remembers a previous life as a boy will insist on dressing as a boy, and I know a couple of them who have got into serious crises at school because the teachers insisted the children came dressed as girls. Some instances of homosexuality may derive from being a person of the opposite sex in a previous life. I think that is a distinct possibility.

It's true that most children remember a previous life in better circumstances than the present one, which has been interpreted as implying the cases might be made up by parents in an effort to exploit the previous family, by extracting money from them. In fact I would almost say that I have never come across any kind of exploitation, except perhaps a few cases where the child has been given some gifts. I think these suspicions are quite groundless.

But why should children mostly remember previous lives in favourable circumstances? It could be something to do with the shock of having been affluent, had a car and servants and lived in a mansion, and then finding yourself in a hovel or a mud hut. The shock might stimulate the memories.

Another point worth remembering is that it's not creditable to remember a previous life in a better family or higher caste, because that implies in the Indian system of Karmic belief that you've been in some way wicked so you have been demoted.

Sometimes spontaneously a child with memories will be able to describe how death occurred in the previous life. That happens in 60 to 70 per cent of cases, particularly if the death has been violent, which is a common occurrence in our cases. Violent deaths vary from one culture to another, as high as almost 80 per cent in Lebanon or Turkey, as low as 25 per cent in British Columbia and around 50 per cent in India. The rate of violent death in our cases is far higher than it is in the general population – a possible explanation is that a violent death is better remembered by the informant. I think violence has something to do with fixing the memories in the child. Violence entails physical suffering and an abrupt termination, which may tie in with this longing that children have to go back to the other family – they seem to want to see how they are doing, and once they meet the other family that sort of desperate nostalgia diminishes.

It's often asked why more children in Asia seem to remember previous lives than Western children. Are the memories fostered by a belief in reincarnation in Asia and suppressed by the disbelief in Western countries? That may explain some of the differences. We hear quite often from the parents of Western children that they wished they'd known about our research when their little boy was three years old because he was saying, 'I used to be a pilot and I was shot down.' 'We told him to stop telling fibs and now he doesn't remember any more.'

The biggest challenge thrown up by the idea of reincarnation is whether people are something more than a combination of genes and the family environment. If you disregard the evidence we have collected, just think of the way the average Western parent regards his or her child – it's exactly the same as one regards an automobile that's come off the factory line. There was nothing before these bolts and bits and pieces of the car were assembled and painted. That is the standard view that Western parents have of their children. They make the child, starting with the genes, the collision of sperm and ovum and that colours their entire relationship with the children they have. If anything goes wrong, somebody has to be blamed. If there's a birth defect, they blame the hospitals or the doctors or themselves.

The attitude is quite different in countries with a belief in reincarnation. In those countries there is this third component, not denying some role to genetics and environment, but there is the component of some existence before the conception of the current body. The child bears some responsibility for what he does and says and how he develops.

It's interesting to see Indian parents talking with some of these children who claim to have had superior status or greater wealth in a previous life. They will say, 'All right, that was the way things were – now you're with us and we're in the jungle and you're going to have to adjust to things the way they are now.' A Western parent with an unusual child doesn't have that kind of defence. The whole thing would be very baffling to them. If the child shows unusual behaviour and claims to remember a previous life, the average Western parent is totally at sea without any kind of sail or rudder.

I think that reincarnation offers a third component to the formation of human persona. If reincarnation occurs, we must be built of layers going back to some remote distance I know not where. But there must be a pre-existence and that pre-existence contributes very importantly to human personality.

CHAPTER NINETEEN

Dead men's hands

It is the secret of the world that all things subsist and do not die, but only retire a little from sight and afterwards return again. Nothing is dead. People feign themselves dead, and endure mock funerals and mournful obituaries, and there they stand, looking out of the window, sound and well in some strange new disguise. RALPH WALDO EMERSON

I n a village in northern Indian we filmed a youth, born with no fingers on his right hand, talking about his previous life as a boy whose fingers had been accidentally cut off by a fodder-chopping machine. Afterwards, we gave him a lift to a house in a village eight kilometres away, where he was greeted as a son by the woman whose own child had died a year after the accident. Both families and the boy are convinced he is a reincarnation of that maimed child. The parapsychologists felt it was a strong case, with one possible weakness – the comparatively short distance between the two villages meant information about the dead child would have been available in the area.

But the coincidence of a boy born without fingers on the same hand as the one mutilated on the unrelated dead child is dramatic. Professor Stevenson told me, 'There is a medical condition called "short fingers" which is extremely rare. Usually cases are born without fingers on both hands – to have just one hand affected is even more unusual. A Danish survey of birthmarks suggested it might occur once in half a million births.'

Stevenson's forthcoming volumes are about dozens of cases like this: children who have not only memories, but birthmarks and deformities corresponding to traumatic injuries sustained by someone, often at the point of death. Such birthmarks may match knife wounds or the points of entry and exit of bullets as recorded in autopsy and other medical records. Stevenson's careful scientific analysis of such compelling evidence should cause a scientific furore. He told me:

I think these are tremendously important cases because they add a more objective element to the kinds of testimony we have heard up to now. The new element is the documentary and medical evidence supporting the idea of seemingly shared physical characteristics between the child and the dead person he claims to have been.

Here, for example, is a photograph of a Turkish child born with one ear virtually absent. He remembered a life as a peasant farmer in Turkey who, at the end of the day, fell asleep in a pasture. A neighbour came along hunting rabbits in the twilight and shot him with a shotgun at point-blank range.

In this case, as with about forty other cases, we managed to get medical documentation of the location and appearance of the wound. In this case, a hospital report showing the man died ten days later of a brain haemorrhage because the pellets had penetrated the skull. This boy had memories of that man's life and because of his birth defect and the medical documents, I consider this one of our stronger cases.

The example we decided to study for our television series was the boy with no fingers on his right hand. At the University of Virginia, Dr Stevenson showed us a photograph of a fodder-chopping machine – rotating circular blades looking like a bicycle wheel mounted on a stand and turned at speed by a handle. A few months later we were filming one of these machines in northern India. It stood ominously in the background as we watched the youth, now aged eighteen, being questioned by the Indian parapsychologist Dr Satwant Pasricha of the National Institute for Mental Health and Neuro-sciences, Bangalore. Pasricha and Stevenson have worked together on many of these cases in India.

The youth's memories of his other life have faded somewhat since his younger days and the earlier interviews with Stevenson and Pasricha. But what he said in Hindi was dramatic enough. 'I died and I was born here. I used to recall it.' He described how he contacted the family of the previous personality.

There was a wedding in our village and my brothers (from the previous life) had come to attend. I recognised them, I knew they were my brothers. My present parents didn't know, but gradually everybody came to know of it. I went to my brothers and recognised them and everyone said, 'Tell us, how was your hand cut?' and my mother (of the previous personality) said they would believe I was their son only if I could show them the machine by which my hand was cut. I went there and the machine was fixed in another room. I showed them the machine and everybody agreed that I was Kamandal's son.

Dr Pasricha asked the youth if he remembered how the fingers had been lost.

> My previous father used to drink and he came home in the evening and rotated the machine and my hand was chopped. I kept standing there and he realised about my hand when all the fingers fell off. Then everybody became concerned. I was taken to hospital for treatment.
> Do you remember what hospital?
> No, I don't remember.
> Do you remember who took you?
> My father – by cart, by bullock cart.

Later that day, we walked across the fields from the boy's village and all drove to a farm eight kilometres distant. The boy entered the house where the dead child had lived. There he greeted his mother and older brother with respect and affection.

Dr Pasricha talked with the mother who confirmed meeting the boy when her family went to the wedding of a relative in his village. Dr Pasricha asked if the boy was truly her son. 'Yes of course he *is* my son. He considers me his mother and I consider him to be my son.' The older son, a security official, was equally convinced.

> He was my brother in the previous life, therefore he is my brother. I remember the wedding ceremony five years ago. I was there with three or four of my brothers and he recognised us. He recognised my mother and my father. He told us how his hand was cut and said people beat him. He said, 'Please take me to live with you,' and I said we would.
> When we were about to leave next morning, his mother stopped us, saying, 'But this is Sanjay.' I said 'That's all right, accept us as your family too – you will now have seven more brothers. He stayed with us for a month.

Today, the young man treats both houses as his home. At his natural home, Dr Pasricha asked him which one he preferred. 'When I go there I long for this house. When I am here, I long for the other one. I like living in both.'

Dr Pasricha told me the researchers had found no similar case of a hand deformity in the village. Accidents with fodder chopping machines were few. They had also researched back some generations into the two families and could find no examples of deformed hands. The weaknesses of the case, she said, were the relative proximity of the two families and the fact that as a child the boy had given few details of his previous life. The strength of the case was obvious to all – the stark testimony of that mutilated hand!

*   *   *   *   *

Back at the University of Virginia, Dr Stevenson showed me photographs of another child born without fingers. This was an equally dramatic case of a young Burmese woman, now married, who remembered a previous life as a man who had humiliated his wife by taking a mistress. The wife committed suicide and the wife's mother vowed vengeance on the husband. She hired professional killers who waylaid him as he was bicycling home from a wedding.

They took him down a slope and killed him with a sword, the principal weapon of murder in Burma. Stevenson continued the tale:

> The last memory of the previous life the subject has is holding up the hands in a gesture of supplication. 'Please don't kill me, spare me.' It also wards off the first blow. To get a good cut at the neck, the swordsman usually chops the fingers and the victim is killed that way.
>
> This child, when she first had these memories, actually remembered the ring that she was wearing and I think a watch. They got into the field of vision of the deceased just as he was going to be killed and somehow got carried over into her memories. We have photographs showing her very badly deformed hands with some fingers seriously mutilated and one or two other marks from sword cuts.

Another case in Burma involved a hanging which was bungled. The person hanged was a notorious brigand, a dacoit who had terrorised the whole territory of upper Burma for a few years. He was captured, charged with murder, convicted and sentenced to death. But the hanging was bungled, so he was hanged twice.

> The subject was born with memories of this brigand and with an almost absent lower jaw – his mandible was exceedingly small and his mouth very narrow and tight, so he really could only take liquid food and couldn't open his mouth very much. I have photographs showing the constriction and his profile shows his lower jaw is very poorly developed.
>
> He had a memory of the first hanging but by the time we met him his memories were beginning to fade. I think it's an authentic case, so if reincarnation is the best explanation then the mental images he had of the tight sensation in his neck, that preceded his death, are the images of the bungled hanging and that somehow became the stimulus for an effect on the body of the person he became in the next life.

Stevenson showed us equally dramatic photographs of another Turkish case, a child who remembered a previous life as a miller. One day, some customers quarrelled – one man wanted his grain milled immediately although there was a queue of other people waiting. The miller became embroiled in the fight and somebody picked up a flour shovel and struck him on the back of the head.

> This child had memories of the deceased miller and a very severe deformity at the back of the head, corresponding to the bashing on the head with the flour shovel. Again, we were able to get a post-mortem report confirming that the miller had indeed died from being hit on the head.

The thoroughness of Stevenson's efforts to get factual verification for his cases was illustrated by photographs of the body of an American who died from being shot in the chest by a shotgun at close range. This showed a circle of small red wounds – but this was not the corpse of someone in a reincarnation case. It was simply Stevenson finding out what someone would look like when shot in the centre of the chest from a certain distance.

> The case was of a boy in India born with an exceedingly prominent birthmark in the centre of his chest, an area of decreased pigmentation. He remembered the previous life of a man who was shot at point-blank range with a shotgun by an unknown assassin. It was probably a case of mistaken identity for the man shot was a harmless Indian villager who seemed to have had no enemies.
>
> We did get an autopsy report from the hospital and the correspondence between the shotgun wounds on the deceased man and the birthmarks is exceedingly close. The weakness of the case is that the deceased man and the boy lived in the same village and there had been some slight acquaintance between the families – but I still consider this a very strong case.

Some of the birthmarks that correspond to memories of another life are moles, blemishes on the skin which Stevenson says might be due to genetics. Certain types of birthmarks are quite common and could by coincidence tie in with the story of someone's death.

> In most of the cases you could not introduce a genetic factor because the families are totally unrelated. Also the birth defects in these cases are uncommon. They are not the sort you find in textbooks or monographs, with rare exceptions.

In particular, we have a collection of about fifteen cases where there are two birthmarks corresponding to bullet wounds of entry and exit. Forensic pathologists know that nearly always when you shoot somebody, the bullet wound of entry is small and round and the bullet wound of exit is large and irregular. That's the way our birthmarks are in about half of these cases. I find that very impressive.

Stevenson is perfectly well aware that many of the cases he has investigated are not perfect, but it does not seem to bother him particularly.

We know some of our cases have what you might call petty blemishes. There may be some exaggeration or distortion, many may have that kind of error. In fact, if they didn't have flaws, you'd be suspicious, wouldn't you? You'd wonder if they had all been cooked up. One of my teachers used to say that if you have the perfect case, you really should be suspicious that it has all been rehearsed. So you kind of expect and welcome a few mistakes – it's a sign in a way that people are genuine and not rehearsed.

CHAPTER TWENTY

Possessed

We may know certain phenomena and even the laws which govern their appearance, but we do not adequately understand a single one of them. To say of a stone which falls to earth that it obeys an attraction, which varies directly as the mass and inversely as the square of the distance is not to understand the stone's fall.

PROFESSOR CHARLES RICHET

On 19 July 1985, Sumitra, a young married woman in Sharifpura, a remote village in northern India, seemingly died. Funeral arrangements were being discussed when she suddenly recovered, but insisted she was someone else. She said the people about her were strangers, and she described the life of another young woman named Shiva who had been murdered on 17 May 1985, two months earlier. Sumitra seemed possessed.

The position remains the same today. Dr Pasricha and our television team arrived unannounced at Sumitra's home and her first words to Dr Pasricha were, 'Don't call me Sumitra. I am Shiva!'

This strange case is one of 350 varied claims of reincarnation Dr Pasricha has studied in India over the past seventeen years. A survey in northern India a few years ago suggested that perhaps one in 500 children may have some memory of another life, but cases of possession are rarer.

At Etawah, a medium-sized town several hours' journey away from the village where the seemingly possessed Sumitra lives, Dr Pasricha talked to the parents of Shiva. The circumstances of her death, in the village where she lived with her husband's family, were suspicious. Shiva, a university graduate, had married into a poorly educated family and there was a history of quarrels before the girl's body was found with head injuries near a railway line. Her in-laws suggested the unhappy Shiva had committed suicide, but Shiva's own family did not believe this story. They hurried to the village to get Shiva's body expertly examined and to press police to investigate, but when they arrived they found Shiva had already been cremated. The husband had not waited for any of Shiva's family to attend the ceremony. Members of the husband's family were arraigned on charges in connection with the girl's death at the instigation of her father, but ultimately there was not enough evidence to convict.

Shiva's father, a school teacher, stood on the roof terrace of his home and told Dr Pasricha a remarkable story. His daughter had died in May and a few months later he heard someone say she had been reincarnated in the village of Sharifpura. By October, he had the address and went to see her.

When I reached the house they called her from the adjoining room. She ran into the room and hugged me. I said, 'How do you know me?' She said, 'You are my papa Ram Sryan Tripathi.' I asked her, 'What is your name?' and she replied, 'Aruna Tripathi.' I said, 'That is what they call you at school, but what is your nickname, what you are called at home?' She replied, 'Shiva Tripathi.'

Then I started weeping and she told me everything. She asked about all the other children at home. I stayed at their house that night and brought her home the next day.

I asked my wife to hide in Shiva's room. There were a number of ladies in the living room and I asked Shiva to identify her mother from amongst these women. She could not. She then went to her own room and hugged and embraced her mother. Then she recognised her brothers and all the neighbours.

I felt as if she was my own daughter, as she had always been. Everything was familiar – the way she walked, sat down, got up. Then she told us some things that were uncanny. There was a road which has been reconstructed and she pointed this out and gave details about what it had looked like before. She recognised her own watch and all her clothes and sarees. I was fully convinced that she was Shiva. We asked her to write letters to us and she wrote her name in the way that our daughter used to and with which we were so familiar. She came home to us for one and a half months and her way of living at home and her manner was the same as Shiva's. We never had any doubts that our Shiva had come back to us.

The girl told the teacher that his daughter had been murdered. There had been a prolonged quarrel with Shiva's mother-in-law over a visit the girl wanted to make to her own family. Eventually, she was asked to come downstairs and talk things over. She was hit on the head with a brick and lost consciousness. She remembered nothing more until she woke up in Sumitra's body.

> Shiva's mother Ram Rani verified her husband's story.
>
> My husband asked her to identify her mother in the crowd of women assembled in our house. She said, 'Mummy is not here.' My husband asked her to find mummy – she ran into the room where I was hiding, embraced me and started crying.
>
> I felt this was my daughter because she remembered us and everything about her life. She was very affectionate towards me, my husband and her brothers. She would talk about her children, her husband's house and her husband. She remembered and talked about her sarees and quite clearly recognised everybody.

Dr Pasricha asked whether she thought someone might have given the girl clues as to the family's identity.

> No. She recognised us very spontaneously. She remembered her parents, her brother, even her uncle. I realised that this was Shiva. Of course, her body had been burned. But her spirit was living on in someone else's body. We still believe she is our daughter – she doesn't look like our daughter but her spirit is still there.

Sumitra's home in Sharifpura is much more remote from Etawah than the distance of sixty-five kilometres indicates. It took us four hours to get there. Single track lanes petered out to nothing and we abandoned our minibus with a flat tyre stuck on a narrow bridge. A farmer's tractor and trailer bounced us for half an hour to this isolated village. It was dusk when we got there and all the village children turned out to cheer. Fortunately Sumitra and her father agreed to talk to us. By the light of candles, her father told us how his daughter had appeared to die on 19 May 1985. She had been subject to attacks, like epilepsy, since the birth of a child.

> It was a Sunday, her problems began at two o'clock and she was dead by four o'clock. We waited for two to four hours and then prepared for the last rites, the funeral. Then she started breathing once again and we were overjoyed.

Dr Pasricha asked, 'How did you know that she was dead?'

> The doctors told us. Her heart had stopped beating. She had no pulse and her body was cold. So we believed she was dead, but after

recovering consciousness she couldn't recognise us. For about four days, we talked with her and she spoke in an unusual manner. It was not the voice we knew. She said, 'This is not my house. I live with my husband and my inlaws in Divyapur. I grew up in Etawah.'

We were dumbfounded. We could not believe what had happened. She said her father was Ram Sryan. We did not know who he was, where his house was, just that he lived in Etawah. Finally, somebody managed to contact him and he came to see her and she recognised him instantly as her father.

We also spoke to Sumitra, seemingly alive and well. She lowered her veil and Dr Pasricha began, 'Tell me Sumitra . . .'

'Don't call me Sumitra. I am Shiva! . . . Tell me, if someone comes to the world with a certain self-identity can that identity ever change?'

Dr Pasricha: 'But yours did change.'

'Yes, but now that I am Shiva, how can I become Sumitra again?'

Dr Pasricha: 'Do you remember your life as Sumitra?'

'I remember nothing. I have no recollection. I have been told about Sumitra, but that has nothing to do with my perceptions or my story. I can only tell you about my life as Shiva.'

Dr Pasricha: 'What do you remember about the life of Shiva?'

'Everything. All of which I have told you before. That I had two children and the way I was murdered.'

Dr Pasricha has gathered some impressive facts about this case – Sumitra named Shiva's father before there was any contact between the two families and later identified 14 members of Shiva's family from photographs. In all she recognised 22 people known to Shiva. Sumitra had never been to any school but taught herself enough to be able to write simple notes to her mother. Since being possessed by Shiva, there has been an improvement in the girl's ability to write and read Hindi. This is not surprising since Sumitra was an illiterate seventeen-year-old when she was apparently replaced by the more educated Shiva, who was twenty-two when she was found dead by the railway line. There have been other differences in the subsequent behaviour of Sumitra – she began dressing differently, wore sandals instead of going barefooted and began speaking to her parents in a more polite and formal way.

Is it possible the whole story is a hoax, a pretext got up by these peasant farmers, perhaps based upon newspaper accounts of the death of Shiva and the prosecution of her in-laws?

Dr Pasricha thinks it unlikely. One newspaper is delivered to the village and is available for anyone to read. Newspaper reports of Shiva's death have been analysed and Sumitra has given sixteen correct items of information not carried in press reports.

How then could Sumitra have acquired her information about Shiva's life? One would need a private detective in Etawah or several accomplices to put together a plot for which no clear motive has emerged in the past five years. The idea of an elaborate con-trick gives a sophistication to simple villagers that is ridiculous to anyone who has been to this inaccessible spot and met them.

*   *   *   *   *

Dr Pasricha also introduced us to a good example of a more orthodox reincarnation case – Manju Sharma, a twenty-year-old girl who remembered an earlier life as a ten-year-old who drowned in a well. Manju, now married with two small children, spent ten years of her life with the parents of the dead girl, where she was known only as Krishna. Today, Manju lives in the town of Brindevan in northern India, whose temples are places of special pilgrimage for Hindus – here the Lord Krishna is reported by the scriptures to have played with the local cow-girls.

The apartment where Manju lives is next door to a shrine. Dr Pasricha talked to her on a balcony overlooking a bustling courtyard, typifying India – children recited holy texts for a teacher, carrots boiled over a smoky fire for a communal stew and an infant shrieked because a large monkey had stolen his banana.

Manju was one of Dr Pasricha's early cases, and the memories have faded a little – she no longer has a fear of wells.

> I was two-and-a-half years old when I remembered I had died by falling in a well in Chaumuha village when I was ten. I was reborn and later I met my uncle Tanji from my previous life. I recognised him and spoke to him. He said, 'No, our child died a while back,' but he promised to send my mother from that life to see me. She came and was very loving and sat me on her knee. Then my brother from that village took me to my parents' house. I stayed there for ten years.

We took Manju, her two little daughters and a young chaperone to meet the parents of the dead girl. The visitors knocked on the front door of a tiny terraced house and were received with obvious joy. The father, who runs a small tea shop, explained, 'We call her Krishna Devi. She is my daughter, she is Krishna. Her children call me grandfather and they call my wife grandmother. When she came last year for two weeks with the children, everything was as normal. They ate, drank and lived with us and played with the other children. They are not outsiders – they are my very own.'

Dr Pasricha asked, 'Do you see her as Krishna? You don't accept her as Manju?'

'Manju means nothing to us,' he replied. 'She is Krishna, she is our daughter Krishna of her previous life. We wait for her to come home.'

It is the clear bond of affection between the girl and a family less well off than her own which Dr Pasricha considers one of the strengths of this case. Manju is a girl from a Brahmin family, the highest caste of Hindu, and chose to live for years with a family from a lower, tradesmen's caste. Critics of these cases sometimes suggest that reincarnates come from poor families trying to scrape up an acquaintanceship with a better-off family. In Manju's case, the opposite is true.

We intended to record another of Dr Pasricha's remarkable case studies and travelled further north to Kanpur to investigate a murder of some years ago. A box was thrown from a train crossing a railway bridge over the river Ganges, but it never reached the water – it lodged in the girders of the bridge. When opened, it contained the dismembered body of a woman.

Later, the woman's doctor husband was charged with her murder, but the trial was abandoned because of his ill health. Around this time, a small child claimed to be the reincarnation of the doctor's wife and made several statements. We arrived in Kanpur in the middle of a riot between Hindus and Muslims. Sixty people were killed in the surrounding areas and smoke from the burning leather market could be seen from our hotel. The army imposed a curfew and it was deemed too dangerous for us to travel any further. The intrepid Dr Pasricha was willing to make the trip, but it was not to be.

As a psychologist, Dr Pasricha is convinced these studies have a relevance beyond the support or otherwise they might offer to the theory of reincarnation. They may also tell us something extra about human personality, revealing a possible extra dimension to all of us. The pioneering work of today's parapsychologists could end in an awareness, if not a theory, of psychic heredity.

CHAPTER TWENTY-ONE

The boy Lama

It were better to live one single day in the pursuit of
understanding and meditation, than to live a
hundred years in ignorance and unrestraint.
THE BUDDHA

A five-year-old boy seated on a high throne in an ornate Tibetan temple gravely blessed every one of hundreds of pilgrims queueing to meet him – he lightly touched each lowered head and put a silk scarf around every proffered neck. Three hours of ceremony marked the entry into Drepung Monastery of the child recognised as the reincarnation of a revered senior Lama, the reborn Ling Rinpoche.

This remarkable child received the homage of a gift from each of the pilgrims, who came from Asia, Europe and America. Most were monks but there were also businessmen, school teachers and a film star from Hollywood. To underline the occasion, each guest was given an envelope containing photographs of the boy and the Dalai Lama's eighty-one-year-old Senior Tutor who died in 1984, an old man and a child who are one and the same, according to the Tibetan theory of rebirth.

We recorded this ceremony on 3 December 1990, at the Tibetan settlement in Mundgod, southern India, where the exiled Tibetans have rebuilt several of the great monasteries destroyed in their homeland by the Chinese invaders. The Tibetans are an example of a culture which not only believes in reincarnation but has its own elaborate methods of identifying reincarnates.

For me, as impressive as any of the evidence, was the behaviour and bearing of this small boy. For the whole of that day of long ceremony, he displayed the dignity expected of a reincarnated High Lama. Throughout the morning, he sat on a small throne just below the Dalai Lama, during prayers for the long life of the spiritual and temporal leader of the Tibetans, who is himself the most famous example of a reincarnate. The Dalai Lama is held to be the reborn Chenresi, God of Compassion, and had also lived before as all 13 previous Dalai Lamas.

Children who are High Lamas reborn are 'tulkus' and are discovered by mystical insights and a series of tests and examinations. Little Ling Rinpoche is one of the best known of recent tulkus. Today, he has servants and lives in a modern bungalow alongside the monastery, but until he was eighteen months old, when he was recognised, he lived in the orphanage at the Tibetan Children's Village at Dharamsala, northern India. His mother was dead and his father was too poor to support him.

In March 1988, I had an audience with the Dalai Lama in his palace, a bungalow and temple complex in Dharamsala. Discussing Tibetan participation in our television series on life after death, the Dalai Lama suggested we consider the case of Ling Rinpoche and told me about his dramatic discovery.

The Tibetan Press Office showed me a video of the child when he was little more than two years old. He was seated on a huge pile of cushions and again blessing an endless line of pilgrims at a round of ceremonies at Dharamsala. He never fidgeted or cried – but between ceremonies was filmed playing with toys on the floor and being dressed and carried around by his servants.

Next day, the Chairman of the Dalai Lama's Religious Council, Kalsang Yeshi, told me more about this reincarnation of the Dalai Lama's Senior Tutor. The old man died on Christmas Day, 25 December 1984. For two weeks after his death, the Tibetans believed he stayed inside his body meditating. His face had been taut with pain before death, but now it was relaxed and there was no pulse or breathing or any sign of life. But his servants noticed there was warmth in his abdomen and for two weeks his body remained like that, in the seated lotus position, with no sign of the flesh beginning to atrophy. Then the warmth disappeared from the abdomen and the Tibetans assumed the spirit had finally left the body.

When a senior Lama dies he sometimes leaves messages if he is to be reborn. A recent High Lama left a series of sealed letters to be opened at various stages in the search for his reincarnation. Often a state oracle, a mystic visionary, is consulted and in a trance he will provide clues to the whereabouts of the tulku. In this case, the Senior Tutor had been so close to the Dalai Lama that His Holiness decided to provide these mystic insights in person.

Last year in Mundgod, I heard the story of the search from one of the men who led it – the present guardian of Ling Rinpoche and long-time servant to the deceased Senior Tutor, Lobsang Lungrig.

I looked to His Holiness for His divine revelation as to whether a reincarnation had appeared yet. He said a reincarnation was already born in the Wood-Ox year of the Tibetan calendar, i.e. 1985. The child was not in any remote place like Nepal but in India itself in the Tibetan settlements.

Two search parties set out on the mission and in one year collected 690 names with all the special signs surrounding their births. Further divinations by His Holiness said that the child was born at Bir, a two hours' drive from Dharamsala, and where ten children were on the list.

We visited Bir once again and carried out investigations. Only three-quarters of the children fared well, some even cried at being pulled close. We were not satisfied, but we noticed only at the last minute that one child was absent. He and his brother had been admitted to the infants' section of the Tibetan Children's Village school in Dharamsala, after their mother passed away.

The next day the Ven. Jhanpa Rinpoche and two attendants went to the school. One child came out and held the hand of one of the attendants and was showing extraordinary cheerfulness, while they were enquiring about the child by name. This child was Tenzin Choephag himself as they realised a few minutes later. Asked if he recognised them, the child nodded as if in affirmation.

They showed the child four rosaries, including one which had belonged to the former master. To the satisfaction of all, the child picked up the genuine one without the slightest hesitation. Not only that, he held it in his left hand and with perfect mastery fingered twenty of the twenty-five beads of it. This reminded the search party of a childhood trait of the past master who was left-handed in his childhood.

This did much to convince us we had located the right candidate – this child of just over one year and nine months old, who was barely able to walk and who could not talk. Next day I went to meet this child and upon seeing me, he showed special liking for me, came close and took hold of my bag. He reached for a pen and made a gesture of writing something on an envelope he took from my bag.

That day we were received by senior staff at the school who arranged some refreshment. We were six or seven persons and all of a sudden the child, of his own accord, rose and distributed the sweets to all present and placed his hand on each head in the manner of blessing.

We went to His Holiness and reported these incidents. He asked us to bring the child to His residence the next day. We told our attendants and the child was happy to accompany them. On the way, one attendant asked where the residence was and the child is said to have pointed in the right direction. When he arrived, the boy exhibited signs of recognition, reminiscent of a child meeting his parents. He sat for an hour on my lap and when he was led to His Holiness he did not show any trait of fear. His Holiness was impressed and even expressed surprise at the small child's acuteness. His Holiness gave him a protection string and some sweets.

Later His Holiness once again did a divination in front of the famous image of Lord Avaloketeshvara, making a final decision on the choice among the last four promising children – again the decision fell in this child's favour.

There were many occurrences that confirmed our belief. His behaviour while eating, his smiling. He does lots of things that are typical of the past master. I served the master ever since he was thirty-four until he died at eighty-one. This child loves me more than his natural father. Every time I visited him he always insisted on accompanying me wherever I went. He always showed sensitivity in recognising past associates and students, especially Western students of the past master. He called some close students by their names.

In a recent book, the Dalai Lama has described the small boy's behaviour.

When I received the boy at my residence and he was brought to the door, he acted just as his predecessor had done. It was plain that he remembered his way round. Moreover, when he came into my study he showed immediate familiarity with one of my attendants, who was at the time recovering from a broken leg. First, this tiny person gravely presented him with a kata (a greetings scarf) and then, full of laughter and childish giggles, he picked up one of Lobsang Gawa's crutches and ran round and round carrying it as if it were a flagpole.

Another impressive story concerns the time he was taken at the age of two to Bodh Gaya, where I was due to give teachings. Without anyone telling him of its whereabouts, he found my bedroom, having scrambled on his hands and knees up the stairs, and laid a kata on my bed.

At Mundgod an American guest at Ling Rinpoche's ceremony, Richard Weingarten, told us that he had met the Senior Tutor some years ago. It was quite a brief meeting, but the Senior Tutor made a very strong impression on him.

I happened to meet the young boy right after he had been identified and he ran up to me and jumped into my arms and patted me on the head. He acted very much like he knew me and although I did not believe in reincarnation at the time, when I met this young child I was absolutely certain it was him, that it was the old man.

One of the reasons for the Dalai Lama's special regard for the Senior Tutor was that back in 1936, he had been part of the search for the reincarnation of the thirteenth Dalai Lama, who had died a year earlier.

There were various mystical signs and clues to lead the searchers, including visions seen in a famous mirror-lake. When the party approached a farmhouse in Eastern Tibet, the leader, Lama Kewtsang Rinpoche pretended to be a servant so that he might eat in the kitchen and study the children of the house. Around his neck, this Lama wore a rosary that had belonged to the Dalai Lama. The youngest son, not yet two years old, seemed to recognise the rosary and wanted to be given it. Later this boy was given a series of formal tests. He was shown two identical black rosaries, one of which had belonged to the Dalai Lama. The boy selected the right one and put it round his neck. They offered him two drums: the first was a very small one which the Dalai Lama had used for calling servants and the second was large and ornate with golden straps. The boy began to beat the small drum in the way drums are beaten during prayers. Then he was shown two walking sticks and the boy touched the wrong one – then he paused and picked up the other which had belonged to the Dalai Lama. Later, the search party discovered that the second walking stick had also been used at some time by the thirteenth Dalai Lama.

Today that boy, the farmer's son, is His Holiness the fourteenth Dalai Lama. I asked if he could recall anything of those tests and the visit by the search party to his parents' farm more than fifty years ago.

One quiet morning, before sunrise, I was disturbed from my sleep and put on some kind of high seat, higher than a member of the search party whose face from that moment is very clear to me – his eyes were round and forceful, an eye like an owl's.

I remember in the kitchen, the leader of the party acted as a servant, but I recognised him as a lama from the Sera Monastery – his body was not fat so he was always very cold and I remember his cold hand touching my baby hands. And then there were tests with a stick and a small drum, but it is not very clear.

I asked the Dalai Lama how he would describe death.

It is just a change of clothes. The being inside, his subtle consciousness continues, but the old cloth is abandoned for new clothes.

CHAPTER TWENTY-TWO

The classic case of Shanti Devi

It is nature's kindness that we do not remember past births. MOHANDAS GANDHI

From antiquity, many people have claimed to remember previous lives, but none was more convincing than an eight-year-old girl in India in 1935. Shanti Devi, born in Delhi, startled the world with her verified story of a past life.

Her claims were widely publicised and for a while she was famous. A crowd of 10 000 fought to catch a glimpse of her when she was taken back to the small northern Indian town of Mathura where she said she once lived as a housewife who died in childbirth. She led the way through streets she had not seen before, straight to the house where the dead woman, Lugdi Devi, had lived.

Shanti recognised and greeted Lugdi's relatives as if she had always known them, and showed where the dead woman used to hide money under the floor. Her knowledge of Lugdi's life and the town of Mathura convinced a Committee of Inquiry. The families of both Shanti and Lugdi accepted her as Lugdi reborn, including the dead woman's former husband, who had re-married.

Professor Ian Stevenson says Shanti Devi is a classic case. No claim by her was shown to be false. Her version was written down before she was taken back to the scene of Lugdi's life, and her claims were investigated, at the time, by a committee of men of good reputation. In February 1988, I went to Delhi hoping to hear her story first-hand, but Shanti had died two months earlier, aged 61. Over tea, I heard the story of Shanti Devi from her brother, Mr Viresh Narain.

In 1935, not everyone had accepted Shanti's case as proof of re-incarnation. A report in Hindi by Mr Bal Chand Nahata the following year, on behalf of the Indian Psycho-Analytical Association, complained there was no psychologist on the committee of inquiry. Nahata interviewed Shanti and found her 'like a child not a re-born adult.' He said the evidence did not prove reincarnation, but he made no effort to talk to any of the known eye-witnesses to Shanti's astonishing walk-abouts in Mathura. A more detailed re-investigation was undertaken and reported in 1939 by Mr Sushil Bose, who sought out all the main witnesses.

From all these sources emerged a story every bit as fascinating as Professor Stevenson had suggested. The life of a grown woman and mother seemed somehow locked in the memory of an eight-year-old girl. Also Shanti told both Nahata and Bose of her experiences between lives – what happened from the moment she died as Lugdi until she was reborn as Shanti.

Today, this reads like a fairly typical Near Death Experience – a sensation of leaving the body, seeing bright lights and meeting archetypal religious figures. But this was half a century before the modern literature on NDEs was written and was received sceptically by both Nahata and Bose.

Bose, whose interviews are recorded in question and answer form, began his inquiry with Shanti's father, Mr Rang Bahadur Mathur, head of a reasonably well-to-do family living in a three-storey house in Cheerakhana, Old Delhi.

Shanti's father said the child began speaking later than his other children. When the others were noisy or misbehaving, Shanti always tried to calm things down and settle disputes amicably. She behaved like a small adult.

Shanti began to speak about a past life from the age of three. Eating and dressing seemed to remind her, and she would tell her mother, 'Mama, in my house in Mathura I was not accustomed to this kind of food.' She also described dresses she used to wear in Mathura. She said her family there had a cloth shop, and lived in a house painted yellow. She often said such things, but her parents did not take her seriously. 'We thought as she grew older she would forget it. Eventually we forbade her to speak about these things, because there is a belief in our sect that a boy or girl who can speak of his or her previous life with accuracy, will not live long. However, ignoring our words, she continued to speak of her desire to go to Mathura, even to neighbours who came to visit us.'

A relative, a teacher at a Delhi high school, heard of Shanti's memories and came to see her when she was about eight years old. He tried to get the child to name her husband in Mathura, Shanti said, 'If I can see him, I will at once recognise him.'

The reports say Shanti was reluctant to give the name because there was a Hindu tradition that a woman should not speak the name of her husband without good cause. The teacher offered the child a bribe. If she told him the name, he would take her to Mathura. Shanti whispered 'Pandit Kedernath Chowbey.'

Shanti's father said, 'None of us had any intention of inquiring about her house at Mathura or her husband. We tried only to make her forget these things.'

Later, the teacher returned with a college principal, Lala Kishan Chand, anxious to meet the child who could remember another life. Shanti described her house in Mathura for him and wrote down the name and address of the man she said was her husband.

Not expecting a reply, Chand wrote to Pandit Kedernath Chowbey at the address given. To everyone's amazement a few days later, Chowbey wrote back saying the description of his house in the letter was 'most exact.' Chowbey asked a cousin in Delhi to visit the girl and test her story. Pandit Kanjimall came to see Shanti, who is said to have recognised him at once as a younger cousin of her husband.

Shanti asked about her son and spoke of the family house and cloth shop in front of the Dwarikadesh Temple. Kanjimall asked questions and was so impressed by the girl's answers, that instead of writing to his cousin, he hurried to Mathura and told Chowbey his wife Lugdi Devi had been reborn.

On 12 November 1935, a rather apprehensive Pandit Kedernath Chowbey came to Delhi to meet the child who claimed to have been his wife. He brought with him the only child of that marriage, Nabanita Lall, a boy who was now a year older than Shanti, and the new wife Chowbey had married after Lugdi Devi's death. When these three and Chowbey's cousin arrived at the house, Shanti was in school, and had to be sent for.

As a test, the cousin told everyone he had brought Chowbey's older brother to see Shanti. The child was told this when she got home from school.

Her father described what happened. 'Shanti bowed her head shyly and stood at one side. She was only nine at the time. Seeing her behaviour, everyone told her, "He is the elder brother of your husband. Why do you feel so shy with him?" Slowly the girl replied, "He isn't my husband's elder brother, he is my husband. I have told you about him many times."'

When Shanti saw her son, she embraced him and wept for a long time. She asked her mother to bring all her toys for the boy, but she was so eager, she could not wait, and ran to get them herself.

Shanti's father continued, 'When Shanti had brought all her toys and given them to her son, who was now older than she, a wonderful expression of motherly love could be seen in her eyes and face. No one seeing that expression could think she was only a child. It seemed she had become middle-aged. She began to shed tears from joy and motherly love, and at times wept aloud. Seeing this the crowd also began to weep.'

Word of this strange family reunion spread. People gathered at the house, curious to see what was going on. Embarrassed by this, Chowbey suggested they go for a ride around Delhi in an open carriage, or tonga. On a wide road, some distance away, Shanti and the boy Nabanita walked hand in hand. They stayed away from the house until the crowds had dispersed.

Shanti asked her mother to prepare a meal and described the foods Chowbey liked to eat. She also pointed to jewellery, which had once belonged to her, now being worn by Chowbey's wife!

After the meal, Shanti looked at Chowbey's wife and said to him, 'Why did you marry her? Didn't we agree that you would not marry again?'

According to Shanti's father, Chowbey hung his head and said nothing. Then he questioned the girl. 'Can you give a description of the Mathura house so that I can really understand that you actually lived in it?' Shanti said, 'In the inner courtyard of the house there is a well. I would usually sit on a stone beside that well and take my bath.'

Chowbey asked, 'How could you recognise this boy as your own son? At the time of your death, this boy was only nine days old, and you only saw him once in your life.'

Shanti replied, 'He is my life. My life has recognised my life.'

It was true that Lugdi Devi had died within two weeks of giving birth to her only child, but identifying the boy was not really difficult. Who else could he be? He was with his father and was clearly the right age to be 'her' son.

Chowbey had another test for Shanti. He insisted on a private talk and afterwards gave his verdict. 'No one except my previous wife and myself could possibly know the detail of the personal talks that we had together. That Shanti is my dead wife, Lugdi Devi, I have not the least doubt.'

So far, the Shanti Devi story is fascinating but largely anecdotal. Shanti had correctly told her mother Chowbey had a mole on the left side of his face, was of a fair complexion and wore glasses for reading, but the witnesses are members of the girl's family. Perhaps Shanti recognised Chowbey because she was told who he was by an onlooker in the crowd —maybe the mole on his face had given him away. Perhaps she had even seen him before. The investigator Nahata had been told Chowbey sometimes went to a sweetmeats shop in Delhi, and Shanti as a child might have seen him there, it was suggested.

But for the next stage of Shanti Devi's story there were thousands of witnesses. Shanti had become a celebrity after the Delhi reunion when the Indian Press printed her story. Even Mahatma Gandhi, father of the Indian nation, came to ask questions, and 'expressed himself well satisfied by her answers.' The schoolgirl had captured the public's imagination. A committee of inquiry, fifteen of Delhi's most prominent and respected citizens, was set up. Members included the editor of a Delhi newspaper *The Tej*, a Member of Parliament, a business magnate, and an eminent lawyer.

They immediately wanted to take Shanti and her parents to Mathura, to see if the girl could identify the places she claimed to remember. At first, Shanti's father refused. 'We entertained a fear in our minds that if Shanti were to go to Mathura, she would be unwilling to return to Delhi after seeing her husband and son. It would create a situation of extreme gravity. The sight of her extreme devotion to Pandit Kedernath and the boy, and her intense desire to return with them to Mathura, had made a deep impression on our minds.'

However, the committee insisted. Eventually, on 24 November 1935, twelve days after meeting Chowbey, Shanti, her parents and the entire inquiry set off by train on the three-hour journey to Mathura. On the train, the committee noted that the girl said in colloquial Hindi, 'It is eleven o'clock and the gates of the Dwarikadesh Temple will be closed.' She said the word 'pot' for 'gate,' which is used by the people of Mathura alone, according to the official report. Shortly before the train reached the station, a committee man told Shanti that Mathura was still a long way off. The girl said she could see from the roads and streets that the centre of Mathura was very close.

It had been announced in the Press that Shanti was being taken back to Mathura and at the station thousands of spectators gathered to see her. Overawed, the child sat on the lap of Mr Deshbandu, the Member of Parliament. Then, says the report, 'a gentleman with a big stick in his hands and a big turban on his head, came in front of Shanti and asked if she recognised him. At the sight of him, Shanti asked Deshbandu to put her down. Then she touched the feet of the turbaned gentleman with great reverence and stood aside, whispering to Deshbandu Gupta, "He is my husband's older brother." Everyone was amazed.'

Coming out of the station, Deshbandu put Shanti in an open carriage, and told the driver to follow her directions. Shanti said the road had not been tarmaced when she knew it, and she pointed out houses recently built. At a junction with two lanes, Shanti jumped from the tonga and led the way towards her house. She greeted an old Brahmin with great reverence and said, 'He is my father-in-law.'

According to the report, 'The neighbourhood had been informed of her coming and the lanes and nearby houses were a mass of seething humanity. A chant of the name of God went up from all lips at the sight of her greeting her father-in-law.'

Shanti pointed out her house. She had said in Delhi that the house was yellow, but it was a different colour. In fact, the house had been rented out and re-painted – when Lugdi lived there it had been yellow!

Inside, Shanti pointed out where Lugdi had slept, and the room where she had kept her clothes. 'Two prominent gentlemen of the locality approached with the desire to test her. They asked if she could point out the "jajarie khann." To an inhabitant of Delhi, this term is meaningless. It is used only by the Chowbeys of Mathura. But to the amazement of all, she descended the staircase and showed the two gentlemen the privy of the house.'

In the crowd, she picked out a twenty-five-year-old man as her brother, and an older man as the brother of her father-in-law. At noon, a committeeman put the child on his shoulders and asked her to show the way to another house, where she and her husband had spent most time. At the end of a lane, she got down and said, 'This is my house.'

In the courtyard, she was reminded she had said there was a well from which she drew water to bathe. There was no well to be seen. 'The girl looked puzzled and grave. She put her foot on a corner of the courtyard and said, "The well was here." A slab of stone was removed from that place and the well was found.'

There was an even more remarkable incident when Shanti went into the room she said was her bedroom. 'Looking hither and thither, she finally pointed to a place on the floor and said, "My money is buried here. If the place be dug up, the money will be found." The place was accordingly opened. Under a stone, a money box was found, but there was no money in it. The girl was stunned for a time, then said, "I kept my money here. Someone must have taken it!" At this, Pandit Kedernath Chowbey, who was present, said, "Shanti, in your previous life you did bury the money here before going to the hospital. But you never returned. You died there. After your death, I removed the money from the box." Shanti was quite satisfied to hear this' says the report.

Leading the committee towards the River Jumna, where she said she used to bathe, Shanti suddenly stopped and pointed to a house she said was the home of her parents.

'Saying this, she entered the house with rapid steps. There were nearly forty or forty-five men, women and children in that house. She picked out her mother and sat on her lap. Her mother embraced her warmly and began to sob aloud. Her father too was recognised and he also began to weep in a way both joyful and sorrowful. The eyes of all men who had gone with Shanti filled with tears. They said to one another – "It is better not to remember one's previous life."'

There were wild scenes as Shanti reached the end of her walk-about. She pointed out the cloth shop owned by the family, and, by the time she reached the bazaar, word of her tour had spread like wildfire. Most of the population had come to catch a glimpse of her.

'Men and women came running to see her from every side. So great was the crowd that the party became separated one from another and some of the group had their clothing torn to pieces. With great difficulty Deshbandu Gupta and others took the girl away in a motor car,' said the official report.

The crowds were so excited that the committee and Shanti's parents refused the many requests for the girl to stay on in the town for a few days more. They got her to the train as quickly as possible. On the journey back to Delhi, Shanti became 'morose and tired.' Shortly after boarding the train, the child fell into a deep sleep. An astonishing day was over!

When the committee met, they were so sure the evidence pointed to reincarnation, they threw the inquiry open. They invited any individual or group of people who did not believe in reincarnation, such as Christians or Muslims, to question the girl for themselves, or offer any alternative explanation. No one stepped forward.

Five years later, the zealous Mr Bose posed some pertinent questions. He asked Shanti's father, 'Did you have any acquaintance or connection with the relations of her previous life? Either you or any family member?'

'Never. We had never heard of them before. Nor did I ever have any occasion to visit Mathura.'

Bose sought out the witnesses of those strange scenes at Mathura. Everyone he spoke to, members of the committee and the people Shanti recognised in the street and at the railway station, confirmed the earlier version of events in every detail.

He went to see the husband Chowbey and asked him bluntly, 'Are you sure your dead wife has been reborn as Shanti Devi?'

'Yes. As to this, I have not the least doubt.'

Bose asked if this certainty was based upon the private talk Chowbey had with Shanti Devi on his first visit to Delhi. He urged Chowbey to tell him about this conversation. 'I have not come to satisfy an idle curiosity, but in a scientific spirit to find out the truth.'

Chowbey said, 'I have not told anyone about the private talks. I am telling you now for the first time.'

Chowbey recalled it had been about one o'clock in the morning. Shanti Devi's family had gone to bed, leaving him with the girl, his present wife and his son, who had fallen asleep. He asked Shanti to tell him something no one else could know, except himself and his dead wife. Shanti suggested his wife should leave the room, but Chowbey said Shanti could speak freely in front of her. The girl said, 'Ask me something and I'll tell you the details.'

Chowbey recalled how Lugdi had been in great pain after gashing her foot on a piece of bone. She was treated in hospital and it was about this time their son was conceived. Chowbey reminded the girl, 'You could not stand erect. You had to slide about on your buttocks. Can you say how, in that condition, conception became possible?'

He told Bose, 'That girl of nine years showed me the position in which it took place. And since then I have had no doubts.'

Bose wrote that Chowbey's eyes became wet with tears as he talked about his previous wife. The researcher went back to Delhi, to see Shanti Devi, now aged thirteen. She told him the memories of her previous life were still 'as clear as if they had happened yesterday.'

He asked Shanti if she remembered how Lugdi had injured her foot. The girl said Lugdi Devi was a devout Hindu, and named five places of pilgrimage she used regularly to visit. At Harihapiri, walking barefoot a hundred times around a sacred shrine, she trod on a piece of bone which caused an infection.

Asked whom she had loved most in her previous life, Shanti replied 'My son.' Had she been thinking of him at the time of her death? She said she had not.

Bose then asked the girl what she remembered from the moment of dying as Lugdi to being re-born as Shanti. This little-known aspect of Shanti's story fits well alongside case studies of modern Near Death Experiences. Back in 1939, it was a remarkable interview.

BOSE Do you remember how you felt at the time of death?

SHANTI Yes. Just before death, I felt a profound darkness and after that I saw a dazzling light. Then and there I knew I had come out of my body in a vaporous form and that I was moving upwards.

BOSE Didn't you see your dead body?

SHANTI No. I didn't look in that direction.

BOSE Did you feel any pain?

SHANTI I did not feel any pain. I simply passed into unconsciousness and at that very moment saw a very brilliant light.

BOSE What happened then?

SHANTI I saw that four men in saffron robes had come for me. They were of the same appearance. All four seemed to be in their teens and their appearance and dress were very bright. After going up for some time, I saw a beautiful garden, the like of which I have never seen in this world. It is beyond description. And I saw a river also.

Shanti Devi said she seemed to be the size of a thumb when she left her body. The four men carried her in what looked like a rectangular cup about ten inches across. They took her to 'the first plane' but there were higher levels. She saw male and female saints, some brighter in appearance than others, and was told there was no difference between souls, such as Muslim, Christian, Hindu, etc.

She said there was no feeling of time, no sun or moon, nothing like night or darkness. 'It was all full of light. It was very soothing, something like the light of a full moon. It was all day and light. Very mild, soothing and enlivening light.'

Eventually, she was told she would have to go back and be re-born in Delhi as a girl. The name of her father was mentioned and so was her address. Then she was taken to a dark room, which had a bad smell, and was made to lie down in a clean place. The descending path to re-birth was in darkness, just as the ascending path from death had been of light.

Even the impassive Bose was moved to scepticism. His next question was almost a speech. 'Whatever we see, hear and smell is with the help of our sense organs. If I am blinded, I will not be able to see you again ... thinking is possible only because we have a brain ... you said you went out of your body in a light-gaseous state devoid of brain and senses. Still you could think, see things, smell things? How is it possible?'

SHANTI I cannot say how it is possible. I am telling you what I have experienced.

BOSE Is there any difference between what one feels with the sense organs and what one feels without them?

SHANTI Yes. Without sense organs the senses become very keen. For example, with my eyes in perfect order, I cannot visualise what lies on the other side of the walls. But without a physical body and the organs of sight, I can. My sight becomes so keen that, penetrating the wall, it sees what is on the other side. And this is true of the other senses too.

The child told her questioners that because of her experience as Lugdi Devi, she would never re-marry. When Shanti died a few years ago, in her early sixties, she was still a spinster. And her brother told me she retained to the end her total conviction of having lived before as Lugdi Devi. She kept in touch with her 'previous family' and was an honoured guest on all their family occasions, such as birthdays, weddings and funerals.

She told her brother, a few days before she died, that she was confident she would not have to be reborn again. Shanti Devi was a school teacher for most of her life. At her funeral were a few hundred friends and mourners – nothing like the thousands who fought to catch sight of her that day in the bazaar in Mathura when a little girl disturbed the thoughts of many.

175

CHAPTER TWENTY-THREE

For whom the bell tolls

God generates beings and sends them back over and over again, until they return to him. THE KORAN

B elief in reincarnation is not limited to Buddhists and Hindus in Asia – it exists amongst North American Indians. Parapsychologists have recorded children in Canada who remember living before and who have birthmarks corresponding to events in previous lives.

Emma Michell, an eighty-two-year-old member of the Wet'suwet'en tribe in British Columbia, told us a powerful story. Years ago, her small nephew Jimmy was playing on the floor when the bell began to toll in the small wooden church next door. The boy asked why the bell was ringing and was told it was because Donald G-, a local man, was dead. The child said, 'That's the one who hired men to beat me up and throw me in the river.' The child was recalling the death of an uncle whose battered body had been recovered from the nearby Bulkeley River before the boy was born.

Jimmy was accepted as the reincarnation of this uncle, but as a young man tragically met a similar death – he too was drowned in the turbulent river that dominates the village. The family say Jimmy has subsequently been reborn yet again as Emma's grandson, who as a small child had some memories of both drowned forebears! He used plaintively to wish he'd been born a girl, and therefore less likely to meet another violent death in the river.

Emma's family was typical of the North American Indian's belief that people are mostly reborn within the same family. This poses a special problem for parapsychologists like Dr Antonia Mills of the University of Virginia, who took us to meet Emma. 'It's very difficult in general to be sure the statement a child makes is not based on knowledge the child could learn from its parents or other relatives.'

Dr Mills said a good case was often a combination of startling statements by the child, sometimes on matters unknown to the parents, and birthmarks, personal characteristics and medical conditions relating to the previous personality.

Today Emma's grandson is a boy of fourteen, whose memories of another life have faded, but his mother and grandmother remember him as an infant. A car that once belonged to the dead Jimmy was standing derelict alongside the house. 'The boy was only two and he'd run around and tell my parents this was his car and the wheels were all flat. He'd kick the wheels and say "Who did this?"'

Today, the youth complains of pains in his feet and knees which have stopped him playing football and meant he had to miss gym classes all last year. He is annoyed about this and has had to consult two doctors. His mother says this reminds her very much of her dead brother Jimmy. 'My brother had a couple of operations and the one side of his foot was flat and he was always talking about his knees hurting him.'

Comparing reincarnation cases in Canada with Asia, there are clear similarities between the cultural beliefs of these North American Indians and the religious doctrines of the East. Perhaps that's not surprising – North American Indians are said to be the descendants of nomadic bands of Asian hunters who crossed the Bering Straits about 10 000 years ago during the Great Ice Age, when Asia and America where temporarily joined between Siberia and Alaska.

Dr Mills pointed out similarities between the Tibetan belief that Senior Lamas may choose to come back as tulkus, and North American Indian High Chiefs who sometimes choose to be reborn to help members of their family or clan. Both cultures also accept reincarnation of animals as well as humans, and these Indians, like the Tibetans, believe the mountains and the forest where they live are inhabited by spirits – their land is a living thing.

We filmed in an area of magnificent forested mountains, lakes and waterfalls, where two small tribes live along the banks of the Skeena and Bulkeley rivers. Traditionally they hunted game in the forest and fished for salmon in the rivers, which still boil with sockeye and spring salmon returning to spawn.

In the rocky gorge at Moricetown, the water breaks over great boulders where gleaming Indian fishermen, half hidden in spray, precariously try to spear the leaping and darting fish. In the flurry of a catch, it's easy to slip off the wet rocks and be swept away – some for safety have a line tied round their waist, with the other end held hopefully by a strong colleague on the shore. These fishing spots are prized, a source of wealth and there is a strict pecking order. A chief of the Wet'suwet'en tribe told me that anyone fishing in his spot would have to move when he appeared.

It had been a dispute between families over fishing rights that led to the murder in the river which Jimmy told Emma about. It was claimed that the drowned man, son of a chief, acted as if he already had the same rights as his father during the chief's lifetime. After a day's fishing, the young man went to collect some traps and was not seen alive again.

Today, there are only a thousand Wet'suwet'en in the valley and about five thousand Gitksan nearby. There is a Christian church in each village and many Indians attend services. It might look as if their old belief in reincarnation has been supplanted by Christianity, but appearances are deceptive. We met numerous Indian churchgoers who believe in reincarnation, and a re-born chief who is also a born-again Christian. The Indians see no contradiction in accepting Christianity and continuing to believe in reincarnation.

There are several distinctive features about reincarnation beliefs amongst the tribes. Often there is an announcing dream by some senior member of the family which reveals the identity of the one who is to be reborn. Sometimes, apparitions of the dead person are seen. At birth, the old people scan every inch of the baby for signs of tell-tale birthmarks and as the child grows up they keep a close watch to see if he or she behaves like the dead person. Sometimes an individual tells a family in advance how he or she intends to be reborn.

For example, Fern was a small child when a member of her clan visited her grandmother's house and announced his intention. 'He was a relative of my grandmother and he just looked at me and said he was going to come back to me, as my child. I was just a young girl, and was terrified of this man. Every time I saw him on the street, I'd hide and wait for him to pass and then run home.'

Years later, Fern had a son and her grandmother told her the child was this man come back. She pointed to birthmarks around the ears of the baby which resembled the pierced-ear marks of a chief. These marks are still clearly visible on Fern's son and Dr Mills photographed them for her records.

Fern said she'd had no idea the old man in question had even had pierced ears. However, she was more impressed by an outburst from her son when he was about three years old. The boy's grandmother, now dead, recorded the incident in a written statement for Dr Mills. The child became furious when he discovered the old man's house had been pulled down and that his widow had remarried. He demanded to know who had taken down the house and said he would kill the second husband. The three-year-old was asked how he proposed to do that – he went to the kitchen and came back with a butcher's knife! Dr Mills commented:

In a number of cases the evidence is difficult to explain. For example, where children have pierced-ear marks, they are not something that would be genetically transmitted or explained by our current understanding of biology. It's interesting in this case that the mother did not know the previous personality had pierced ears, so it's not a question of a mother willing it – not caused by a maternal impression which is an alternative explanation for birthmarks.

A man who was having his pierced-ear marks photographed by Dr Mills told us about an experience with an apparition. In 1969, when he was a boy, his uncle Carl was missing and there was a big search. Carl's body was eventually found hidden amongst logs in the dock at Prince Rupert – he'd been murdered, but the body wasn't found for three weeks and the family became very anxious. One day, the telephone rang. The twelve-year-old boy picked it up and heard his uncle Carl ask if there had been any messages for him. The boy was shocked and held the telephone away from his ear. 'Carl had a kind of hysterical laugh when he thought there was something funny, and my father and others around the room heard him laughing down the telephone.' Some nights later, the boy believed he saw Carl come through a glass door and stand in front of him and again ask if there had been any telephone calls. Then he vanished.

At a chief's house, Dr Mills talked to a small group of women, all chiefs and all reincarnates. Dr Mills asked a woman how she knew that her daughter Barbara, who was present, was reincarnated. 'By her thumbnail. My grandmother had an accident and it split her thumbnail and lasted all her life.'

Barbara showed us her thumbnail – a very clear ridge runs down it, which we filmed. She accepted she was her own great-grandmother and said as a child she had a special relationship with the son of the dead woman. 'He knew a lot of things and had ways of knowing I was his mother. He just assured me of his love for me.'

In her own life, Barbara has found herself retracing old steps. The great-grandmother was leader of a local rebellion and a healer. Today, Barbara is a leader of the blockade movement pressing for land reform and she helps run a centre for holistic healing.

Barbara's grandson, now aged eleven, is believed to be the reincarnation of an hereditary chief named Peter Milton, who told three cousins before he died that he intended to come back.

On the morning the child was born, in another part of Canada, one of the cousins told Barbara's mother she had just had a dream announcing that Peter Milton had been reborn. A little later, a telephone call said a baby boy had been born – he had three pierced-ear marks, similar to the earrings worn by Peter Milton.

When the child was about three, he was brought to the area and he showed some interest in seeing where Peter Milton had lived. The infant was in his family home when there was a knock at the door – it was Alice, one of the three cousins Milton had spoken to about coming back. The child had never seen her before.

> We were here in the kitchen and Aunty usually knocked and walked in. As soon as she opened the door, the little boy walked up to her and gave her a punch. Georgia was very upset, but Alice said, 'Don't be upset, I have something to tell you.' She gathered us around this table and told us that before Peter Milton passed away, his cousins had asked how they would recognise him when he came back. He said 'I'll give aunty Alice a punch!'

Dr Mills' research followed in the footsteps of Dr Ian Stevenson in British Columbia. They have made several surveys of reincarnation cases amongst the Indians and I asked Dr Mills for her conclusions:

> I began seeing that the belief in reincarnation among the Indians suggested a totally different concept of personality than the concepts I had been trained to think of. They talked about personality in terms of who they were before – they were saying a person comes back bringing the traits they had at the end of their previous life.
>
> The Beaver Indians particularly think when a person dies violently or suddenly, he or she has a hard time finding the trail to heaven. When the person dies in a confused state, they linger around as discarnate beings, a kind of ghost. A lot of people see apparitions of such a person until the person is reborn. They believe people who find the trail to heaven and stay there for a considerable time, also come back, but it is so long after their death on the earth plane, they no longer have any memories of a previous identity. But their personality characteristics are still the result of who they were before. So even when they don't know who they were before, their personality is an accumulation of qualities from previous lives. This was a very interesting world view.
>
> Some of the more difficult cases are explained by the native concept of reincarnation. The question is whether reincarnation is the only explanation that would account for these phenomena. I have not been able to think of an explanation for the phenomena in some cases other than reincarnation – but what reincarnation is, how it operates, that's not fully understood.

Most anthropologists approach the beliefs of native people in terms of 'What does a tradition give a people?' They have not looked at whether there is any validity to these beliefs and sometimes they assume they are in fact incorrect. I don't think we're justified in making those kind of assumptions. This belief deserves a careful analysis.

We're only on the threshold of understanding the impact on people of culture, of mind, of what people believe. We are past the colonial era where we can presume to know better.

CHAPTER TWENTY-FOUR

A fear of thunder

End and beginning are dreams,
Birthless and deathless and changeless
Remaineth the spirit forever.
Death hath not touched it at all,
Dead though the house of it seems.

BHAGAVAD GITA

(THE SONG CELESTIAL, TRANSLATED BY
SIR EDWIN ARNOLD)

In a tropical thunderstorm, a frightened three-year-old girl told her parents she had been killed in a previous life by a landslide caused by torrential rain. From her account, researchers identified a disaster some years before, in which twenty-eight people died, and they found a victim who matched the child's description of this earlier life.

This was one of four dramatic stories of previous lives which sent us to Sri Lanka in November 1990. These were strong cases because each child's memories were written down before anyone discovered whose lives they might be talking about. And it was the researchers, mostly by good detective work, not the families concerned who identified the dead people the children remembered.

Two of the cases were investigated by Dr Ian Stevenson of the University of Virginia and both were children who recalled earlier lives in poor circumstances, a blow to those who pretend Stevenson's cases are all about poor families trying to scrape up an acquaintance with wealthier ones. The other cases, equally fascinating, were researched by Professor Erlendur Haraldsson of the University of Iceland.

Stevenson's second case was another three-year-old girl who said she was the daughter of a flower seller and had drowned after being pushed into a river by a dumb boy. It sounded an unlikely scenario but the researchers verified the facts. Stevenson's published verdict on both cases was that the evidence showed the children obtained correct information about deceased persons 'by some paranormal process.'

Our introduction to the child who remembered a landslide disaster was dramatic. We arrived at the parents' home in Sri Lanka in mid-afternoon to record an interview with Subashini, now aged ten, when she arrived home from school. Her schoolteacher parents, well educated and quite prosperous, live in a pleasant house at the end of a forest track. Their daughter still has a fear of thunderstorms and, as we were talking to her parents, a tropical storm broke. The father took a large umbrella and rushed off to meet his daughter as the track swiftly turned into a stream. When Subashini arrived, sheltering close, against her father, we talked to her about her phobia as the storm raged in the background.

Today Subashini's memories have almost completely faded, but her parents' recollections are vivid. They talked to Godwin Samararatne, a skilled researcher frequently used by Dr Stevenson to investigate Sri Lankan cases. The parents recalled that their daughter was three years old when she began to speak of another life as the daughter of tea-pickers on a plantation at Sinhapitiya, Gampola, almost 100 kilometres from their home.

The child said that one night in a great storm there was a noise like 'gudu, gudu' and her mother told her to take a torch and go outside to see if the mountain was falling down. The child said simply, 'I took a torch and went outside and came here.'

Subashini had described tea bushes, which she could not have seen growing anywhere near her home, and made gestures to show how tea was picked. She said that tea-pickers lived in 'lines,' rows of terraced shacks. She talked about Tamil workers, who are the poorly paid descendants of Hindus from India, brought over in the nineteenth century by British tea planters as cheap labour for their highland estates.

She talked so frequently about Tamils that the neighbouring children began teasing her, saying she had been a Tamil in a previous life. Little Subashini got very angry and made it clear that her family had been Sinhalese Buddhists.

The child was still only three when Dr Stevenson's other researcher in the area, Tissa Jayawardane, heard about her story, visited the family and began to record her statements. Subashini described life in the 'lines' in some detail – there was a water tap in the yard that irritated her mother because it would not stop dripping, her father had a pot-belly, she had an older brother and sister as well as a younger brother and sister. On the night of the storm, her older brother returned home but left because his supper wasn't ready and so escaped the disaster. Outside the shack, in the dark with her torch, the child had become 'trapped.'

Subashini had named the area where the disaster occurred and her schoolteacher father was then told by a relative about a serious accident on a tea plantation in that district some years before. The father was invited to a wedding in this area and thought it would be a good opportunity to investigate.

Stevenson's written report says, 'Subashini's father took her along a road on the tea estate where he had been told the landslide had occurred. However, Subashini became frightened, screamed and refused to go on, saying she was afraid of being trapped. They turned back and did not meet any of the families who had lost members in the landslide.'

It didn't take Stevenson's researchers long to get to grips with the facts of the disaster which happened in October 1977, just over two years before Subashini was born. The *Ceylon Daily Mirror* carried a story and a picture of coffins of those victims they managed to find after a landslide that killed twenty-eight people. The researchers established that there had been no other landslips in the area within living memory.

The report of the official inquiry into the disaster yielded an important fact – there was just one Sinhalese Buddhist family living in the lines alongside Tamil families. The mother and father of this family were killed and so were their three youngest children. One was a little girl, Devi Mallika, aged about seven who seemed to fit Subashini's descriptions. On the night of the storm, an older brother had returned home but had gone out again before the landslip occurred and escaped unharmed, as did another sister who was not at home that evening.

Godwin Samararatne analysed Subashini's thirty-two recorded statements of fact and found that twenty-five fitted the life of Devi Mallika, according to surviving relatives and a family friend. Of the seven other facts, some were simply unverifiable – like the child's claim that her mother had asked her to take a torch and look outside. No one from the house survived to bear witness. The child had correctly said that an older brother left the house before the disaster, but the boy told researchers he left at the request of his father, not because his supper was not ready. This largely accurate statement was therefore classified as unverified, which indicates how scrupulous the researchers were in weighing the facts.

In 1986, Samararatne and Jayawardane tried an experiment. They took Subashini and her parents to the plantation manager's office where she met a group of people, including surviving relatives. Would she be able to identify relatives from the previous life? It was a partial success.

Subashini, whose memories might have been starting to fade at the age of six, said nothing about her sister or a neighbour, but correctly said a young man present was her older brother. It was an important identification but it was flawed, as Stevenson acknowledged. 'Subashini's recognition of the brother was marred because he pushed himself forward from a group and stood in front of her. Godwin Samararatne then asked her "Who is he?" Thus, although she had no verbal clue to his identity she might have inferred that he was an older member of the family.'

To capture something of that terrible night in October 1977, our team visited the landslide site. The manager, Mr I. B. Herath, drove us up a steep mountain path in a four-wheel drive vehicle. The hillsides were covered with neat, low bushes of tea all the way up to the mountain tops – the higher the tea grows, the better the quality and the higher the price. Nothing seemed to have changed. The workers, nearly all Tamils earning low wages, lived in 'lines,' squalid rows of shacks on small plateaus cut into the hillside. Chickens strutted about the yards, outside taps seemed still to drip, and children with large brown eyes gazed back at us from every doorway.

The site of Devi Mallika's home was completely overgrown. Herath told us what happened on the night of the disaster. After four days of rain, there was a thunderstorm about eight o'clock in the evening of 27 October. Suddenly huge granite boulders, weighing several tonnes, went slithering down the mountainside in a tide of mud. The lines were engulfed and partly swept down the hillside for another 250 yards and buried. Half the bodies were never recovered, including those of Devi Mallika and her family.

The older brother and sister still work on the plantation and we talked to them alongside the disaster area. They showed us how their family, when drinking tea, put a little sugar on the palm of the hand and lick it as they drink – the family couldn't afford to buy enough sugar to put in a cup. This was the way Subashini drank tea at home when she was small, which used to baffle her present parents.

I couldn't help thinking that the Subashini I met in her school uniform, protected against the rain by her father's umbrella, has a much better deal from life than the child whose bones were somewhere down the hillside below us, probably under one of those neat tea bushes.

*   *   *   *   *

In the second Stevenson case, we looked at Thusitha, the three-year-old daughter of a village tailor who heard someone mention the name 'Kataragama' and said 'I used to live there.' She was referring to a town 200 kilometres distant from her home at Payagala, near Colombo. In 1984,

Thusitha told her parents her father had sold flowers near a Buddhist temple, which she named. She had lived near a river and a dumb boy had pushed her in, and she drowned.

Within a year, Tissa Jayawardane heard about Thusitha and began to record her statements. He went to Kataragama, a place of pilgrimage famous for its Buddhist and Hindu temples, with a river running through the middle.

At the police station, Tissa asked if there was anyone who sold flowers, perhaps had a dumb boy in the family. He was directed to lines of stalls near a Buddhist temple. At one of them he was told the flower seller's daughter Nimalkanthi had drowned in the river in 1974 when she was nearly two years old. She had been playing with her two brothers – one of whom was dumb!

Godwin Samararatne also recorded information from Thusitha. The child spoke of dogs which were tied up near her home and fed meat, which sounded most unusual because Buddhists do not usually eat meat and rarely keep dogs as pets. In Sri Lanka there are many dogs, but they are usually strays who scavenge for food. However, the child was correct – a neighbour of Nimalkanthi's family was a hunter who kept his dogs tied up and fed them on the meat he caught.

The child also described how her father was a part-time priest in a temple and took part in coconut-smashing ceremonies. The child waved her arms about to show how it was done. In Kataragama, we filmed at the temple where the dead girl's father assisted at ceremonies – coconuts were set on fire and then ceremonially smashed in the way the child had described, symbolising the solving of life's problems.

To make sure they had found the correct family, Stevenson went around every one of the twenty stalls in the road and asked each family if they had a dumb boy or had lost a child through drowning. Thusitha made thirty statements of fact, of which twenty-eight were verifiable, and twenty-three were correct for the life of Nimalkanthi.

At the flower stall we filmed a sad-faced young man cleverly opening out the petals on blooms and making a vivid display. He was the dumb brother. The most poignant moment for us came when Nimalkanthi's mother led the way across the field to a river and showed us where she had been washing clothes on the bank while the little girl played with her two brothers. Sixteen years on from the day of the tragedy, the dumb boy, who had been unable to tell his mother of the terrible accident, looked on sadly and there were tears in the mother's eyes.

✳   ✳   ✳   ✳   ✳

Our quartet of Sri Lankan children who seemed to remember previous lives was completed by two remarkable six-year-olds. Duminda, a serious little boy, chanted obscure Buddhist texts in Pali, a language used only in religion, and behaved like the abbot he might once have been. Dilukshi, a little girl treasured by two sets of parents, pointed to the river where she says she drowned in an earlier life.

We were introduced to them both by Professor Erlendur Haraldsson of the University of Iceland, who emphasised that the children's recollections were recorded well in advance of any previous personality being found.

Both sets of parents tried initially to play down their children's stories. Duminda's tale seemed most far-fetched. The little boy recalled the life of a monk who had a motor car, an elephant and a money bag. Property is routinely forbidden to monks, so it was an unlikely description, but Dr Haraldsson found a corresponding real life version.

For Dilukshi, a matching past life came to light only after her story was published in a newspaper and read by the father of a drowned girl.

Dilukshi, an only child, was two years old in 1986, when she began to upset her parents by refusing to call them mother and father – she called her mother 'Clooche' or aunt. The infant wanted to be taken to her real mother and her real home in Dambulla, over one hundred kilometres distant. Her parents scolded the child to get her to stop this talk, but she replied that her real parents never shouted at her – they used to call her 'darling' or 'sweet little daughter.' Dilukshi insisted she had once drowned in a river near Dambulla.

Eventually her worried parents contacted the high priest of the Dambulla temple. His enquiries came to nothing and he passed the problem to a feature writer with the newspaper *Weekend*, Mr I. W. Abeypala, who printed a full account of the girl's story. This was read by a man in the Dambulla district. Dilukshi's story of a drowning echoed the circumstances of his own daughter's death in September 1983, one year before Dilukshi was born. He and his wife wanted to meet the girl who might be the reincarnation of their daughter Shiromi.

In a busy newspaper office in Colombo, Abeypala told the story of how he took Dilukshi and her parents to meet the other family. It was a long walk along rutted paths to the remote house where Shiromi had lived and little Dilukshi led the way confidently. She was met by a group of people. Abeypala said, 'This was a very strange story – to be born again and go in search of the parents of the previous life. It occurs rarely in Sri Lanka. But I was there and saw the child herself identify the parents of her previous birth. She recognised the parents, the brother, the sister, her aunt, her grandmother. I saw with my own eyes how she recognised them, so I accept that as proof.'

Inside the house, clothes and toys belonging to the dead girl were fetched from a cupboard and Dilukshi was invited to inspect them. 'She recognised not just her parents but her clothes, her school flask, her sunglasses, her slate and pencils. She identified all these and there was a drawing book which she took hold of and turned the pages to a half-finished picture – and then she completed it,' Abeypala said.

Dr Haraldsson was not present at this meeting and for him this identifying of clothes was unscientific. 'As a test of recognition it was useless. If we had done it, we would have mixed Shiromi's possessions in with items belonging to other children, and we would have had someone running the test who did not know which items were which. As it was, everytime something was picked up, you could say she had identified an object of Shiromi's.'

Over the fields, behind the house, Dilukshi led the way to the river where nine-year-old Shiromi had drowned. Abeypala said, 'Then she went to the place where she had fallen into the stream. She went there and hit it with stones, threw stones at the water, saying "This is the place." Children have a habit of hitting a place where an injury occurred and she did just that. Hence, I believe what she says.'

For Haraldsson the value of Abeypala's intervention is that the reporter's notes and published report provided a record of Dilukshi's claims which could confidently be compared to the facts of Shiromi's death, especially since the notes were made before Shiromi's father came forward.

Standing on the river bank, Haraldsson told us the location fitted in well with both versions. Dilukshi had said she drowned near a footbridge over a river close to where her father owned paddy-fields. Haraldsson pointed to the same stretch of water Dilukshi had indicated. 'This is where Shiromi drowned and there isn't a footbridge here now, but there was in Shiromi's time. And the paddy-fields just by here are owned by Shiromi's father. All Dilukshi's statements about the stream fit the death of Shiromi.'

We filmed another aspect of Dilukshi's tale that described where Shiromi lived. The child remembered playing with her brother on a small outcrop of rock they called 'the little Dambulla rock' and she said from here they could see the roof of their parents' house through the trees. There was a small rocky outcrop halfway between the river and Shiromi's house. We filmed a new generation of children spontaneously playing there, and clearly visible over the treetops was the roof of one house – Shiromi's.

It was clear Shiromi's parents accept Dilukshi as their daughter returned. We took the child and her parents there, to film the two families together, and they made a party of it. Dilukshi was totally at home and brought small presents for the younger brother and sister of her previous life. It was a reunion that was somehow both happy and sad.

Haraldsson's statistical assessment of the case is that Dilukshi made seventeen verifiable statements and thirteen of them were at least partially correct for the life of Shiromi – but four were wrong. The inaccuracies were names of people. For instance, Dilukshi gave wrong names for two of Shiromi's brothers – although the dead child had playmates with those names.

As we were leaving, Haraldsson confirmed another tie-in between the lives of the two girls. Dilukshi had said that near her previous home was a vegetable shop run by 'a very thin boy.' Near Shiromi's home was one shop that fitted the description, but it had closed some years ago. We were taking some shots of it, when the former shopkeeper turned up, quite by chance. He spoke with Haraldsson – yes, he had sold vegetables in those days – yes, he was known as 'the thin brother' – he even remembered the drowned girl Shiromi coming into his shop. Dilukshi seemed to have got that right too.

      *   *   *   *   *

Haraldsson's other case in Sri Lanka was equally compelling – a little boy who walked about with the gravity of an old man and chanted Buddhist texts in Pali, the ancient language of Sinhalese Buddhism. Duminda's chanting is the equivalent of a six-year-old Western child chanting parts of the Roman Catholic Mass in Latin.

He began this chanting at the age of three and his mother, the wife of a former bus driver who runs a small poultry farm, was at first anxious to suppress his strange behaviour in case the child should leave her and enter a monastery. Today, three years on, she is reconciled to the idea and we were told there are plans for Duminda to become a boy monk in another year or so.

Duminda was brought up a few miles from Kandy, the old capital of the island and famous as a religious centre – there, the Temple of the Tooth houses one of the most famous relics of the Lord Buddha, and nearby is the Asgirya monastery.

The boy has grown up at his grandparents' house. From an early age, he draped a piece of yellow cloth over his shoulder in the fashion of a monk, and made twice daily visits to a small shrine in the area, where he chants

Pali texts. He told his family he had been a monk at the Asgirya temple. His grandfather said, 'From the age of three, he used to urge us "Come on, lets go to the Asgirya temple." He'd get up early, wrap himself in a towel for a robe and go outside. If he saw a priest going for a bus, he used to cry out, "There, the priests are going. I too want to go to the Asgirya, let's go!"'

The child also refused to eat a main meal after eleven o'clock in the morning, as is normal with monks. He was extremely clean and asked his mother not to touch his hands when she helped him to wash – women are not supposed to touch the hands of a monk. He did not play with other children and asked his family to call him 'Podi Sadhu' or 'little monk.' Duminda's mother, not surprisingly, sought advice and took the boy to see a monk at a nearby temple, Ven. Jinorase, who told Haraldsson that the boy asked for a fan, such as monks use. The child held it in front of his face, in traditional style for a monk and recited a stanza. The boy told the monk he too had been a monk at Asgirya, and he had a room at the monastery and some belongings there. He wanted to go to see the temple and his motorcar.

The monk's verdict was that the boy behaved 'like no other boy' and he did not believe the parents could have taught him this behaviour. The monk suggested Duminda be taken to the Asgirya monastery. This visit was arranged and one Sunday in October 1987 Duminda was taken there. A journalist from the newspaper *Island*, Oliver Silva, who had heard about the story, was also present. According to the witnesses, the boy seemed to know his way around. He said a traditional prayer at a stupa and told a monk, Ven. Wimalakeerthi, that he had worshipped there before. The monk asked if he knew where the bodhi tree was? This special shrine under a tree was only partly visible, above them on a hillside, but un-hesitatingly, Duminda ran up the winding steps to the bodhi tree.

There are seventeen residences at the monastery complex and Duminda entered the one next to the temple. He said he had lived there before. Inside the building, he was invited to sit down but waited until a white cloth was placed over the seat, as is traditional for a monk.

All the monks present agree that the boy had gone upstairs to a large room and identified a bed in a corner as his, and said a large, old wooden box had once been his property, but had not had a lock on it in those days. Duminda had said he died as a monk after falling down with pains in his chest and being taken to a hospital. The journalist Silva discovered that a senior monk, Ven. Rathamapala, had lived in the residence identified by Duminda, and died of a heart attack in 1975. He concluded the child was this monk reborn.

Almost a year later, Haraldsson arrived on the scene and sensed that this identification was too hasty. There were some statements by Duminda which did not fit – there was no evidence that this particular monk owned a red motorcar, had an elephant or money and a moneybag. The breakthrough came with an old photograph of a dozen monks. Haraldsson was told that Duminda had pointed out someone he knew on that picture but nobody seemed sure who that had been. Haraldsson, who did not know the identity of anyone in the photograph, took it along to Duminda's home – the small boy pointed to a monk and said, 'This was me.'

Two old monks and the present high-priest confirmed the man in the picture had been the chief high-priest, Ven. Gunnepana, who died in 1929. It was the first time Haraldsson had heard this name, but suddenly the facts began to fit. He found that Abbot Gunnepana had had money and a moneybag and had been the first monk in Kandy to own a motorcar. Two very elderly monks even remembered it as red or brownish!

Other pieces of evidence dropped neatly into place. It was found that a disciple of Gunnepana had owned an elephant, which the old man took a great interest in and regarded as his own. Gunnepana was also famous for his knowledge of religious chants. He had even died of a heart attack, but the two old monks remembered that he died in the monastery and they did not believe he had been taken to hospital, as Duminda said.

There was another seeming mistake. Gunnepana's residence was not the one specified by Duminda – it was the one next door. It is possible, says Haraldsson that the monk had lived in a different residence at some earlier stage in his career. The child might also have been confused between buildings that are quite similar on the inside and next door to each other. We filmed Duminda, watched by Haraldsson, going back to the residence. Again, he went into the same building, climbed the stairs and pointed to where he said he used to sleep. He showed where he used to keep his clothes – but it was still in the wrong house, as far as we could tell.

We filmed the child walking home alone from school. He put a piece of cloth over his shoulder and, holding a fan before his face, went to the local shrine and sang some texts in Pali. Next day we went with Duminda to the temple and there, before the altar, he began chanting more texts.

There was some excitement when he chanted a text which the onlookers had not heard before. For a comparison, we went to a nearby monastery and filmed a group of monks whom we asked to chant the seven texts Duminda had sung. When they came to the little-known chant, only the abbot was able to continue, but he had looked it up in a book beforehand.

This text seemed to dispose of one theory that Duminda had picked up his knowledge from an early morning radio programme that began with chants at five o'clock every day. Haraldsson took a tape to the radio station and they confirmed they had never played this particular chant.

But Haraldsson was then told by the grandmother that she and her daughter both knew this chant and several more besides. However, they insisted they have never taught Duminda any chants – in fact, they say he has taught them one! Duminda's two brothers, who have been brought up with him, show no signs of any special chanting ability or knowledge of chants, and researcher Godwin Samararatne asked the boy directly, 'Where did you learn the chants?' Duminda's measured reply was, 'I have not learned them.'

Haraldsson is satisfied the only normal explanation for Duminda's chants in Pali is that he has somehow learned them from his grandmother or mother. On the other hand, Abbot Gunnepana would certainly have known them all, including the little known chant which is sung mainly in the Temple of the Tooth, Kandy, where Gunnepana was in charge.

These four children, along with the others we filmed in India and Canada, together made an impressive statement on behalf of the parapsychologists whose work they represent. Of course, today's sceptical scientists are not particularly impressed with spectacular individual cases, which might be caused by chance or freak circumstance. They prefer the safe statistical conclusions which can be drawn from large numbers of similar cases.

The good news is that Dr Stevenson and his colleagues have done all that. What I have written about is just the tip of their statistical iceberg. There are hundreds of other similar cases, analysed with tables and charts and statistics in the academic papers and books the individual scientists have published – and there is more to come. There are even parapsychologists in this area whose work I haven't mentioned so far, like Dr Jurgen Keil of the university of Tasmania, who has investigated reincarnation claims in countries such as Thailand, Burma and Turkey.

A good case for reincarnation as a form of survival after death seems to have already been made out. The problem is that the critics seize on the weakest aspect of any case, which the parapsychologists as good scientists always include, and publicly deride that part of the material and pretend the rest of the evidence doesn't exist.

The case for survival is stronger than is generally realised. There is even a range of relevant circumstantial evidence, about science and the nature of reality, which we haven't touched on yet.

CHAPTER TWENTY-FIVE

Quantum leaps

**The concepts which now prove to be fundamental to
our understanding of nature seem to my mind to be
structures of pure thought ... the universe begins to
look more like a great thought than like a great
machine.** SIR JAMES JEANS

Half a century ago, quantum physicists exploded the idea that the
universe is a predictable place whose secrets are well understood
by the scientific heirs to Sir Isaac Newton. What was perceived
as reality is now a great mystery.

The old materialist theory was that all matter obeyed cause and effect
laws like balls on a billiards table. Quantum physicists, looking at matter
on the micro-scale of atoms and electrons, found the old rules for billiards
did not apply. Matter is patterns of energy, electrons can behave like
waves, and nuclear particles fired from a common source in two different
directions, no matter how far apart, are somehow still in touch. Any
change to one set of particles causes a similar change in the other – action at
a distance.

Also, the observer seemed to influence his own experiment, altering the
result just by watching – matter was perhaps responding to consciousness
or Mind. It was all very paranormal!

It was so contrary to established science that even Albert Einstein in
1935 was unhappy with the implications of 'spooky actions at a distance.'
If an observer was producing a physical reality just by watching, Einstein
asked if it meant the moon was there only when he looked at it!

Today, quantum theory is understood by so few people and the speculative theories are so strange and controversial that most of us know little
or nothing about them. Some scientists are happy with this state of general
ignorance. They pretend quantum doesn't exist and they have all the
answers – for them the old Laws of Nature are still intact and not a bucket
with a hole in the bottom. The fear of some hardliners is that any scientific

acceptance of action at a distance or mind effecting matter opens the door to the world of psi and even the possibility of survival.

On the other hand, some scientists, familiar with quantum and the best research in parapsychology, see the need for a new science, perhaps free from the old straitjacket of no-go areas imposed at the time of the Reformation.

Quantum has demonstrated that the old mechanistic ideas about reality and the universe have only limited validity. But there is still no overall theory to put in their place, even after fifty years, although there are some exciting alternatives. For instance, one quantum effect is that matter can appear to be in two places at the same time, so there is a theory of parallel universes – there might be alternative worlds to our own, near mirror-images of our lives taking place in a dimension we are unaware of. Now that is what I call 'spooky.'

Also, because consciousness comes into the quantum equations, comparisons have been made with Eastern mysticism, and there is the suggestion that reality might be thought itself or consciousness – which might explain paranormal phenomena like psi, as well as apparitions and even survival.

To learn more about quantum and these fascinating speculations, I went to several experts, including the 1973 Nobel Prize winner for physics, Professor Brian Josephson of the Cavendish Laboratory, Cambridge. He told me it was sometimes assumed that quantum effects occurred only on the smallest sub-atomic scale, but in superconductivity experiments, electromagnetic tests at low temperatures, he had witnessed it on a scale big enough to see.

> Quantum has made the whole world seem very mysterious and almost unvisualisable. It is incomprehensible even to the scientists. We can only make calculations and predict the results of experiments. We don't have a clear mental picture of what is going on.

What kind of hypotheses are currently available to explain these quantum effects?

> For a lot of people it is sufficient to make equations which seem to explain nature. But the mysterious thing is that the observer himself has to be put into the physics to get answers out. Different people have different attitudes to all of this and you could say the theory is not completely logical. One speculation is the idea there are a lot of parallel universes. Another is that Mind is ensuring there is only one universe at a time. A theory popular amongst some people is there is a sort of

hidden reality behind that which we can see. That's a very interesting hypothesis because, if you try and explain what you see in terms of a hidden reality, you find you can't explain what is observed without putting in action at a distance – this is significant because experiments on things like telepathy suggest there really may be 'action at a distance.'

Does all this put Mind or man, however we define ourselves, more at the centre of things?

Well, it suggests that maybe Mind is important. There's another line of reasoning which people call the anthropic principle. There are a large number of coincidences necessary for life to exist. For example, if certain numbers didn't work out right, the universe wouldn't last long enough for life to have evolved. The universe would expand so quickly you couldn't get the kind of world we have. One way of explaining these coincidences is to say that Mind is in the background keeping its eye on things and adjusting the properties of the universe so that it will be right for some future life.

Does this tend towards the possibility of survival?

If you wanted an explanation for survival in science, you could call upon a number of things. The fact that according to some versions of physics, the observer has to be put in. Or you might say the universe is a lot more subtle than we thought, and so there may be some kind of energy that could survive death.

At the moment, science is fairly neutral I would say on the possibility of survival. We know that nature is not just lumps of matter, it's some kind of energy pattern. So, in principle, survival would be possible if some kind of energy pattern could survive the absence of a body to support it. But that's purely speculative at the present time.

Is it a realistic question that man might be a thought-form in a universe that was made of thought?

It has been suggested by some people that the universe is made of thought. The scientist says everything is made up out of fields. It's somewhat parallel that a field might be a thought and then you could arrive at the conclusion that everything is made of thought. Certainly things are not made up out of particles, so I think to show it was made up of thought, you'd need to show that something like a thought process was going on, and we really don't have that picture yet. But we do have some sense that observation might help to construct reality, and that comes close to the idea that thought is involved in the nature of reality.

How would you compare scientific speculation today about the nature of reality, and the insights that religion claims to have? How certain can we be about scientific values?

Well, there are all sorts of things that scientists claim that are really acts of faith, just as much as religious belief. When a scientist says, for example, 'We understand how the brain works,' or 'We understand how man came into existence through natural selection,' that's an enormous extrapolation. The kind of thing that happens is somebody writes a computer programme that can understand simple sentences and then says, 'We understand the principle of language and so we understand how our minds work.'

Similarly, somebody produces a theory which explains a little piece of evolution, like changes in colour of a moth as the background changes, and scientists may then say, 'We understand how evolution works.' To apply this to the evolution of man or to say how man's mind works involves an enormous leap of faith, which I'd say is almost bigger than the kind of faith involved in religious belief.

Some people have the idea that science is reaching its climax, and will soon find the right equation that will explain everything. But I don't think we are in that sort of situation, because I don't think we really understand Mind. That, in turn, means we don't really understand life. Neither does science really take into account the concept of meaning.

Science has advanced a lot in the direction of taking things to bits, but it's not advanced nearly so far in finding out how things work as a whole. I think science will ultimately have to move in this direction. It may have to develop new means of exploring nature in this direction, and I don't mean new tools.

What about parallels in Buddhism, in mysticism, to aspects of quantum theory? They seem to have been saying some approximately similar things?

You have to be a little careful in trying to connect science and mysticism. Some features of mysticism can be connected quite well with properties discovered by science, but I think mysticism goes beyond science. I believe aspects of nature, deeper than those discovered by science, are understood in mysticism. It's as if science has just scratched the surface of the Mindlike aspects of nature. And because Mind is fundamentally more elusive than matter, the methods of science have so far failed to grasp the subtleties in the way mystical experience has. In the last decade, there's been a lot of talk among ordinary people about connections between science and mysticism. The reaction of a vast number of scientists has been to say this is nonsense, it's pseudo-science!

I think this is a wrong conclusion, and we will in future see this kind of thing becoming routine science. The statement is often made that when something unorthodox comes up, scientists first of all ignore it and then say it's nonsense. Eventually they say it's obvious, and it was obvious all the time. I think we'll get that happening in the areas that you're exploring in your programme.

CHAPTER TWENTY-SIX

Scientific no-go areas

Newton forgive me. You found the only way that, in your day, was at all possible for a man of the highest powers of intellect and creativity. The concepts that you created still dominate the way we think in physics, although we now know that they must be replaced ... if we want to try for a more profound understanding of the way things are inter-related.

ALBERT EINSTEIN

'Is there life after death?' is a question which has been a no-go area for science for 300 years. There is a modern scientific assumption that we are machines made of flesh, which crumble to nothingness at death, but the mass of scientific research directly addressing the question is by parapsychologists and fellow-travellers, the sort of people mentioned in this book, who frequently come to very different conclusions. So, who is right?

Classical science has sat on the fence since the seventeenth century when Galileo, Descartes and Newton agreed that consciousness lay outside the remit of science. Our subjective reactions to the environment were non-scientific and irrelevant to the scientific task of measuring and analysing the objective realities of the universe. Descartes defined all a scientist needs to know about consciousness 'I think therefore I am.'

Nowadays, the cracks are apparent in the great edifice of Reformation science which brought order and reason to the 'collection of curiosities' of mediaeval science. Einstein and Relativity and the effects of quantum physics have shown that the observer cannot be left out of modern scientific equations, and many informed minds today are seeking a new branch of science, perhaps a science of the Mind.

Are we on the brink of an historic scientific change? I talked to the consultant neuro-psychiatrist Dr Peter Fenwick.

The science we have today is basically Reformation science dealing with shape, motion, weight and so on. Subjective qualities like redness, love, truth, beauty are non-scientific and that has been a principle of our science.

The whole of neuro-science is brain function. The five senses are not represented in science, only the pathways, the area of the brain in which the five senses are structured and how they come into consciousness. What is not represented is the quality of the experience itself. One theory is that we don't need anything else, because qualities are just the brain's subjective view, in other words the internal view, a model or representation. But the people who hold that view have no way of explaining it directly. So science describes the mechanism and describes it beautifully, but it can't explain qualities. It cannot explain this rich, perceptual world in which we live.

We recognise the brain as a machine, and know a great deal about its structure. We can talk about a red patch of light which strikes the retina, which then comes through the optic nerve to the cortex at the back of the brain. And there science stops, puts its finger to its mouth and is silent. We cannot talk about redness because that is non-scientific and there is no theory. This follows from what Galileo said, so we talk about movement and chemical change but not about the subjective experience of redness.

Can existing sciences be expanded to cope with these questions, or do we need a new science?

We certainly need a new science to understand the true nature of the universe. The mechanical aspects of the universe we've now got nearly tied up. In terms of the nature of man and his subjective experience, we haven't even begun. We cannot say what man's place is in this mechanical universe, there is no proper definition of consciousness, nor explanation of why in mystical experience and in Near Death Experiences we see the universe as composed of love. We need a science of values and with that will come a much better appreciation of man's place in the universe. So morality and experience come into science where they are not at the moment.

The exciting thing is this new science is almost here. Physics is already pointing the way and I think psychology will also start to go along that line. Then we will have the beginnings of a science of Mind.

Despite the seeming evidence for psi powers, like telepathy and action at a distance, the belief is widespread that mind is just an aspect of the working of the brain. Of course, the brain itself is composed of atoms and so the quantum effect of non-locality might therefore apply directly to it, holding out the possibility that one day physics will not only accept psi but is already part way to understanding how it works. However, it is certainly true that most people not only know nothing about quantum but if Isaac Newton has fallen off his throne they have not been told.

Should we accept the 'scientific view' that we are machines made of flesh run by a brain which is a glorified computer? Dr Roger Penrose, an Oxford professor of mathematics who has recently written a book on quantum, told me he did not share the view that the brain was a computer. It could be demonstrated that certain mathematical insights could not be obtained by calculation or computation. Science was a long way from understanding the nature of consciousness – 'We don't have the physics yet.'

Dr Fenwick speculated that the knowledge waiting for us around the next scientific corner might be that the universe was not a solid and material place but composed of 'love, consciousness and mind-stuff.' He fell back on more orthodox science when I asked for his assessment of life after death.

> If you are asking a scientific question then you are tied up with genes, hereditary factors, brains, bodies and it's quite clear they don't survive. If you are talking about subjective experience, you are asking a non-scientific question and the answer will be non-scientific. There is no reason why personal experience in some form or other should not continue. The only reason we think it doesn't is that we link it quite incorrectly with modern-day science. Now, if you take that away it's equally likely that some part of personal experience may have a wider distribution than just in the brain – there is no evidence either way and maybe some of the studies now taking place may push one to the conclusion that some form of survival will turn out to be more likely.

Today, the majority of scientists definitely seem happier with Reformation science than quantum theory. According to the polls, only one in five scientists accepts the possibility that their mechanical universe may be prone to paranormal phenomena. Things have not changed. Back in 1953, the famous biologist, Sir Alister Hardy of Oxford University, gave four reasons why his scientific colleagues would not accept the findings of psychical research.

Firstly, the experiments often could not be repeated in a laboratory – which is perhaps a less valid objection today after years of Ganzfeld experiments. Secondly, the scientists suspected the phenomena were caused by fraud. Hardy acknowledged there were charlatans who pretended to have supernatural powers but told his colleagues, 'The great science of chemistry sprang from the cradle of alchemy, some of whose exponents were genuinely striving after the transmutation of metals and the elixir of life, while others were as rank impostors as any false medium or fortune-teller of today.'

Sir Alister was too polite to mention that Sir Isaac Newton himself was an alchemist, or that numerous orthodox scientists have been caught cheating and falsifying their results.

The third objection was that parapsychologists seemed to want a particular result to their experiments, making critics suspicious of their findings. Were they biased and ready to arrive unwittingly at false conclusions? Hardy said, 'If we say science must only be concerned with experiments about whose results we have no emotional feelings, then we can never hope to come to a real understanding of living things.'

Finally, orthodox scientists could not bring themselves to look at psi research because they believed it to be 'impossible and a waste of time.' Hardy's reply was that to refuse to investigate telepathy because it did not appear to fit the framework of present-day science, was to be the same as those bigots in the seventeenth century who condemned Galileo for his experiments and conclusions.

Some parapsychologists today have faced opposition reminiscent of the old days of Galileo and the Inquisition. Dr Michael B. Sabom of Atlanta, a well known researcher of Near Death Experiences, has faced critics and made a relevant observation in the *Journal of the American Medical Association* in 1980. 'Dr Blacher points out that the physician must be especially wary of accepting religious belief as scientific data. I might add that equal caution should be exercised in accepting scientific belief as scientific data.'

Most scientists who concede the possibility of the paranormal do so from some personal experience and not because of the strength of the evidence. Sir Alister Hardy was a case in point. He came to believe in telepathy because of two experiences during the First World War. He was serving with a Cyclist Battalion in England, when he went to tea with a Mrs Arthur Wedgwood, an amateur medium. This lady knew that Hardy's brother was a prisoner-of-war in Germany, and she told the young officer she could see his brother in a little room, with a camp bed, sitting at a table. 'On a large sheet of white paper I see him painting what seems to be squares and oblongs of red and blue.'

Hardy was surprised, because Mrs Wedgwood had described exactly what Hardy himself had been doing that afternoon. His colonel had asked him to prepare illustrations for a lecture on the Franco-Prussian War.

'That afternoon I had been cutting out squares and oblongs of card painted red and blue to represent various units of infantry and cavalry. I spent the afternoon in my rather bare room with a camp bed, looking at a map and moving red and blue cards about. I then went straight on my bicycle to have tea with Mrs Wedgwood and am absolutely certain no one could have told her what I had been doing.'

Could it have been coincidence? A year later, Hardy was again having tea with Mrs Wedgwood in London. He was now a camouflage officer with the Royal Engineers and that afternoon had been doing experiments in dazzle effects. He had painted a large sheet of white cardboard with vivid pink distemper and watched it dry on a table in front of him. As soon as he sat down opposite Mrs Wedgwood, she said, 'What have you been doing? I see a large pink square on the table in front of you.'

Some scientists simply cannot understand how others can be so foolish as to have such beliefs. Dr Fenwick commented, 'You have to understand cognitive dissonance. I know that smoking may kill me, but it doesn't mean I stop smoking. Many scientists hold opposing views at the same time. Scientists live in a world of mechanical fact.

They cannot square their science with their own perception of the world, so they compartmentalise: on the one hand, a Christian and on the other hand a scientist. However, I know of no scientist who really believes the Communion wine turns into blood, and they are not prepared to do an experiment to see if they can find haemoglobin present. That would be inappropriate.'

Looking for white crows

Concepts which have been proved to be useful in ordering things, easily acquire such an authority over us that we forget their human origin and accept them as invariable. ALBERT EINSTEIN

Does this book's collection of strange lives and events, supported by the testimony of scientists, amount to a plausible case for life after death? The primary concern of the scientists was always the integrity of their research – they always seemed aware of possible alternative explanations like hallucination, extraordinary coincidence, self-deception, fraud or telepathy. But if the subjects, unwittingly or wittingly, deceived themselves and us, it wasn't apparent from their evidence or attitudes – Western adults often had to overcome a fear of being ridiculed to speak out about their experiences, and there was the shy assurance of Asian children who behaved and spoke like older persons whose life and death they remembered.

Fortunately, all the cases don't have to be equally strong to undermine the materialist rule that death annihilates life. The nineteenth-century American psychologist William James said that to demonstrate all crows were not black, you need only find a single white crow – just one was enough. On the face of it, the parapsychologists have a flock of white crows.

Credibility and crows to one side, the first thing we tested in this project was psi. If Survival was possible, we needed to show that a human being was more than flesh and cerebral cortex – all destroyed at death. ESP, telepathy and clairvoyance were tell-tale signs of some mind-force that might exist outside the brain, perhaps even capable of surviving the death of the body.

Charles Honorton's computerised analysis of years of Ganzfeld Remote Viewing tests seemed to demonstrate statistically that psi was real. In labs across the country, blindfolded subjects had correctly picked one of four targets with a one-in-three frequency, a clear improvement on chance – and some of the individual successes were impressively detailed.

Our own recorded Remote Viewing test, supervised by parapsychologists Dr Keith Harary and Dr Nancy Sondow, was an astonishing success. Tessa Cordle of the BBC 'saw' an unknown location with the clarity of a genuine eye-witness and drew, on a single sheet of paper, the salient features of the small park where Dr Sondow was standing. Nothing was drawn that was not represented on the target site. It was every bit as impressive as Mrs Wedgwood's demonstration of psi for Sir Alister Hardy. By Ganzfeld standards, of a single picture on a slide, she scored five hits in one, since she separately identified a T-shaped path, a small park with trees, a structure with steps and a pointed roof, a shop with a red and white striped awning and the statue of an angel turning green.

Psi seemed effectively demonstrated, but Dr Honorton raised a serious doubt about what it might mean for life after death. Telepathy is a double agent – it makes survival seem plausible by identifying a force which could operate separately from the brain, but Honorton suggested telepathy might also produce the evidence that is generally taken to indicate life after death. It's easy to see how this might apply to seances. Mediums who tell sitters strange truths they seem to have no normal way of knowing, may be getting the facts telepathically from the minds of the sitters. It was more difficult to relate Honorton's theory to Dr Stevenson's cases of small children who recall previous lives of people they and their family know nothing about. Is it feasible for a child to have unconscious access to some general pool of information about dead people? If the child telepathically gets such information, why should the infant imagine he or she had once been that person? Dr Stevenson also pointed out that these children mostly show no other signs whatever of telepathic ability.

In the second of our searches, there were compelling narratives about apparitions and Near Death Experiences. Dr Melvin Morse has a powerful collection of drawings by children close to death and was critical of routine scientific explanations that NDEs were hallucinations in a dying brain or some re-living of the birth process.

It was difficult to doubt the sincerity of witnesses whose brush with death in many cases seemed to change their lives. Particularly significant was the hospital worker's story of recovering a shoe from a ledge, after it was seen by a patient having a heart-attack, who simultaneously found herself floating out-of-body around the outside of the hospital. This seemed to corroborate the claim that an NDE is at least a genuine out-of-body experience and not a simple hallucination.

This non-locality, the ability to be in two places at the same time, was central to much of the evidence we looked at. Is there now hope of a scientific framework for this concept in quantum physics? In 1964, the physicist Dr J. S. Bell published a mathematical paper which offered this possibility, and numerous eminent physicists today think Bell's Theorem is supremely significant.

Dr Brian Josephson told me, 'It is one of the most important results in science in recent decades – you compare it with things like quantum theory itself or relativity. In Bell's Theorem, things in different places can be directly connected. One consequence which might be relevant to Survival is that a well defined structure doesn't really have to exist in any particular place. It can be spread around everywhere, interacting with itself through the kind of connections Bell discovered.'

Quantum theory is a minefield of possibilities. The paranormal has not been accepted into the body of science, but that remains a possibility for the future – partly because quantum has blown apart the certainty of traditional scientists that such phenomena were beyond the bounds of credibility. Another eminent physicist, the Rev. Dr John C. Polkinghorne, the President of Queen's College, Cambridge, gave me a view of quantum and Survival.

Quantum mechanics has taught me something very surprising: the world that seems so solid and reliable in everyday terms is in fact made up of particles which are elusive and fitful in their behaviour, when we get down to the atomic and sub-atomic level. It's taught us two things – the world is full of surprises and is more subtle than we might have expected. Secondly, whatever the world is, it is not merely mechanical. The physical world of ourselves is part of something more subtle, more interesting, more open to the future than elaborate pieces of clockwork.

If you're going to discuss the question of destiny beyond death, you have to decide what might have a destiny. Some people believe the 'real me' is some sort of spiritual ingredient, a separable soul which is sitting here inside the body – it is indestructible and therefore survives death.

I don't think human beings are like that, I don't think we are apprentice angels – I think we are minds in bodies and that is the soul if you like. The 'real me' is not an extra, spiritual ingredient but is the infinitely complex information-bearing pattern within the matter of my body.

Perhaps the most intriguing idea to come out of a mass of speculation about quantum is that reality might be consciousness or thought. The old idea that matter was composed of particles has given way to the idea of fields – Einstein referred to matter as 'frozen energy.' If the energy in the fields is thought, does that mean each of us is a thought-form?

Thought is a force which might operate independently from the brain, producing telepathy, apparitions and out-of-body experiences. At death it presumably quits the body and perhaps find a new body – a reincarnation, or it simply moves to a dimension of Mind, inaccessible to our five senses.

So what should we make of it all? If the stuff of the universe is 'mind-stuff,' as Sir Arthur Eddington said, then the observer may indeed interact with the experiment. The physicist Niels Bohr said, 'We are both onlookers and actors in the great drama of existence.' Quantum science may be telling us that our individual consciousness, some part of our mind, is our own little bit of eternity, a fragment of the underlying reality of the universe. Of course, as Dr Josephson pointed out, mystics have been telling us something like that for many centuries. The main difference is that they called the fragment 'soul.'

But these are areas of speculation and belief a long way from where most of the scientists dropped us. Whether the evidence has demonstrated psi, life after death, or reincarnation is clearly for each of us to decide individually. My own beliefs have changed somewhat in the two years it took to make these programmes and in an unexpected way.

I was on holiday in Spain with my family in 1990 and spent every afternoon working in a hotel room. I had with me Tegwyn Hughes' account of his apparitional experience in a Malta convoy, when the destroyers *Arethusa* and *Orion* were attacked. I was also researching the complexities of the cross-correspondence 'The Ear of Dionysius,' a series of communications to mediums.

One morning in a Spanish market, I saw three blackened coins on a stall. I was told they were Roman. I liked one and bought it, with no other ideas about it. I kept it with other coins in my pocket. Months later, we were filming with Dr Antonia Mills in British Columbia, Canada, and in the library of an academic, my assistant Tessa Cordle, with no specific aim in mind, pulled a book from one of many shelves and opened it. On the page were pictures of my coin – a head on one side and a racing chariot on the other. The caption said it was a fifth century B.C. coin issued by Dionysius, the tyrant of Syracuse. The head on the coin was the goddess Arethusa – that day in Spain I had unknowingly picked up an object specifically bridging the two separate stories I was working on.

Carl Jung had a theory of Synchronicity to link up coincidences which sometimes made the past appear to overlap the present. He wrote that the coincidences may be so extreme that 'their unthinkability increases until they can no longer be regarded as pure chance but, for lack of a causal explanation, have to be thought of as meaningful arrangements.' The coin came to symbolise the project, a true talisman – even the place and manner of its identification by my 'psychic' colleague seemed significant.

Today, I believe in the possibility of life after death and reincarnation as perhaps a next stage in the evolution of human consciousness. But I am convinced of two concepts: telepathy and synchronicity. I have seen both in action and have my copy of Tessa's drawing and the coin in my pocket to remind me – the world is full of surprises.

Bibliography

BADHAM, PAUL & LINDA *Immortality or Extinction* (S.P.C.K. London 1984)

BAIRD, A. T. *Richard Hodgson* (Psychic Press, London 1949)

BANCROFT-HUNT, NORMAN *People of the Totem* (University of Oklahoma 1988)

BASSETT, JEAN *100 Years of National Spiritualism* (The Headquarters Publishing Co, London 1990)

BELOFF, JOHN *The Relentless Question, Reflections on the Paranormal* (McFarland and Co., North Carolina and London 1990)

BERGER, ARTHUR S. *Evidence of Life after Death: A Casebook for the Tough-Minded* (Charles C. Thomas, USA 1988)

BUTLER, JOHN *Exploring the Psychic World* (Oak Tree Books, London 1947)

CARPENTER, EDWARD *From Adam's Peak to Elephanta* (Allen and Unwin 1911)

CARRINGTON, HEREWARD *The Coming Science* (Werner Laurie, London 1908)

CRANSTON, SYLVIA AND CAREY WILLIAMS *Reincarnation – a new horizon* (Julian Press, New York 1984)

DALAI LAMA OF TIBET *My Land My People* (Potala Corporation 1983)

ENCYCLOPAEDIA OF OCCULTISM & PARAPSYCHOLOGY (Gale Research Co., Detroit, USA 1990)

EVANS-WENTZ, W. Y. *The Tibetan Book of the Dead* (Oxford University Press 1927)

EYSENCK, HANS L. AND CARL SARGENT *Explaining the Unexplained* (Weidenfeld and Nicolson, London 1982)

FEILDING, EVERARD *Sittings with Eusapia Palladino* (University Books, USA 1963)

GALLUP, GEORGE JNR. *Adventures in Immortality* (McGraw Hill, New York 1982)

GAULD, ALAN *Mediumship & Survival* (Paladin 1983)

GURNEY, EDMUND, F. W. H. MYERS AND F. PODMORE *Phantasms of the Living*, two volumes (Kegan Paul, London 1918, original 1886)

HARALDSSON, ERLENDUR *Encounters with the Dead* (Luce et Ombre 1989)

HARARY, KEITH AND PAMELA WEINTRAUB *Mystical Experiences in 30 days* (St Martin's Press 1990)

HARDY, ALISTER, ROBERT HARVIE AND ARTHUR KOESTLER *The Challenge of Chance* (Random House, New York 1973)

HEAD, JOSEPH AND S. L. CRANSTON *The Phoenix Fire Mystery* (Julian Press, New York 1977)

HILL, DOUGLAS AND PAT WILLIAMS *The Supernatural* (Aldous, London 1965)

HYSLOP, JAMES H *Contact with the Other World* (The Century Co., New York 1919)

INGLIS, BRIAN *The Hidden Power* (Jonathan Cape, London 1986)

JAHN, ROBERT G. AND BRENDA J DUNNE *Margins of Reality* (Harcourt, Brace, Jovanovich, New York & London 1987)

JAMES, WILLIAM *The Mrs Titus Case* (Proceedings of the American Society for Psychical Research Vol 1, part 2, 1885)

JUNG, CARL *Man and his Symbols* (Picador 1978)

Memories, Dreams and Reflections (Fontana 1962)

KOESTLER, ARTHUR *The Act of Creation* (Hutchinson 1965)

The Ghost in the Machine (Penguin, London 1967)

LODGE, OLIVER *Past Years* (Hodder and Stoughton, London 1931)

MARTIN, EVA *The Ring of Return* (Philip Allan, London 1927)

MCCLENON J. *A Survey of Elite Scientists* (Journal of Parapsychology 1982)

MOODY, RAYMOND *The Light Beyond* (Macmillan, London 1988)

MORSE, MELVIN *Closer to the Light* (Villard Books, USA, Souvenir Press UK 1990)

MURPHY, GARDNER *The Challenge of Psychical Research* (Harper and Brothers, USA 1961)

NAHATA, BAL CHAND *The Evidence for Survival from Claimed Memories of Former Incarnations* (Indian Psycho-Analytical Association 1935)

OSIS, KARLIS AND ERLENDUR HARALDSSON *At the Hour of Death* (Hastings House, New York 1986)

    Deathbed Observations of Physicians and Nurses (Parapsychology Foundation 1961)

PASRICHA, SATWANT *Claims of Reincarnation* (Harman, New Delhi 1990)

PEDLER, KIT *Mind over Matter* (Eyre Methuen, London 1981)

PICKNETT, LYNN *Encyclopaedia of the Paranormal* (Macmillan, London 1990)

REES, W. DEWI *The Hallucinations of Widowhood* (British Medical Journal 1971)

RHINE, J. B. *New Frontiers of the Mind* (Farrar and Rinehart, New York 1937)

RITCHIE, GEORGE, *Return from Tomorrow* (Chosen Books, Virginia, USA 1978)

SABOM, MICHAEL *Recollections of Death* (Corgi, 1982)

    Letter published in Journal of the American Medical Association 1980

SALTMARSH, H. F. *Evidence of Personal Survival* (Bell and Sons, London 1938)

SPENCER, A. J. *Death in Ancient Egypt* (Penguin 1982)

STEARN, JESS *Adventures into the Psychic* (Coward McCann 1969)

STEVENSON, IAN *Twenty Cases Suggestive of Reincarnation* (University Press of Virginia 1966)

    Telepathic Impressions (University Press of Virginia 1970)

    The Explanatory Value of the Idea of Reincarnation (Journal of Nervous and Mental Disease 1977)

    Cases of the Reincarnation Type (three volumes) (University Press of Virginia 1980)

    Children who Remember Previous Lives (University Press of Virginia 1987)

    Birth Marks, Birth Defects – A Study of their Etiology (University Press of Virginia 1991)

TERRY, MAURY *The Ultimate Evil* (Bantam 1987)

THOMPSON, ROBERT J. *The Proofs of Life after Death* (Werner Laurie, London 1902)

ULLMAN, MONTAGUE, S. KRIPPNER AND A. VAUGHAN *Dream Telepathy* (McFarland, reprinted 1989)

WEST, D. J. *Psychical Research Today* (Macmillan 1954)

WILSON, COLIN *Mysteries* (Grafton, London 1989)

Index